Exploring music with the BBC Micro and Electron

Kevin Jones

Exploring music with the BBC Micro and Electron

Pitman

PITMAN PUBLISHING LIMITED
128 Long Acre, London WC2E 9AN

PITMAN PUBLISHING INC
1020 Plain Street, Marshfield, Massachusetts 02050

Associated Companies
Pitman Publishing Pty Ltd, Melbourne
Pitman Publishing New Zealand Ltd, Wellington
Copp Clark Pitman, Toronto

First published in Great Britain 1984

British Library Cataloguing in Publication Data
Jones, Kevin
Exploring music with the BBC micro and electron
1. Music–Data processing 2. BBC Microcomputer
3. Electron Microcomputer
I. Title
780'.28'5404 MT723

ISBN 0-273-02214-8

Text set in 11 on 13pt Plantin by
Dobbie Typesetting Service, Plymouth, Devon
Printed and bound in Great Britain at The Pitman Press, Bath

Contents

per una compiuta donzella

Preface

This book is aimed both at musicians who may know little about computers, and at seasoned computer users who may know little about music. As a result it ought to be suitable for a comparative beginner in either field. I hope that experts will be patient when simple ideas are explained, for I am sure that they will find much to interest them as well.

The main purpose of the text is to explore creative ways of using the computer to make music, rather than just as a passive sound synthesizer. In doing so we are scratching the surface of the world of artificial intelligence. Some of the programs try, in a simple way, to make the computer produce music which copies certain distinctive styles. They take into account choices which a composer might make as he puts together a piece of music.

Musical applications which fit awkwardly on to a computer are avoided; there is much music best made without a computer. On the other hand, there are many musical tasks and styles to which a computer is ideally suited. Sometimes we can even go so far as to start with an abstract computer programming idea to see what musical effects it can produce. That way we may produce new and unexpected sounds. As a result many of the programs in the book are quite short.

The range of musical styles covered in our exploration is wide. It includes "serious" and pop music, folk music, classical and modern music. This includes the wierd and wonderful electronic sound effects much used in contemporary music and which are perhaps the most obvious part of a computer's musical repertoire. Music from non-European cultures also features strongly, and there are many examples of how the computer can be used to help teach music.

I have tried to make the book suitable for dipping into, which is the way I tend to use books myself. Where immediate explanations are not given, or are not adequate, cross-references and use of the index should help you find your way around the book. Complete beginners will find it useful to start with Chapter 2. The chapters which follow introduce new musical and programming ideas. You do not need to worry about the first chapter unless you are interested in some of the background acoustics.

If you are new to computers, and some of the programming or occasional appearance of mathematics seems daunting, do not despair. Just jump in and try it out! Many apparent difficulties become much clearer and disappear once a program is seen in action.

Much of the material covered will work quite well on the ELECTRON as well as the BBC computer. In some cases slight modifications will need to be made and the sound quality will not be so good. Regrettably, the Electron will only produce one channel of sound. Any programs which involve the simultaneous use of all three channels will only work on the BBC machine. An appendix gives more details about how to adapt programs, where necessary, for the Electron.

1 Introducing sound and computer music

simple acoustics and background to computer sound generation

By way of introduction, this chapter describes how the BBC computer produces its sounds. You do not need to understand how it works in order to use the machine to make music, so if you want to start immediately move on to Chapter 2.

How we hear sound: the duck pond

If you twang a ruler on the edge of a table it moves backwards and forwards very quickly. We say it **vibrates**. Any sound is caused by vibrations. When a piano or guitar note is played, a string vibrates. When you speak, your vocal chords vibrate. When a trumpet is played, the player's lips vibrate. These vibrations make the neighbouring air molecules vibrate. As each molecule pushes and shoves his neighbour, the vibrations pass through the air until they reach our ears and make the ear drum vibrate. This is registered in our brain as a sound. The air itself does not move across from the sound source to the ear. The message comes in the form of a wave.

This is rather like a small stone being thrown into the middle of a pond. Waves will spread out from the centre and cause ducks sitting on the edge to bob up and down.

The water itself does not move out from the centre of the pond. If it did, water would be sucked from the middle of the pond and the hapless ducks would shoot out over the edge. The water only moves up and down as the waves spread out.

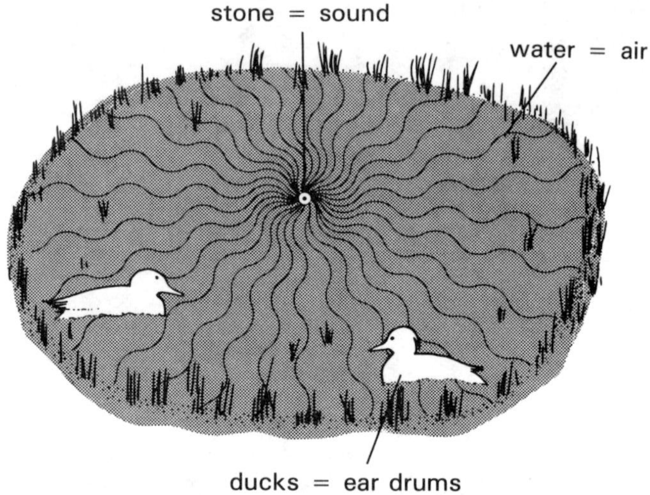

Sound works in the same way. The stone corresponds to the sound being made, the pond water to the air through which the sound travels, and the ducks to our ear drums.

When a ruler or plucked string vibrates, it moves backwards and forwards in the air. The air molecules are alternately squashed together and stretched out. This produces tiny changes in the air pressure. Scientists have designed an instrument which will sense the pressure change as a sound wave passes through a particular spot, and then display a wavy line representing the changes. It is called an **oscilloscope**. When the air pressure goes up, the line on the oscilloscope moves up. When the air pressure goes down, the line moves down.

This diagram represents changes in air pressure as a sound wave passes by. The pressure is greater where the air molecules are squashed together, and less where the molecules are thinned out:

Where the molecules are closer together, the line on the oscilloscope will move up. Where the molecules are further apart the wavy line will move down:

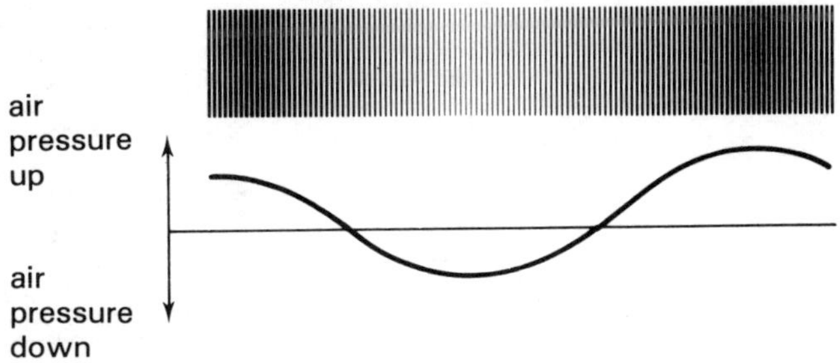

The shape of the wavy line is known as the sound's waveform. You should notice that this representation of a sound wave is rather similar to the shape of the waves produced on the duck pond.

Waveforms

Different types of sound produce different sorts of vibration and so have differently shaped waveforms.

Sometimes the sound goes steadily from high to low pressure, then suddenly changes direction to move back to the opposite level, like this:

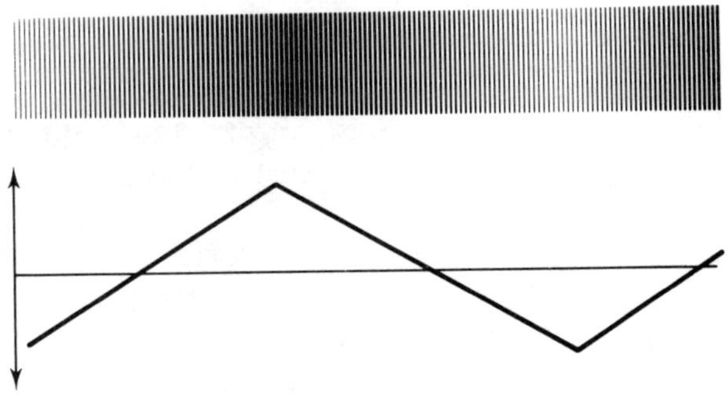

This is called a **triangular wave**. It is a characteristic shape associated with most musical sounds such as those from a violin or clarinet, for example.

Alternatively the pressure might jump immediately from high to low, stay like that for a moment, then jump back again:

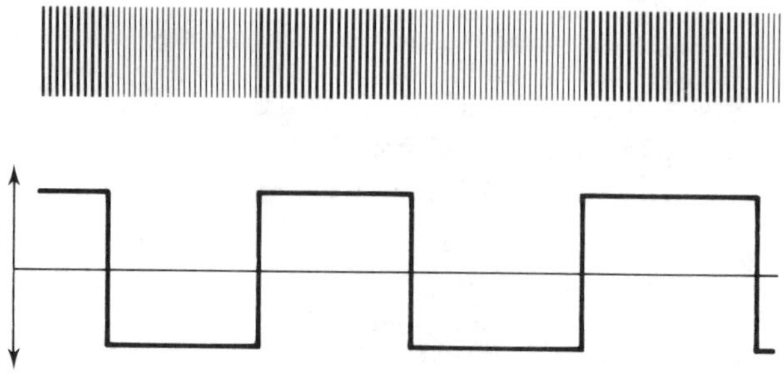

This is called a **square wave** and is characteristic of rougher, brassy sounds. The sound produced by most microcomputers is closest to a square wave.

Halfway between a triangular and a square wave is a situation where pressure may change gradually from high to low, then immediately jump to high again, to keep repeating the pattern:

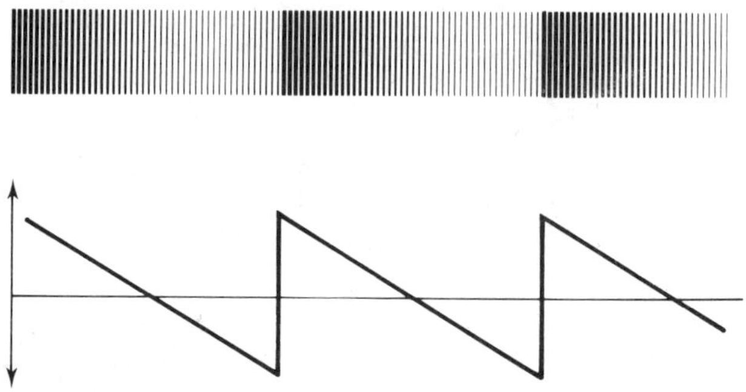

This is called a **sawtooth wave**. Like its shape, its sound is between that of a triangular and a square wave.

Another waveform which moves evenly from high to low, but then smooths out as it passes through each limit, looks like this:

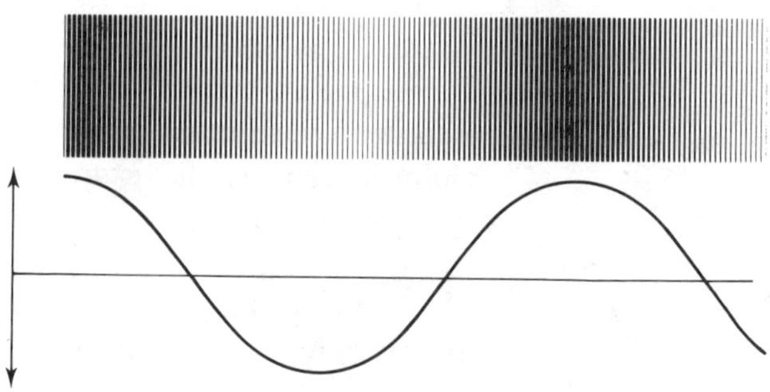

This is called a **sine wave**. It is the same as a sine curve in mathematics. Many natural objects allowed to move or vibrate freely will produce this waveform.

The movement of a swing follows the same shape.

A swing does not move at an even speed from one side to the other and then suddenly change direction to return, as it would if it followed a triangular waveform pattern. Instead, starting at one side, it gathers speed to reach its fastest as it crosses the lowest point in the middle. As it rises on the other side it will gradually slow down again until it reaches the opposite limit. It is stationary for just a tiny moment, as it changes direction, then the speed will increase again as it heads once more for the other side. The Latin word for a swing is **oscillum** which gives us the word **oscillate**. The term **oscillation** is often used by engineers and technicians to refer to musical vibrations and also gives the **oscilloscope** its name.

There is just one type of musical instrument where no vibration of strings, reeds or lips is used to make a sound. Instead, the air is pursuaded to vibrate directly by blowing gently. It is, of course, the flute, or even more effectively, the pan pipes. These instruments produce a sound which is closest to a pure sine wave.

The different waveforms we have just described are ideal shapes. They are useful for dividing sounds into categories. When such perfectly shaped waveforms are synthesized electronically the result will always sound artificial. The waveform of a natural musical sound would be much more complicated, like this perhaps:

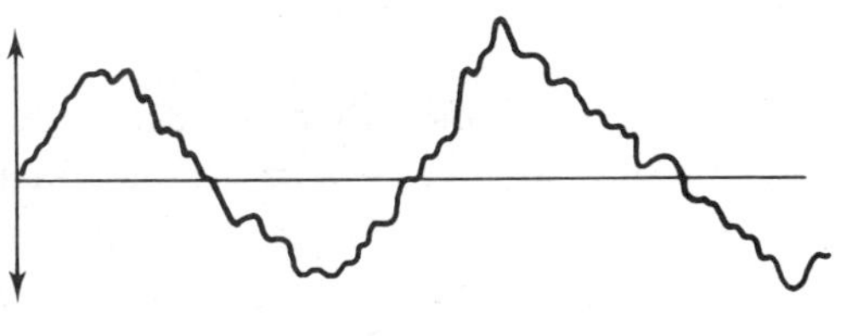

Computer sounds

The sounds made by most microcomputers consist of square waves. These are the easiest for a computer to produce. It is simply a matter of continuous switching between two limits to produce a regular pulse. On some computers, those capable of producing just one note at a time, this is done by linking a single "bit" in the computer to a small loudspeaker. The bit can have just two values, 0 and 1. As it switches from one to the other a pulse is sent to the loudspeaker which makes it twitch. Repeated switching leads to repeated twitching and, if done fast enough, the resulting vibrations are heard as a pitched sound. If done slowly they are just heard as clicks. Changing the speed of the switching will vary the pitch of the sound.

On the BBC computer a special sound chip is used which is capable of producing three separate channels of sound. Even though the basic square waves which it produces may sometimes sound coarse, much can be done to shape and control them and so produce some quite sophisticated results. Unfortunately, because of the way the controlling software is designed, higher pitches become slightly distorted and can sound out of tune. Much of the time this does not matter, but musicians with sensitive ears may find themselves wincing when an occasional jarring pitch occurs.

A computer such as the COMMODORE 64 has a capacity for generating different waveforms and so, in theory, should produce better quality sound. In practice these facilities turn out to be rather difficult to program and control.

Where the BBC computer scores is in the sophistication of its software to control the sound generators. Not only are there useful sound commands built into BBC BASIC, but the language itself offers an extensive range of additional facilities not available on most other comparable machines. It means that many interesting musical tasks can be done simply and efficiently.

Some other small computers have special add-on sound generators, most of which are very effective in their own way. The APPLE computer does particularly well with ALF, Mountain Hardware, Sound Chaser and other systems, all of which will plug in, or interface, to the Apple and produce reasonably good quality results. Nevertheless there is still a limitation in that these systems come pre-packaged with their own controlling software, which makes it difficult to adapt them to different tasks. Sometimes it is not possible to use a multi-purpose language like BASIC with them at all. Unless you want your machine to slavishly play pre-programmed sounds, it is much more fun to be able to experiment with your own composing programmes and have the possibility of also adding graphics and text, for example.

Some powerful add-on synthesizers are now appearing, which can be easily interfaced to the BBC computer. Welcome as they are, there are still limitless possibilities for creating interesting music with the BBC computer just as it stands.

Enhancing the BBC computer's sound output

One slight modification worth doing is to feed the computer's sound output into a separate amplifier and speakers. Suitable modifications have been published in various user-magazines, but these are best carried out by those competent in electronics and usually risk invalidating your purchaser's warranty. One possibility is to buy a kit, such as the MICROVOC marketed by MICROADVENT. This enables the sound output to be routed via a jack socket to two external speakers. It includes a useful control knob for the volume level which can be fitted on to the back of the computer, and of course, the jack socket can be used to feed the sound into an amplifier, tape recorder, or any other studio device.

When larger speakers are linked to the computer, bass sounds tend to come into their own. Although the resulting sound is "bigger" and better there is a disadvantage. Unwanted bass interference, which may not be noticeable on the small internal speaker, will make itself brazenly conspicuous on large speakers.

Even if you do not want to make modifications, it may be worthwhile to open the machine to adjust the volume control which is hidden inside. Before removing the lid make sure that the power is turned off and all leads disconnected. The four fixing screws for the lid are situated two at the back, and two at the front by the rubber feet. You will find the tiny device which controls the speaker volume underneath the back of the keyboard, roughly below the red f0 and f1 keys. It looks like this drawing.

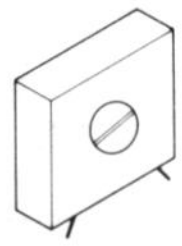

With a long thin screwdriver gently turn the small screw fully clockwise.

After replacing the lid and switching on the power, the easiest way to make a sound to check the volume is to press CTRL and G at the same time. If there is no response your volume control must work in reverse. (Machines do vary, and it may be anticlockwise on yours.) Repeat the operation, this time turning the screw fully *anti*clockwise.

2

Tuning up

the SOUND statement: coding tunes

Sound commands

In the BBC BASIC programming language there are two special commands for producing and controlling sounds. These commands are SOUND and ENVELOPE.

The SOUND command is used to instruct the computer to play a note. The ENVELOPE command is used to give it information about the way to change the sound quality of the notes. Each command is followed by some numbers, separated by commas, which are used to give the computer information about the sound required. The SOUND command is followed by four numbers. For example, it might look like this:

```
SOUND 1,-15,97,10
```

In a command of this sort the numbers are known as **parameters**. The ENVELOPE command has 14 different parameters which makes it a little more complicated. Its use is explained in more detail later on (see Chapter 8). We start by looking at the simple SOUND statement.

The SOUND statement

We will use different letters to refer to each of the four parameters following the SOUND command to help us remember what each one controls. The SOUND command, then, will have this form:

```
SOUND C,V,P,D
```

where C stands for channel number
V stands for volume
P stands for pitch
D stands for duration

channel number This can be 0, 1, 2 or 3. It is possible to use up to three channels of sound at the same time. This means that three-note chords may be used or music with up to three different simultaneous streams may be played. We often refer to these separate musical strands as **voices**.

Channels 1, 2 and 3 produce pitched musical notes. Channel 0 produces noise and is useful for making bangs, crashes and whooshy sounds for games, and for imitating percussion instruments like drums and cymbals. Chapter 11 expands on ways of using this noise channel. For now we will just use channels 1, 2 and 3.

For many of the programs in this book only one voice or channel is needed. We would usually use channel 1, then move on to 2 and 3 when we need to add other simultaneous parts.

volume This can range from 0 (silence) up to −15 (loudest). It seems odd that we have to put a minus sign in front of the number here. The reason is that this second parameter can also be used to specify an envelope if required. Envelopes are referred to with positive numbers: 1, 2, 3 etc.

Usually we will want maximum volume, so this parameter will nearly always be equal to −15. Notice that to our ears these values do not appear to go down in even steps. There will seem to be a bigger difference between −15 and −14 than between −7 and −6. The words **amplitude** or **intensity** are often used by musicians when referring to volume.

pitch This means how high or how low the notes are. The pitch value may be between 0 and 255. Higher pitched notes have higher pitch values, lower notes have lower pitch values. (This may seem obvious but it is not the case with sound generators on all computers.)

Musicians scale note-pitches using tones and semitones. A semitone is the smallest gap between two notes, for example the pitch gap between a white note and its black note neighbour on the piano. A tone is twice as big as a semitone.

Some of the adjacent white notes on the piano are separated by tones and some by semitones depending on whether a black note sits in between them or not. The smallest gap between pitches on the BBC computer is one-quarter of a semitone, or one-eighth of a tone. This means that to play notes corresponding to the semitone steps our ears expect, we have to count up in fours. This figure shows how the notes on the stave correspond to the pitch numbers used in the computer's SOUND command.

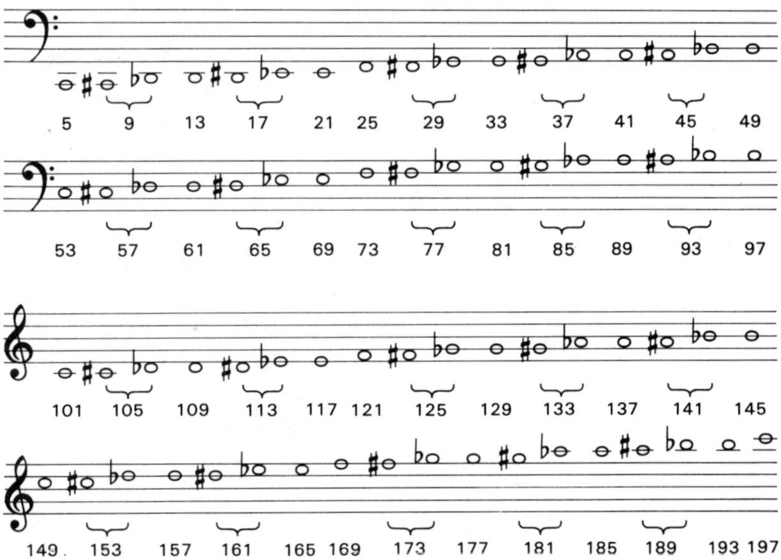

This chart gives the same information, but in terms of letter names:

	Octave			
note	**lower**	**lower-middle**	**upper-middle**	**upper**
C	5	53	101	149
C# or D♭	9	57	105	153
D	13	61	109	157
D# or E♭	17	65	113	161
E	21	69	117	165

(continued overleaf)

(chart continued)

note	Octave lower	lower-middle	upper-middle	upper
F	25	73	121	169
F# or G♭	29	77	125	173
G	33	81	129	177
G# or A♭	37	85	133	181
A	41	89	137	185
A# or B♭	45	93	141	189
B	49	97	145	193

It is even possible to pitch out-of-tune notes. Thus middle C has a pitch value of 101. A pitch value of 100 will give a slightly flat middle C.

Remember that the pitch values in these lists actually give notes one octave higher than proper "concert" pitch (like a descant recorder). It is reasonable to adopt this convention since it makes better use of the range of pitches used in most music.

duration

The duration value can range from 1 to 255 and represents how long the note is to last in twentieths of a second. A duration value of 20 will produce a note lasting one second; a value of 100 will give a note lasting five seconds. There is one special case: a duration value of 255 will give a note lasting for ever, unless you switch the computer off or take steps to stop it.

Musicians do not usually measure note lengths in fractional parts of a second, but in the traditional notation of quavers, crotchets, minims and semibreves (known in the USA as eighth-notes, quarter-notes, half-notes and whole-notes respectively). Their relationships are shown by this table:

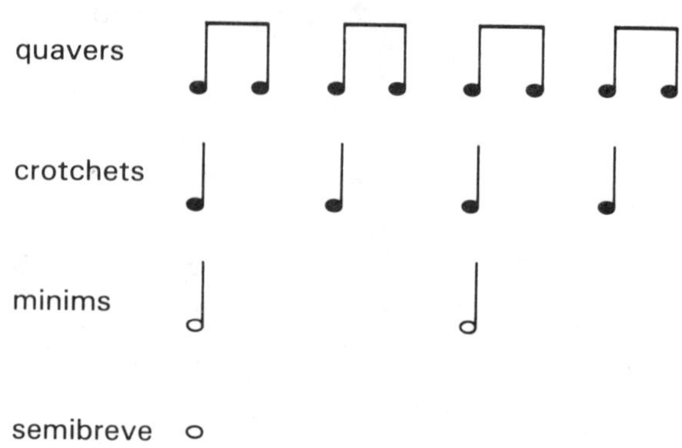

Since these notes represent proportional relationships their actual durations will depend on the tempo of the piece. At a fast tempo there may be eight quavers to a second, at a slow tempo there may be only two. A reasonable value to use for a quaver is 4. This has the advantage of being easily divided up for time units less than a quaver, such as a semiquaver.

This table of suitable values includes dotted notes. (A dotted note is equivalent in length to one-and-a-half times the original note.)

semiquaver	𝅘𝅥𝅯		2
quaver	𝅘𝅥𝅮		4
dotted quaver	𝅘𝅥𝅮.	(= 𝅘𝅥𝅮 + 𝅘𝅥𝅯)	6
crotchet	𝅘𝅥		8
dotted crotchet	𝅘𝅥.	(= 𝅘𝅥 + 𝅘𝅥𝅮)	12
minim	𝅗𝅥		16
dotted minim	𝅗𝅥.	(= 𝅗𝅥 + 𝅘𝅥)	24
semibreve	𝅝		32

If you prefer a slower tempo you could use 3 for a semiquaver, 6 for a quaver, and so on. If a piece contains nothing smaller than a crotchet there is no reason why you should not use an odd value like 9 or 11 for it. The important thing is to decide what the value of the shortest note is going to be and then double it for the other main values consistently.

Here then is a typical SOUND statement:

SOUND 1, – 15,101,32

channel 1 : maximum volume : middle C : about 1½ seconds long

which will produce this note:

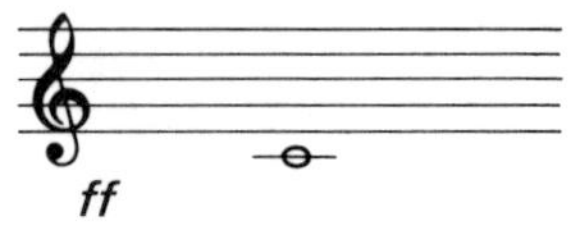

and another:

SOUND 1, – 7,45,12

channel 1 : softer volume : low B♭ : about ½ second long

which will produce this note:

This statement will play the highest note:

SOUND 1, – 15,255,100

and this the lowest:

SOUND 1, – 15,0,100

Type them in (press RETURN at the end of each line) so that you can hear the result.

Coding a simple tune

To get the computer to play a tune we can write a short BASIC program consisting of SOUND statements. The lines in a BASIC program are usually numbered in tens. The computer will work through the program is sequence doing what each line instructs. In this case each line will make it play one note of the tune.

We will begin with the theme that is always used to announce the villain in a spoof Victorian melodrama:

When coded into SOUND statements this becomes:

```
10 SOUND 1,-15,109,12
20 SOUND 1,-15,117,4
30 SOUND 1,-15,121,8
40 SOUND 1,-15,109,8
50 SOUND 1,-15,133,32
```

Notice that these lines are very similar. You can use the editing (arrow) keys and the copy key to speed up the process of typing them in.

Once you have typed the program in (pressing RETURN at the end of each line) type RUN to hear it work.

If you prefer it a little slower, we can make a quaver equal to 6, so that a crotchet will become 12 and a semibreve 48. We can also change the volume levels in each line to make it start softly and gradually get louder:

```
10 SOUND 1,-7,109,18
20 SOUND 1,-9,117,6
30 SOUND 1,-11,121,12
40 SOUND 1,-13,109,12
50 SOUND 1,-15,133,48
```

Here is another, slightly longer tune. It is the beginning of the Christmas Carol *We Three Kings of Orient are*:

(If you are not very familiar with music notation, notice that the seventh note is the same as the fifth. The # applies to them both.)

```
10 SOUND 1,-15,145,16
20 SOUND 1,-15,137,8
30 SOUND 1,-15,129,16
```

```
40 SOUND 1,-15,117,8
50 SOUND 1,-15,125,8
60 SOUND 1,-15,129,8
70 SOUND 1,-15,125,8
80 SOUND 1,-15,117,24
```

The second phrase of *We Three Kings* is exactly the same as this first phrase. If we add this line:

```
90 GOTO 10
```

then when the program reaches the end, it will jump back to the beginning of the program and repeat the tune. The only problem is that it will keep on repeating it indefinitely; it does not know when to call a halt. You will have to press ESCAPE to stop it.

Riffs and rests

A small group of notes repeated over and over again is known in jazz as a **riff**. Riffs are also the basis of much contemporary pop music. Since they do not get bored, computers are ideal machines for producing endlessly repeated riffs (remember *We Three Kings*). Here is a common riff pattern:

which when coded becomes:

```
10 SOUND 1,-15,33,12
20 SOUND 1,-15,33,4
30 SOUND 1,-15,49,8
40 SOUND 1,-15,61,8
50 GOTO 10
```

Run this program and listen to it carefully. What do you notice? According to the music and the program there should be four notes being repeated, but you can only hear three. The first two notes have become merged into one. The second note begins immediately the first one ends and because they both have the same pitch it is impossible to distinguish between them. We could solve this problem by using an envelope but there is an alternative solution which saves us worrying about envelopes for the time being. All we need to do is to introduce a gap or rest between the two notes, like this:

becomes

We replace the dotted crotchet with a crotchet followed by a quaver rest. They will still be equal in total time value, and the notes will still start in the same place which is what is important in recognizing a rhythm.

To code a rest into the program we simply use a SOUND statement with zero volume. The pitch value used in the statement is immaterial, since the note is not heard. Any value will do, but using 0 helps to identify its rest status. Changing the program, line 10 will become:

```
10 SOUND 1,-15,33,8
```

and we will slip an extra line in between 10 and 20 for the quaver rest. This will be line 15:

```
15 SOUND 1,0,0,4
```

(You now see why we began numbering lines in tens. It allows us the freedom to add extra lines if required. If you are not familiar with the computer, notice that all you have to do is type in the revised or additional lines and the computer will automatically replace the old ones and slip new lines into position.)

The full program will now look like this:

```
10 SOUND 1,-15,33,8
15 SOUND 1,0,0,4
20 SOUND 1,-15,33,4
30 SOUND 1,-15,49,8
40 SOUND 1,-15,61,8
50 GOTO 10
```

Here is another riff pattern; it starts with a rest this time:

```
10 SOUND 1,0,0,4
20 SOUND 1,-15,129,4
30 SOUND 1,-15,145,4
40 SOUND 1,-15,129,4
50 SOUND 1,-15,149,4
60 SOUND 1,-15,145,4
70 SOUND 1,-15,129,4
80 SOUND 1,-15,109,4
90 GOTO 10
```

Using a duration variable

If we decide that the riff just programmed needs to be a little slower it is rather tedious to have to go through every line of the program changing each 4 to a 5, say. All we need do is replace the duration value at the end of each SOUND statement with a variable, instead of a fixed number. The letter D is a suitable variable name for duration. We then allocate a value to D at the start of the program. Whenever the computer comes across a D in the program it will look in its memory to see what its current value is, and use that value in obeying the command. We give D its value at the beginning of the program simply by stating D=5, or whatever value we require. So the program becomes:

```
5  D=5
10 SOUND 1,0,0,D
20 SOUND 1,-15,129,D
30 SOUND 1,-15,145,D
40 SOUND 1,-15,129,D
50 SOUND 1,-15,149,D
60 SOUND 1,-15,145,D
70 SOUND 1,-15,129,D
80 SOUND 1,-15,109,D
90 GOTO 10
```

If we now want to speed up the riff we just change line 5:

```
5 D=3
```

Experiment with different values of D. If D=1 it becomes so fast that the riff is no longer a short melody but a repeated wobbly splodge of sound.

Look back at the first riff again. It is not quite as easy to adapt this one in the same way since there are two different note lengths being used. If we are using D to represent the length of a quaver, then a crotchet, which is twice as long, will be represented by D*2. (Notice that computers use a star * to represent multiplication.) Substituting D and D*2 into the program gives us:

```
5  D=4
10 SOUND 1,-15,33,D*2
15 SOUND 1,0,0,D
20 SOUND 1,-15,33,D
30 SOUND 1,-15,49,D*2
40 SOUND 1,-15,61,D*2
50 GOTO 10
```

Loops

As they stand, these riffs repeat indefinitely, but it is not difficult to make them do a fixed number of repeats. We use a programming loop, which looks something like this:

```
FOR I=1 TO 8
       :
(rest of program)
       :
NEXT I
```

In this case, whatever is inside the loop between the FOR . . . and NEXT . . . lines will be repeated eight times.

This is how it works. When the computer reaches the line:

```
FOR I=1 TO 8
```

it recognizes the start of a loop. It sets the variable I equal to 1 and then goes on and does the intervening lines of the program until it reaches the line:

```
NEXT I
```

which is the end of the loop. At that point it makes I one bigger and hops back to the FOR . . . line at the beginning of the loop. Here it checks to see if I has gone past the upper limit (8 in this case). If not the computer keeps repeating the loop, making I one bigger each time until it reaches the limit. At that point, realizing that the loop has been done the required number of times, the computer leaves it and carries on to the next line (or finishes, if it is the end of the program).

To make the first riff repeat eight times we top and tail the sound statements with the appropriate loop statements:

```
5  D=4
7  FOR I=1 TO 8                          loop starts here
10 SOUND 1,-15,33,D*2
15 SOUND 1,0,0,D
20 SOUND 1,-15,33,D
30 SOUND 1,-15,49,D*2
40 SOUND 1,-15,61,D*2
50 NEXT I                                and ends here
```

Here is another fragment of music:

It consists of two alternating low notes a semitone apart repeated many times. The two notes are:

```
SOUND 1,-10,5,6
SOUND 1,-10,9,6
```

To make them repeat, say 16 times, we would use a loop like this:

```
10 FOR I=1 TO 16
20 SOUND 1,-10,5,6
30 SOUND 1,-10,9,6
40 NEXT I
```

The sound this makes should bear a faint resemblance to part of the background music to the film *Jaws*.

READ and DATA statements

You will have noticed in the programs which we have encountered so far that most of each line is the same. We usually have:

```
SOUND 1,-15,
```

followed by two numbers, the pitch and the duration, which change for each note. We can save ourselves having to type this in for every note we use, and make the coding more efficient by using a loop and two other BASIC commands, READ and DATA.

READ is used to instruct the program to look at a list of numbers, called the data, and give a value from that list to whatever variable is specified after the READ command.

DATA is used to identify the list of numbers which are being read by the READ command.

We have already used the variable D to stand for the duration of a note, in addition we will use the variable P to stand for the pitch value. Here is a simple example:

```
10 READ P,D
20 SOUND 1,-15,P,D
30 DATA 97,40
```

Line 10 instructs the computer to look at the first number in the DATA statement and give that value to P, then to look at the next number and give that value to D. Proceeding to line 20 it will then make the sound with whatever values of P and D it has just read.

The DATA statement can go anywhere in the program, though it is usual to put it at the end of the program lines which make use of it. The numbers in the DATA statement should be separated by commas.

Now look at the *We Three Kings* program once again. It contains eight notes. We can set up a loop which will do the READ and SOUND commands eight times:

```
10 FOR I=1 TO 8
20 READ P,D
30 SOUND 1,-15,P,D
40 NEXT I
```

Then all the pitch and duration values can be put one after the other in a DATA statement at the end:

```
50 DATA 145,16,137,8,129,16,117,8,125,8,129,8,125,8,
        117,24
```

As the program runs it will work through the numbers in the DATA statement two at a time reading them as pitch and duration values each time the SOUND statement is obeyed. If for any reason there are not enough numbers in the data list and the computer attempts to read a number which is not there, it will come up with an "out of data" error. If, on the other hand, there are more numbers than needed the extra ones will just be ignored.

Courante

With a longer tune the advantage of using loops and data statements is more obvious, especially if the durations are the same throughout. In such a case only the pitch changes for each note. An example of an interesting "classical" piece where all the notes have the same duration is the opening of the *Courante* from J. S. Bach's *Third Suite* for solo cello:

Except for the last one, all the notes are quavers so we need only set the duration once at the beginning. We can use a READ and DATA loop for the first 43 notes, and then tag the last note on at the end with an extra SOUND statement of its own:

```
10  D=4
20  FOR I=1 TO 43
30  READ P
40  SOUND 1,-15,P,D
50  NEXT I
60  DATA 101,101,81,69,53,33,21,5,101
70  DATA 109,101,97,101,109,97,81,61
80  DATA 49,33,25,109,101,97,89,81
90  DATA 101,97,89,81,73,69,73,61,33
100 DATA 89,81,73,69,61,53,49,53,33
110 SOUND 1,-15,5,D*3
```

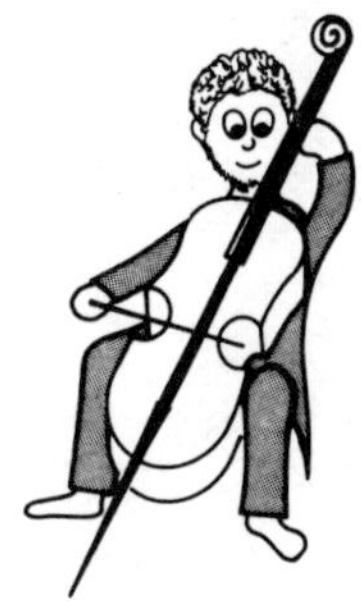

There is quite a lot of data here. It looks neater if it is broken up over a number of program lines, each beginning with the DATA command.

Notice that if you try to put GOTO 10 at the end to make the music repeat, you will be rewarded with an "out of data" message. The computer does not know that when it returns to the start of the program it must also return to the start of the data. It will try to read the next number after the end of the data list and, of course, find nothing there. To rectify this we can use another command RESTORE which tells the computer to start reading data from the beginning again. To make the music repeat *ad infinitum* we can add these two lines:

```
130 RESTORE
140 GOTO 10
```

As before, you can experiment with setting different values of D in line 10 to change the speed.

Introducing envelopes

The quality and interest of the sounds being made can be improved by using envelopes. The ENVELOPE command is dealt with more fully in Chapter 8, but it is quite possible to use envelopes without needing to know how or why they work. We just need to put an extra line at the beginning of a program like this:

```
5 ENVELOPE 1,1,0,0,0,0,0,0,40,-1,-1,-1,126,100
```

You do not need to understand what this does; just remember that it works.

Now wherever −15 occurs, showing the volume level in a SOUND command, replace it with a 1 which tells it to use envelope number 1 (which we just defined in line 5) instead.

To improve the sound of the *Courante* program above, in addition to adding line 5, we must change line 40 to:

```
40 SOUND 1,1,P,D
```

Try substituting 1 for −15 in some of the earlier programs and see what difference it makes.

(Incidentally, once you have defined an envelope in one program, if you type in, or load, a different program without an envelope definition, even if you press BREAK, the computer will still remember the old envelope. You do not have to define it again unless you switch the machine off.)

We can use the envelope to play this familiar riff as an endless loop. It is the opening of Mike Oldfield's *Tubular Bells*:

```
10  ENVELOPE 1,1,0,0,0,0,0,0,40,-1,-1,-1,126,100
20  D=4
30  FOR I=1 TO 30
```

```
40  READ P
50  SOUND 1,1,P,D
60  NEXT I
70  DATA 117,137,117,145,117,129,137,117
80  DATA 149,117,157,117,145,149,117
90  DATA 137,117,145,117,129,137,117
100 DATA 149,117,157,117,145,149,117,145
110 RESTORE 70
120 GOTO 30
```

Notice the symmetry and repetition in this music. It can be used to code the music more efficiently, as we will see in later chapters.

Sailor's Hornpipe

The *Sailor's Hornpipe* is another good tune which works well on the computer. It was designed as a single melody line without accompaniment and so is effective when we are just using one voice.

This piece is a mixture of crotchets and quavers, so it is not quite as easy to deal with as was the *Courante*. But we can still save ourselves the labour of specifying two numbers, pitch and duration, for each note. You can see that the crotchets and quavers come in alternating groups. At the beginning there are two quavers followed by three crotchets, followed by ten quavers, and so on. The groups have been marked in the music above. If we can get the computer to recognize them, then it can do a quaver group with constant durations, then a crotchet group with a different duration constant, and then go back to keep repeating alternating quaver/crotchet groups. We can tell the computer how many notes there are in each group by putting the number in as an extra data item before the pitch values. It is simpler and reduces the likelihood of making mistakes if we use a separate line of data for each group. The data statements will start off looking like this:

```
120 DATA 2,149,145
130 DATA 3,149,101,101
140 DATA 10,129,121,117,129,149,145,149,165,157,
         149
150 DATA 3,157,109,109
       :
       etc.
```

When we come to write the program to read these values and make the required sounds, we have to put in an extra line which will read the number of notes in that group. Starting with quavers, we can call the variable used to store the number of quavers in the group NQ:

```
10 READ NQ
```

The value of NQ is then used as the upper limit of the loop, so that it reads in all of the pitch values which come after it in the line of DATA:

```
20 FOR 1=1 TO NQ
30 READ P
40 SOUND 1,1,P,4
50 NEXT I
```

The first time, this loop will only be done twice, but you can see that a little later there is a much longer run of 26 quavers.

Next we come to crotchets. We will use NC to stand for the number of crotchets. The program will read in this value and then, as before, go on to read in the equivalent number of crotchet pitch values which follow it in the data statement. This time a crotchet duration value of 8 appears at the end of the SOUND statement instead of the quaver loop's value of 4:

```
60  READ NC
70  FOR I=1 TO NC
80  READ P
90  SOUND 1,1,P,8
100 NEXT I
```

After that the program is instructed to go back to the beginning ready to tackle the next group of quavers:

```
110 GOTO 10
```

There is one remaining problem. How does the computer know when it has reached the end? If we leave things as they are the computer will print an "out of data" message when it discovers that there are no more numbers for it to use. This may not worry you as long as the program works, but it is rather untidy. To get round this we can put in a dummy value of 0 to identify a non-existent group of quavers at the end of the data. At the start of the program we can then add a test to see if the end of the data has been reached by checking to see if NQ is equal to 0:

```
15 IF NQ=0 THEN END
```

This line uses a new BASIC command: IF . . . THEN. The computer will check to see if NQ is equal to 0 and end the program if it is. If not, it will just carry on.

It is important to use an envelope in this program so that neighbouring notes of the same pitch will be heard separately. We have already used 1 instead of −15 in the SOUND statements listed above. It only remains to add an envelope definition at the beginning. The standard envelope introduced in the previous section will do:

```
5  ENVELOPE 1,1,0,0,0,0,0,0,40,-1,-1,-1,126,100
```

As we did before, we can also use a duration variable D at the end of the SOUND statements to allow us to change the speed easily if we want. It must be set at the beginning:

```
7  D=4
```

and the SOUND statements changed to:

```
40 SOUND 1,1,P,D
90 SOUND 1,1,P,D*2
```

Here then is a listing of the *Sailor's Hornpipe* program with the complete set of data:

```
  5 ENVELOPE 1,1,0,0,0,0,0,0,40,-1,-1,-1,126,100
  7 D=4
 10 READ NQ
 15 IF NQ=0 THEN END
 20 FOR I=1 TO NQ
 30 READ P
 40 SOUND 1,1,P,D
 50 NEXT I
 60 READ NC
 70 FOR I=1 TO NC
 80 READ P
 90 SOUND 1,1,P,D*2
100 NEXT I
110 GOTO 10
120 DATA 2,149,145
130 DATA 3,149,101,101
140 DATA 10,129,121,117,129,149,145,149,165,157,
         149
150 DATA 3,157,109,109
160 DATA 4,109,101,97,109
170 DATA 2,129,129
180 DATA 26,137,145,149,145,137,129,137,129,121,
         117,121,117,109,101,101,97,89,81,89,101,
         97,109,101,117,109,121
190 DATA 3,117,101,101,
200 DATA 10,129,121,117,129,149,129,117,129,149,
         129
```

```
210 DATA 3,137,121,121
220 DATA 10,137,129,125,137,157,137,125,137,
         157,137
230 DATA 4,145,129,129,117
240 DATA 24,121,117,121,129,137,129,121,117,121,
         117,109,101,101,97,89,81,89,101,97,109,
         101,117, 109,121
250 DATA 3,117,101,101
260 DATA 0
```

More tune ideas

You should now be in a position to encode a wide variety of different tunes. Those which were originally designed as solo pieces without accompaniment work best, and those with long repeated groups of similar note durations involve the least labour to program. Good sources of melodies are books of Scottish fiddle and pipe tunes. The *Irish Washerwoman* works well:

For the more serious minded Bach's unaccompanied suites for cello and violin are good sources. The Prelude from the 3rd violin partita in E major is quite well known and has long passages in even semiquavers.

Most music involves much repetition. By identifying the repetitions in a piece, encoding can become even more efficient, as we will see in later chapters.

Chords and music in two parts

To sound a chord, a different pitch value can be sent to each of the three sound channels. This short program will produce a chord containing the notes C, B♭ and E:

```
10 SOUND 1,-15,53,20
20 SOUND 2,-15,93,20
30 SOUND 3,-15,117,20
```

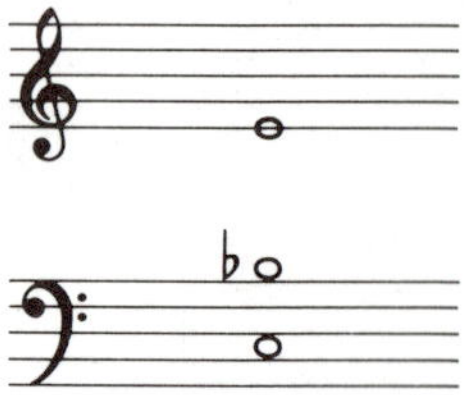

Even though the SOUND statements appear one after the other in the program, they begin to sound as fast as the computer takes to send the instruction to each sound channel in turn. That happens almost immediately, and so the notes are heard as a single chord.

To program music in two or three simultaneous voices involves quite complicated problems of co-ordination. It is necessary to match up the durations in each stream of notes with care.

Each SOUND channel has a buffer which can store up to four notes at a time. This means that in a program up to four notes can be specified for one channel before needing to go on and specify the notes for another channel which are to be sounded at the same time. Examples of music using two or three channels appear in later chapters. As a simple demonstration to conclude this chapter, we can make the two riffs we used earlier sound simultaneously, simply by listing one set of notes after the other. Conveniently, they both have the same length, equivalent to eight quavers, or a semibreve. The first riff will be played on channel 1. For the second riff, channel 2 will be used:

```
10  ENVELOPE 1,1,0,0,0,0,0,0,40,-1,-1,-1,126,100
20  SOUND 1,1,33,12
30  SOUND 1,1,33,4
40  SOUND 1,1,49,8
50  SOUND 1,1,61,8
60  SOUND 2,0,0,4
70  SOUND 2,1,129,4
80  SOUND 2,1,145,4
```

```
90  SOUND 2,1,129,4
100 SOUND 2,1,149,4
110 SOUND 2,1,145,4
120 SOUND 2,1,129,4
130 SOUND 2,1,109,4
140 GOTO 20
```

You can experiment to see what happens if the lengths of each riff do not match up. For example, try removing line 60. With the channels out of synchronization, the buffers juggle the notes about for a while, but eventually manage to settle down into a repeated pattern.

A similar effect will occur if different note lengths are specified in the three-note chord we first used above:

```
5  ENVELOPE 1,1,0,0,0,0,0,0,40,-1,-1,-1,126,100
10 SOUND 1,1,53,18
20 SOUND 2,1,93,20
30 SOUND 3,1,117,22
40 GOTO 10
```

This sounds rather like church bells on a Sunday morning in Salzburg. Some more creative uses of repeated simultaneous riffs of different lengths are explored in Chapter 15.

3 Random selection

using random numbers to generate sounds and music

Random numbers

In the previous chapter we saw how the computer could be used to play simple tunes when they are coded in the form of a BASIC program. The computer can also be used to make decisions about what sounds are to be produced; in other words to have a hand in composing the music. In later chapters we will see how it can produce some quite interesting results if programmed with the right idea. To start, we look at some short, simple programs which show how the computer can be used to produce continuously differing output.

We will be making use of **random numbers**, using an expression which looks like this:

```
RND(N)
```

Whenever the computer comes across this expression it will think of a number, at random, between 1 and N inclusive.

The expression RND(6) will simulate a dice throw. It could deliver any number between 1 and 6. RND(2) is like the toss of a coin. It could produce a 1 or a 2. (This gives us a useful way of making the computer choose between two alternative options.)

So what has this to do with music? We can use random numbers to stand for parameter and control values in SOUND statements and see, or rather hear, what happens. Some quite interesting effects can be produced. Random numbers are a way of producing variety with comparatively little effort. The computer takes its first, hesitant steps in thinking and being creative!

Random pitch and duration

We will begin by making the pitch random. The pitch value can be anything between 1 and 255, so we can put RND(255) in at the appropriate place in the SOUND statement:

```
10 SOUND 1,-15,RND(255),4
```

Each time this command is carried out, and a sound is made, a different pitch will be produced. Adding an extra line will make it cycle indefinitely:

```
20 GOTO 10
```

(Press ESCAPE to stop it.)

If we shorten the duration to 1 a bubbly effect is produced:

```
10 SOUND, 1,-15,RND(255),1
20 GOTO 10
```

This is rather like the voice of a little robot we could call Solar Teedo. We will meet him again later.

We can also make the note durations random, although it is rather tedious waiting for the next note to appear if we choose anything longer than 30. We will use RND(30) in the duration position which will give us random numbers between 1 and 30:

```
10 SOUND 1,-15,RND(255),RND(30)
```

This gives the result a curious, disorienting rhythm. But music is built up from more than just durations; it needs a beat or metre. Using such a large range of durations makes it difficult to listen to. A more interesting result is achieved by limiting ourselves to just two durations, quaver and crotchet: a 4 and an 8. We can let the computer choose between one and the other. This is programmed using RND(2). By itself it will produce a 1 or a 2, so multiplying whatever it gives by 4 means that we end up with 4 or 8:

```
10 SOUND 1,–15,RND(255),RND(2)*4
```

This produces a more reasonable rhythm and is easier to listen to. It will generate rhythmic patterns which look like this in conventional notation:

. . . etc.

Over a period of time there should be a roughly equal number of crotchets and quavers. It is possible to build in a bias to one or the other; we will consider biased probabilities later. As before, the speed can be altered by changing the 4 to a 6, say, or some other suitable value.

Limiting the pitch range

We can limit the pitch range within which the random notes are generated. For example, we could make the pitches stay within the boundaries of the top and bottom notes of the double stave from bottom F (25) to top G (177):

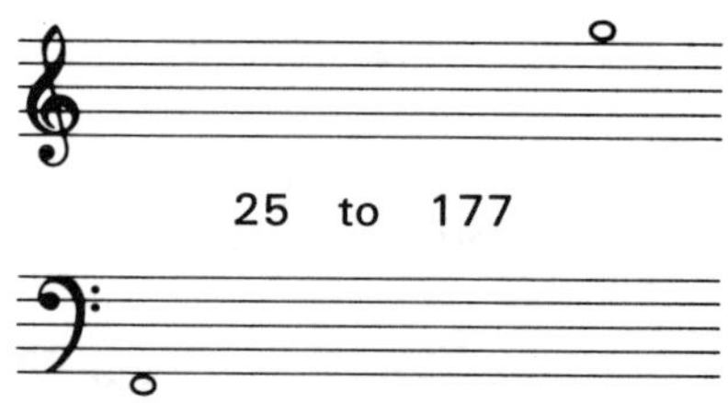

Using RND(177) would give us numbers between 1 and 177, but we want numbers no lower than 25. The difference between these two limits is 152. If we set 24 as the bottom limit then add a random number to it between 1 and 152, we get the required range:

```
24+RND(152)
```

Incorporated into the SOUND statement it becomes:

```
10 SOUND 1,–15,24+RND(152),RND(2)*4
20 GOTO 10
```

If you listen to the result you should hear that we have chopped off the top and bottom ends of the range.

So far, we have been hitting not only all the musical notes in the range, but also all the microtones that lie in between them. You remember from Chapter 2 that the pitch values come in eighth tone steps. To make our pitches land on even semitones, to correspond to the usual set of musical pitches, all the pitch values must be multiples of 4.

We can treat the pitch values here as we treated the duration values before. There are 39 notes between our chosen limits. We choose one at random:

```
RND(39)
```

multiply it by 4 so that it is on an even semitone step:

```
RND(39)*4
```

then add 21 to make the smallest possible value be equal to 25 (which happens when RND(39)=1):

```
21+RND(39)*4
```

A quick calculation will verify that the largest possible value will be 39*4+21 which is 177.

The complete SOUND statement will then be:

```
10 SOUND 1,-15,21+RND(39)*4,RND(2)*4
20 GOTO 10
```

We are now producing sounds which fall on precise, chromatic notes. Represented in conventional notation a typical output might look something like this:

As with durations, given long enough we would expect all notes to be equally represented. In the short term, though, you will notice if you listen carefully that it is not unusual for the same note to be repeated alternating, perhaps, with another one:

It is an interesting exercise in aural concentration to listen out for these patterns.

Monkeys and arrows

You may know the story of the monkeys and the typewriters. The theory is that if you sit enough monkeys at enough typewriters and leave them for a sufficiently long time (a few centuries or so) you will eventually find amongst all the worthless output the complete works of William Shakespeare. This assumes that the monkeys type at random and do not, for example, insist on repeating their favourite key. Replace the monkeys with a fast, reliable computer and maybe Shakespeare will appear more quickly.

This may sound rather dubious but the analogy is that if you generate enough random sounds with our random note program you may end up with a theme from, say, a Beethoven symphony. The greater the number of restrictions that are designed into a program to limit or direct the notes produced, the more likely we are to achieve a result sounding like a familiar tune. You will see this, for example, in some of the melodies generated in Chapter 6.

As far as pitches are concerned, we began by allowing ourselves complete freedom over the pitch-value range. Using random numbers to choose from this range can be likened to shooting arrows at it evenly:

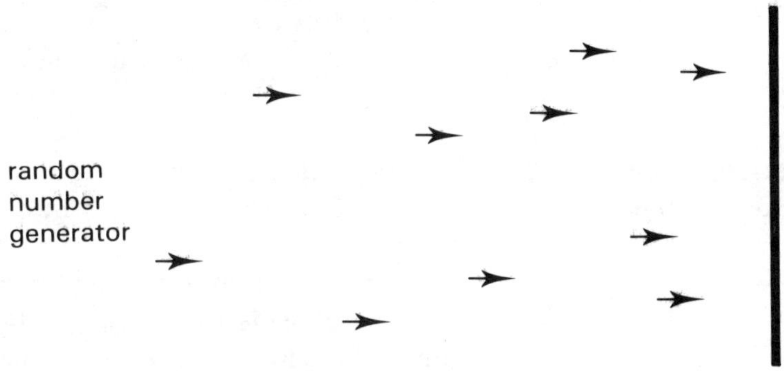

When we reduced the pitch range we chopped the ends off the target:

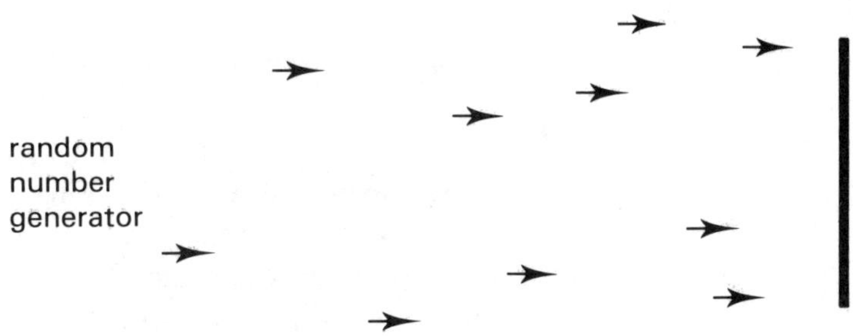

Then selecting multiples of 4 was rather like sticking small wedges on to the target to force the arrows into the valleys between them:

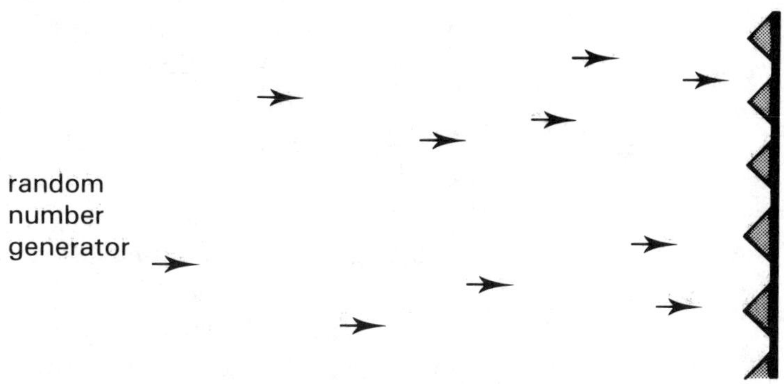

Mathematicians use the word **stochastic** to describe this idea of starting with completely random numbers and then introducing some sort of pattern or shape on to the result by controlling the randomness. It comes from an ancient greek archery term for **target**, hence our arrow diagrams above. The random numbers, like the arrows, are directed or shaped to fit a particular target or aim. One of the first to use this term for music was the composer Xenakis, who was also one of the first to compose with the help of a computer, in 1962.

Random volume and channels

Having randomized pitch and duration, we can then also randomize the volume. We will choose a random value between 1 and 15, and still keep the minus sign in front of the number chosen. (It is important that the minus sign does not appear inside the bracket as RND(−15) does something quite different. Try it and see what happens.)

```
10 SOUND 1,-RND(15),RND(180),RND(10)
20 GOTO 10
```

Notice that we have changed the other limits as well for variety.

It is usually very difficult for a composer to achieve precise control over volume. With pitch and duration he can give quite specific instructions, but with volume it is all relative. It is up to the performer how he interprets the markings in the music. With a computer, of course, much greater accuracy is possible, but since our ears are not at all used to such fine nuances in volume it may be wasted on them.

We have randomized three of the four parameters so it only remains to randomize the channel number as well. We can choose between channels 1, 2 and 3:

```
10 SOUND RND(3),-RND(15),RND(180),RND(30)
20 GOTO 10
```

You might expect a sound to be generated from each channel in turn. For example, a note from Channel 1, followed by one from channel 3, then from 1 again, then perhaps 2, and so on. If each channel waited until the note had been played on the previous channel it would sound as if just one channel were being used, since all the sounds come from the same loudspeaker. Instead, as soon as a note has started on one channel, the next channel begins its note, so that they overlap. This gives a pleasing three-voice sound texture which is rather more interesting to listen to than the single lines we had before.

To try and control three channels in a more sophisticated way can become quite tricky. This is considered in more depth in later chapters. This simple example gives us some idea of how the channels sound if doing different things simultaneously and sorting out their own queuing and buffering problems.

Pietro Grossi, one of the pioneers of computer music in Italy, heads a research group in Pisa. It has been rumoured that the only music he now listens to is authentic randomly-generated sounds, similar to those we have just been making, anything else being too "predictable". This sounds like the ultimate in computer music snobbery but I suspect the report is exaggerated.

By choosing pitch values that are multiples of 8 we can make the notes generated fall on even whole-tones:

```
10 SOUND RND(3),-15,RND(20)*8,RND(2)*2
20 GOTO 10
```

This produces a result rather like some of the music written by the French composer, Debussy, who often used notes from the whole-tone scale.

Solar Teedo: random loops

You remember the little robot sounds which we made at the beginning of the chapter. They came in a continuous stream which only stopped when the program was interrupted. For a more authentic Solar Teedo "voice" we need to break the sound up into smaller bursts of bubbly notes separated by silences. We can do this using a loop, like those introduced in Chapter 2:

```
10 FOR I=1 TO 35
20 SOUND 1,-15,RND(255),1
30 NEXT I
```

This will produce a sequence of 35 random pitches; and we then follow it with a short silence:

```
40 SOUND 1,0,0,40
```

and go back to repeat it over again:

```
50 GOTO 10
```

This produces very regular blocks of bubbly sound. To improve the effect we should make the durations of the blocks, and of the gaps in between, of random length. We can replace the loop limit, 35 in this case, with a random value and give the silence at line 40 a random value as well:

```
10 FOR I=1 TO RND(50)
20 SOUND 1,-15,RND(255),1
30 NEXT I
40 SOUND 1,0,0,RND(60)
50 GOTO 10
```

You can experiment with the limits to produce short bursts of sound with long silences:

```
10 FOR I=1 TO RND(10)
          :
40 SOUND 1,0,0,RND(90)
```

which sounds like Solar Teedo in a sulky mood—or long bursts of sound alternating with short silences:

```
10 FOR I=1 TO RND(90)
          :
40 SOUND 1,0,0,RND(10)
```

which sounds like Solar Teedo in an exuberant mood.

It is possible to set a variable in the program to represent Teedo's mood, and then use its value to make the required lengths of sound and silence. We will call the mood variable M and let it take values between 1 and 100. The higher the value of M, the more exuberant Teedo becomes.

If the sound loop is done M times:

```
10 FOR I=1 TO M
```

then we will make the silence last for a duration value of 100−M:

```
40 SOUND 1,0,0,RND(100−M)
```

Here is the complete amended program with line 5 added to set an initial value for M:

```
5  M=50
10 FOR I=1 TO M
20 SOUND 1,−15,RND(255),1
30 NEXT I
40 SOUND 1,0,0,RND(100−M)
50 GOTO 10
```

We can make the program rather more interesting by making the pitch values also depend on M. When M is smaller, we would like a lower range of pitches. When M is larger we would like a higher range of pitches. If we use:

```
M+RND(155)
```

for pitch values, then when M is at its maximum, that is 100, the pitches will be between 100 and 255. When M is at a minimum, that is 1, then pitches will be between 1 and 156; and it will cover appropriate ranges in between. So, line 20 will be replaced with:

```
20 SOUND 1,−15,M+RND(155),1
```

Finally, we can even make the mood depend on a random choice:

```
5  M=RND(100)
10 FOR I=1 TO M
20 SOUND 1,−15,M+RND(155),1
30 NEXT I
40 SOUND 1,0,0,RND(100−M)
50 GOTO 10
```

Using an INPUT command

Rather than changing line 5 each time we want to vary the mood, we can use an INPUT statement. When the program comes across an INPUT statement in a program, it will stop, print a question mark on the screen, and wait for the user to type in a number (followed by RETURN). Whatever value is typed in at that point will be allocated to the variable name which followed the INPUT command. So, if the program line is:

```
5 INPUT M
```

When it reaches line 5 the computer will print:

```
?
```

If you type in 67 at that point, then M will be given the value 67.

In this form the program is fine if you are using it for your own benefit; but what if someone else wants to use the program? If they are not sure what it does and are faced with a bald question mark, they have no way of knowing whether the computer is expecting a single or a six-digit number.

Whenever a program expects a response from the user, it is a good idea to print on the screen an explanation of what the program does and what sort of responses are expected. This can often make the program rather long, but it is a fairly routine task. We need to use a PRINT command followed by whatever we want to print in inverted commas. These lines would print some appropriate instructions for our Solar Teedo program:

```
30  PRINT "SOLAR TEEDO SOUND ALIKE"
40  PRINT "----- ----- ----- -----"
50  PRINT "Type in a number between 0 and 100 to
          represent"
60  PRINT "Solar Teedo's mood, then press RETURN"
70  PRINT
80  PRINT "These values are examples of the mood
          range:"
90  PRINT "0 dead"
100 PRINT "1 struggling"
```

```
110 PRINT "10  sullen"
120 PRINT "20  sulking"
130 PRINT "30  off-hand"
140 PRINT "40  reserved"
150 PRINT "50  contented"
160 PRINT "60  happy"
170 PRINT "70  cheerful"
180 PRINT "80  jolly"
190 PRINT "90  exuberant"
200 PRINT "100 ecstatic"
```

Note that line 40 has the effect of underlining the title, and line 70 prints a blank line.

It is best to clear the screen first before printing. This is done with the command:

```
20 CLS
```

We have now used up line numbers less than 50, so the rest of the program will need to be renumbered to fit at the end:

```
240 INPUT M
250 FOR I=1 TO M
260 SOUND 1,-15,M+RND(155),1
270 NEXT I
280 SOUND 1,0,0,RND(100-M)
290 GOTO 250
```

If the program is run in this form, then each time we want a different mood it is necessary to first interupt the program with ESCAPE, then type RUN followed by RETURN and finally input another value. However, if we make use of another BBC BASIC command which can be put at the start of the program:

```
10 ON ERROR GOTO 20
```

then whenever ESCAPE is pressed, instead of stopping the program the computer will jump to line 20 (or whatever line number happened to be specified) and continue with the program from there. In this case it means that pressing ESCAPE will interupt whatever sound is being produced and straightaway set the computer up ready to receive the next "mood" number. We can add an extra line at the end of the instructions to explain this:

```
210 PRINT
220 PRINT "Press ESCAPE to finish"
230 PRINT
```

The only problem with this method is that you now have to use BREAK to exit the program completely. You can then type OLD to recover the program if you want to correct or develop it. Notice also that once you have put this ON ERROR command into a program, any mistake you make will not be reported and the program may act very strangely!

Here then is the complete program:

```
10  ON ERROR GOTO 20
20  CLS
30  PRINT "SOLAR TEEDO SOUND ALIKE"
40  PRINT "_ _ _ _ _ _ _ _ _ _ _ _ _ _ _ _ _ _ _ _ _"
50  PRINT "Type in a number between 0 and 100 to
          represent"
60  PRINT "Solar Teedo's mood, then press RETURN"
70  PRINT
80  PRINT "These values are examples of the mood
          range:"
90  PRINT "0 dead"
100 PRINT "1    struggling"
110 PRINT "10   sullen"
120 PRINT "20   sulking"
130 PRINT "30   off-hand"
140 PRINT "40   reserved"
150 PRINT "50   contented"
160 PRINT "60   happy"
170 PRINT "70   cheerful"
180 PRINT "80   jolly"
190 PRINT "90   exuberant"
200 PRINT "100 ecstatic"
210 PRINT
220 PRINT "Press ESCAPE to finish"
230 PRINT
240 INPUT M
250 FOR I=1 TO M
```

```
260 SOUND 1,-15,M+RND(155),1
270 NEXT I
280 SOUND 1,0,0,RND(100-M)
290 GOTO 250
```

Using the loop variable inside a loop

It is possible to use the loop variable (I in the examples we have had so far) inside the loop. As the value steps up one at a time, it can make something else go up a step at a time. For example it could be **pitch**:

```
10 FOR I=1 TO 255
20 SOUND 1,-15,I,2
30 NEXT I
```

This short program will run quickly through all the pitch values starting at 1 and going up to 255.

To make it clearer what is being controlled, we do not always have to use the letter I for the loop variable. If we are changing pitch, P would be an appropriate choice.

There is also no reason why we have to start the loop at 1. We could start with a higher value and move through pitches in a smaller range. For example:

```
10 FOR P=101 TO 149
20 SOUND 1,-15,P,2
30 NEXT P
```

will play all the pitch values from middle C to the octave above.

We could also use the loop variable to control **duration:**

```
10 FOR D=2 TO 20
20 SOUND 1,-15,RND(255),D
30 NEXT D
```

This produces a succession of random pitches with gradually lengthening durations giving the impression of slowing down.

Finally, we can use the loop variable to control volume. This program makes a sequence of random pitches which reduce in volume and produces quite an interesting effect:

```
10 FOR V= -15 TO 0
20 SOUND 1,V,RND(255), 1
30 NEXT V
40 GOTO 10
```

Notice that in line 10, V starts off as a negative quantity, −15, and then counts up one at a time: −14, −13 . . . etc. until it reaches −1 and finally 0. When substituted in line 20 it has the effect of reducing the volume by one step, each time a new note is played.

This chapter has shown just a few of the simple possibilities for using the random number function to make sounds. Many of the ideas can be combined with each other and similar patterns explored. Later chapters show how more complex musical ideas can be assembled from these building blocks when they are linked and controlled by appropriate programming logic.

4 Steps and glissandi

Stepping up and down

In Chapter 3 we saw how loops could be used to move through a sequence of rising pitch values, like this:

```
10 FOR P=101 TO 149
20 SOUND 1,-15,P,2
30 NEXT P
```

As it stands this will move through each pitch value one by one. If we wanted to make it move through a sequence of pitches separated by even semitones, in other words to produce a chromatic scale, we need to pick out only every fourth pitch value. We can do this by specifying a STEP size at the end of the FOR . . . TO command like this:

```
10 FOR P=101 TO 149 STEP 4
```

which makes P go up through the sequence 101,105,109 . . . etc. and so play a chromatic scale from middle C to the C above:

We can use a negative step size to make the sequence go down:

```
10 FOR P=149 TO 101 STEP -4
```

This will reduce the value of P by 4 each time and so give us a descending chromatic scale:

We cannot use this technique to make the computer produce a standard major scale, all the white notes in sequence for example, since the step size keeps changing. (It is necessary to store a series of values in advance and then choose from them; this is explained in Chapter 5.) However, it is easy to generate a sequence of notes separated by tones, that is a step size of 8:

```
10 FOR P=53 TO 149 STEP 8
20 SOUND 1,-15,P,3
30 NEXT P
```

In conventional music notation it would look like this:

This is the same whole-tone scale, arranged in ascending order, from which notes were chosen to make the Debussy-like music in Chapter 3. When the notes come as a straight scale, as here, the sound is like that often heard introducing the appearance of a conjurer or magician on TV. Because the whole-tone scale ambiguously drifts between different keys it produces a strange air of mystery.

Random limits

We can use random limits on these loops. There are a number of possibilities. We could have a random lower note to a fixed higher note:

```
10 FOR P=RND(149) TO 149 STEP 4
20 SOUND 1,-15,P,3
30 NEXT P
40 GOTO 10
```

which gives us a series of musical stalactites:

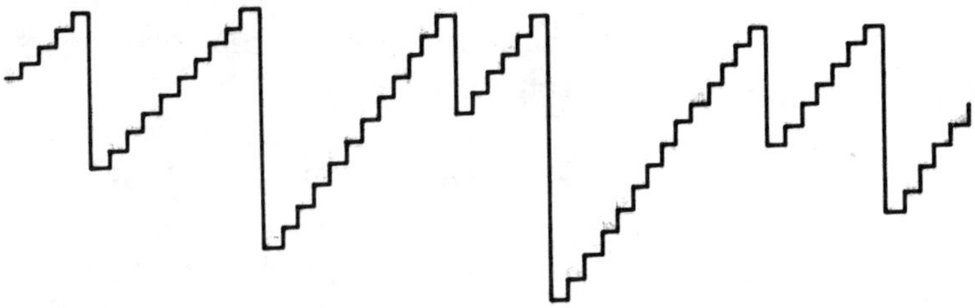

or alternatively a fixed lower note to a random higher note:

```
10 FOR P=101 TO 101+RND(48) STEP 4
```

which generates musical stalagmites, or a series of saw-tooth fins with a different number of notes ascending from middle C each time:

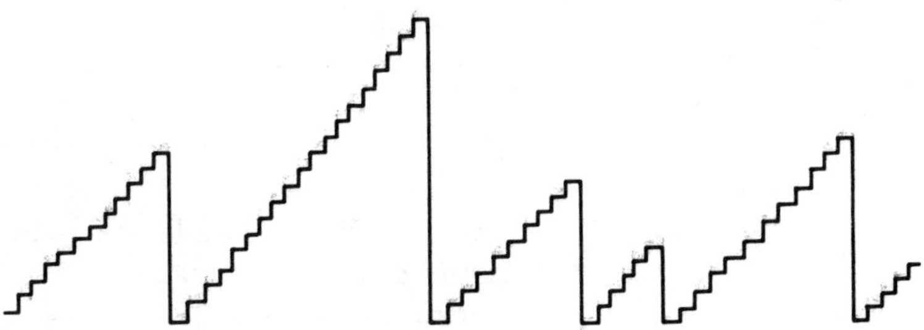

In conventional music notation it would look something like this:

We can even use a random step size if we want. It works best if we avoid the smallest step sizes, less than 4. Here we will get a step size between 5 and 55:

```
10 FOR P=1 TO 255 STEP 5+RND(50)
20 SOUND 1,-15,P,2
30 NEXT P
40 GOTO 10
```

If we want to choose random lower and upper limits at the same time we have to work out their values first in order to avoid having an upper limit that proves to be lower than the lower limit! If the computer was faced with this command:

```
FOR P=100 TO 50 STEP 4
```

It would first check to see if the upper limit for P of 50 had been reached, discover it had (since P=100 at the start) and so end up doing nothing. It is not clever enough to deduce that perhaps you wanted it to go down with a step size of −4. So first we choose the lower limit. We can call it L:

```
10 L=RND(255)
```

After which we want the upper limit, which we can call H, to lie between the value of L and 255:

```
1. . . . . . . . . . . . L . . . . . . . . . . . . 255
                                  ↑
                           H somewhere here
```

There are 255-L possible values for it to take, so if we generate a random number between 1 and 255-L, and then add it to the value of L, it will end up inside the required limit:

```
20 H=L+RND(255-L)
```

The values of L and H can then be put in appropriate positions in the FOR . . . TO loop:

```
10 L=RND(255)
20 H=L+RND(255-L)
30 FOR P=L TO H STEP 4
40 SOUND 1,-15,P,2
50 NEXT P
60 GOTO 10
```

This program will keep doing random snippets of the chromatic scale. Diagrammatically the result could be represented something like this:

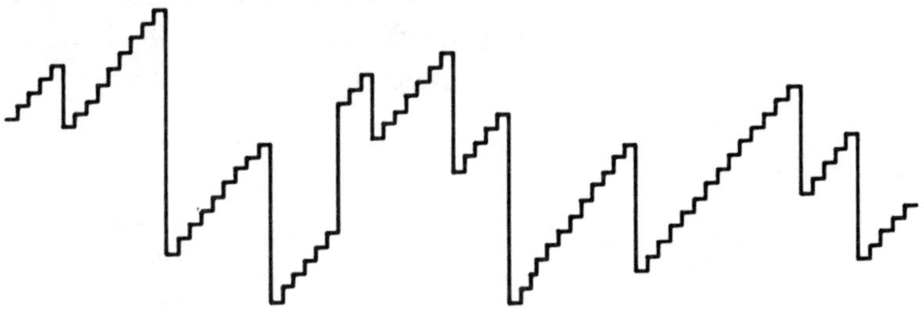

Looping the loop

It is possible to put loops inside other loops. For example, we could make a sequence of short chromatic scales with the starting note, or root, a few steps higher each time. The first loop will increase the root of each scale segment. We can use a step size of 12 (one-and-a-half tones) to move the root up each time:

```
10 FOR R=1 TO 100 STEP 12
```

This will make the root proceed through the sequence 1,13,25 . . . etc. Another loop will make use of the current value of R as its starting point, and then step by semitones up to, say, an octave above R to make the actual notes:

```
20 FOR P=R TO R+48 STEP 4
30 SOUND 1,-15,P,2
40 NEXT P
```

We then close off the R loop with its matching NEXT statement:

```
50 NEXT R
```

This is how the complete program looks:

```
┌─10 FOR R=1 to 100 STEP 12
│┌20 FOR P=R to R+48 STEP 4
││ 30 SOUND 1,-15,P,2
│└40 NEXT P
└─50 NEXT R
  60 GOTO 10
```

We say that the P-loop is nested inside the R-loop. In the listing above the brackets show how they relate. Diagrammatically the sound output of the program could be represented like this:

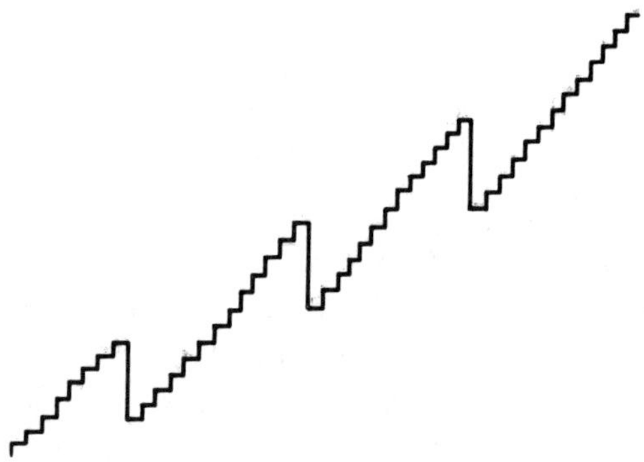

In a similar way we could program cascades of falling musical waterfalls by stepping down descending scales. This time we have used the variable T for the top of the scale which steps down, and have used a shorter note duration:

```
10 FOR T=200 TO 100 STEP -12
20 FOR P=T TO T-48 STEP -4
30 SOUND 1,-15,P,1
40 NEXT P
50 NEXT T
60 GOTO 10
```

In diagrammatic form the output could be drawn:

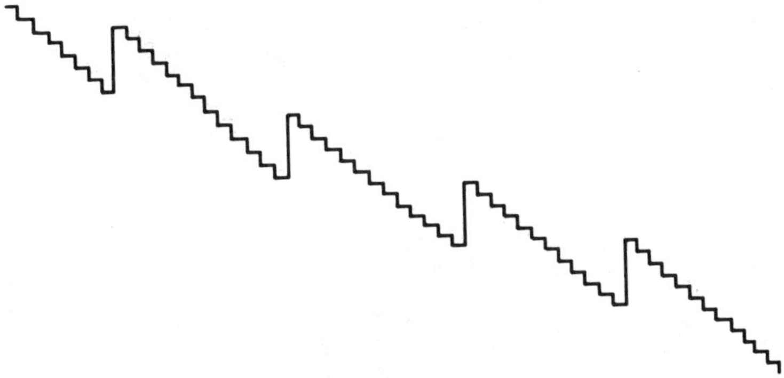

You can experiment with different limits and step sizes in these programs.

So far we have only used loops to control the pitch. We could also use an additional loop to control the volume, for example, and make a revolving scale pattern get softer with each repetition. Here is the "conjurer's" whole tone scale which we had before with its limits adjusted slightly and lines renumbered:

```
20 FOR P=100 TO 200 STEP 8
30 SOUND 1,-15,P,1
40 NEXT P
```

We can now construct a loop and use it to change the volume a step at a time. The volume-loop variable, V, will also need to be incorporated into the SOUND statement at line 30:

```
10 FOR V=-15 TO 0
20 FOR P=100 TO 200 STEP 8
30 SOUND 1,V,P,1
40 NEXT P
50 NEXT V
```

The first time the scale is played the volume V will be at its maximum, −15. The next time it will be a step softer at −14, and so on until it reaches silence. This is quite an interesting and useful effect.

Glissandi

Some of the sounds we have been making in this chapter are examples of what musicians call **glissandi** (from an Italianized French word meaning **slides**). A **glissando** is when a group of notes in ascending or descending sequence are played so quickly that the individual elements merge into one continuous movement. On a piano, dragging the back of a finger up the white notes or across the bare strings will produce a glissando effect. With the voice, or instruments like the violin, trombone and swanee-whistle (a pipe with a plunger that moves in and out) it is possible to get proper glissandi which slide through all intervening pitches as well, in a continuous, smooth motion. It is quite hard for musicians to produce well-controlled glissandi, though some modern composers use them frequently in their music. On a computer, glissandi present no problems.

The speed of the glissandi we have been making so far has been limited by the length of the shortest duration value we can use in the SOUND statement, which is 1. But we can get even shorter notes, and so make faster glissandi. If these two characters:

```
&1
```

are inserted immediately in front of the channel number, then the note specified by the SOUND statement will start straight away without waiting for the full duration of any previous note to be completed. This means that when used inside a loop the sounds will be redefined, and thus change, as fast as it takes for the program to move from line to line at its usual operating speed. The SOUND statement will then typically look like this:

```
SOUND &11,-15,P,1
```

The last duration parameter is redundant; it makes no difference what value is put there, but a 1 will do. Incorporated into a loop we could have, for example:

```
10 FOR P=1 TO 255
20 SOUND &11,-15,P,1
30 NEXT P
```

This sound sweeps swiftly through the whole pitch range.

It is worth going through some of the short programs in the earlier part of the chapter substituting &11 for the channel number in each of the SOUND statements and seeing what effect it has. It is possible to experiment with different loop limits and step sizes to produce a wide range of effects.

Using repeated glissandi of varying lengths will generate a series of warbling sounds rather like bird song. Higher pitches tend to work best:

```
10 FOR P=200 TO 200+RND(50)
20 SOUND &11,-15,P,1
30 NEXT P
40 GOTO 10
```

Varying the limits changes the overall sound quality to a different sort of bird, or to an insect-like sound:

```
10 FOR P=150 TO 150+RND(50)
```

Making the glissandi go down gives a subtly different sound which is perhaps more authentic:

```
10 FOR P=250 TO 250-RND(50) STEP -1
20 SOUND &11,-15,P,1
30 NEXT P
40 GOTO 10
```

Rampant Budgies are on the move! As before, it is possible to play around with the limits. We could try dropping up to 100 steps down:

```
10 FOR P=250 TO 250-RND(100) STEP -1
```

You could write a program, similar to the Solar Teedo mood program in the previous chapter, which enables the user to input a value specifying a bird-type. Alternatively, we can make the limits themselves subject to random choice. It will produce something like a sound-picture of a digital jungle which keeps swapping from one bird or insect to another. We need to select a starting pitch (S) at random, say between 150 and 250. We also select the maximum amount (F) for the pitch to fall:

```
10 S=150+RND(100)
20 F=RND(100)
```

The glissando loop itself needs to be repeated for a certain number of times which means putting it inside another loop. Up to 40 repeats is reasonable:

```
30 FOR I=1 TO RND(40)
```

Then comes the main glissando loop which will go from the starting pitch down to a random value below it:

```
40 FOR P=S TO S-RND(F) STEP -1
50 SOUND &11,-15,P,1
60 NEXT P
```

Finally, the outer loop is closed, and the program repeated over again, which will work out different random limits and so sound like another "bird":

```
70 NEXT I
80 GOTO 10
```

In full this "Tropical Forest" program looks like this:

```
10 S=150+RND(100)
20 F=RND(100)
30 FOR I=1 TO RND(40)
40 FOR P=S TO S-RND(F) STEP -1
50 SOUND &11,-15,P,1
60 NEXT P
70 NEXT I
80 GOTO 10
```

(You may hear the occasional hint of a distant police-car siren amongst the exotic fauna. Perhaps the forest is in Florida.)

It is possible to do a version for ascending glissandi, or perhaps to merge both types for an even more authentic sound where ascending and descending versions alternate. In the light of some of the melody programs in Chapter 2 and elsewhere in the book, I wonder whether the animals in the trees of this digital jungle have a Bach worse than their byte?

Wolf whistle

A sound well known to most of us which does, in fact, consist of glissandi is the familiar wolf whistle. It has a rising sweep followed by a short silence and then a rising and falling shape. We could represent its "pitch contour" like this:

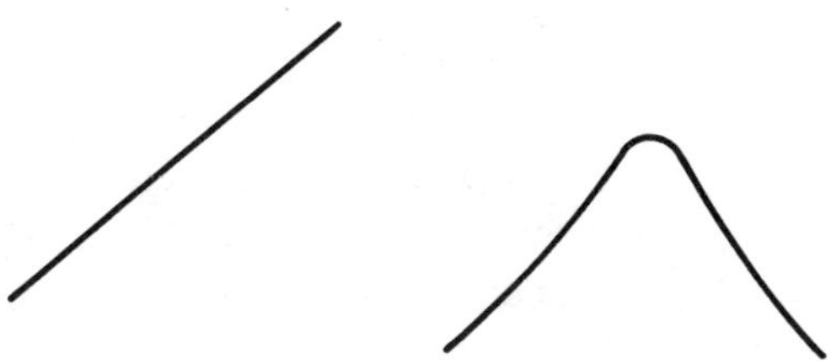

These shapes can be programmed into the computer using three glissando loops. We need to work out the pitch limits for starting and ending the glissandi. These values seem to work reasonably well:

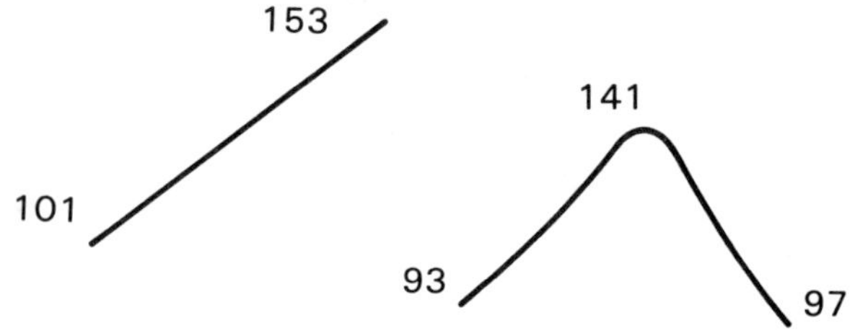

Programmed into loops we get:

```
10 FOR P=101 TO 153
20 SOUND &11,-15,P,1
30 NEXT P
40
50 FOR P=93 TO 141
60 SOUND &11,-15,P,1
70 NEXT P
80 FOR P=141 TO 97 STEP -1
90 SOUND &11,-15,P,1
100 NEXT P
```

Notice that we have left room at line 40 to specify the short rest. If, as we did for rests before, we try putting in a line like this:

```
SOUND 1,0,0,10
```

the command will appear to be ignored. This is because the &11 which appears in the next SOUND command (line 60) will make it immediately interrupt the silent "note". Instead, we can use a different technique which holds up the computer for a short time to prevent it going straight on to the next instruction.

One way of doing this is to use an INKEY command. This command is normally used to read the keyboard to see if a key has been pressed (see, for example, Chapter 9). Its value for our present purpose is that a length of time can be specified after the command, in brackets, which tells the computer how long it has to wait before carrying on if no key has been pressed. We also need to use a dummy variable which would have taken the value of the key pressed if the command had been used for its main purpose. This line will do the job and hold the computer up for a fifth of a second:

```
40 A=INKEY(20)
```

If you now run the program you will discover that the glissandi are much too fast. In order to slow it down we can use fractional step sizes in the loops. It will not make any difference to the pitches which will be rounded to the nearest whole number. For example, a step size of 0.2 will sound the same pitch value five times before going on to the next one and so the glissando loop will be five times slower. Similarly a step size of 0.5 will halve the speed, and so on. Experimenting with the wolf whistle shows that the three glissandi actually need different speeds. For the first one a step size of 0.4 seems reasonable. The second glissando needs to be slower, so a step size of 0.3 is used. The third glissando should be fast again, so here a step size of 0.5 is used. Incorporating these changes into the program it becomes:

```
10 FOR P=101 TO 153 STEP 0.4
20 SOUND &11,-15,P,1
30 NEXT P
40 A=INKEY(20)
50 FOR P=93 TO 141 STEP 0.3
60 SOUND &11,-15,P,1
70 NEXT P
80 FOR P=141 TO 97 STEP -0.5
90 SOUND &11,-15,P,1
100 NEXT P
```

A sensitive ear may still think that this is not as convincing a wolf whistle as the real thing. For increased accuracy it may need more control over the individual glissando slopes. For example, a slope could be broken into two segments with different step sizes for each, so that it starts off steeply and then levels out:

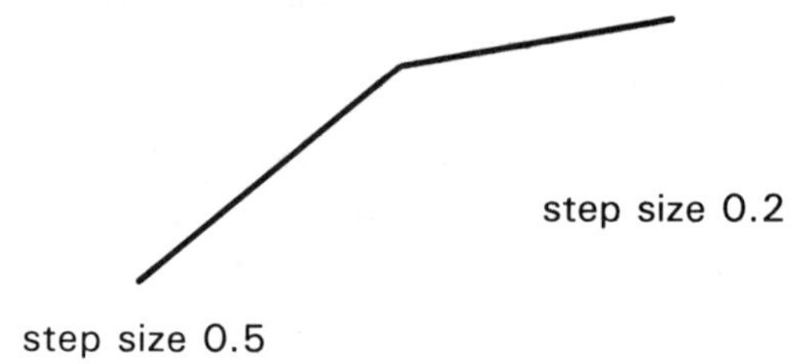

Musical mountains: plotting the sound

We have been drawing diagrams which help to show how a particular pattern of glissandi may appear to go up or down. It is not difficult to get the computer to plot on its screen (or the TV monitor) a representation of the sound being produced. We will build on some of the ideas we have developed so far to generate a sequence of up-and-down glissandi, or musical mountains, like this:

We first choose a low pitch (we will use the variable LO) and use that to choose a high pitch (HI) in the space between LO and the upper limit of 255, as we did before on p.50:

```
10 LO=RND(255)
20 HI=LO+RND(255-LO)
```

Then we have the loop for the first ascending glissando:

```
30 FOR P=LO TO HI
40 SOUND &11,-15,P,1
50 NEXT P
```

In order that the next descending glissando joins exactly on to the end of its predecessor we need to start with the last HI value and this time choose a new LO value between it and 0:

```
60 LO=RND(HI)
```

These values are then used for the descending loop:

```
70 FOR P=HI TO LO STEP -1
80 SOUND &11,-15,P,1
90 NEXT P
```

To do the next ascending part we must start with the same value of LO and choose a new HI value. Instead of returning to the very beginning of the program it cycles back to line 20:

```
100 GOTO 20
```

Here then is the sound-making part of the musical mountains program with brackets drawn in to show how the loops and sections relate:

```
10 LO=RND(255)
20 HI=LO+RND(255-LO)
30 FOR P=LO TO HI
40 SOUND & 11,-15,P,1
50 NEXT P
60 LO=RND(HI)
70 FOR P=HI TO LO STEP -1
80 SOUND &11,-15,P,1
90 NEXT P
100 GOTO 20
```

If you try running this as it stands it will go too fast to give any reasonable idea of what is happening. Once the plotting commands are added you will find that it will slow down to a more reasonable pace.

On the BBC computer we need first to make sure that the computer is in a suitable mode for doing graphics. Since we will only be plotting white on black, and we are not fussy about memory space, we can use MODE 0 which will give us the most detailed resolution. MODE 1 or MODE 4 would do just as well but there would be a slight "chunky" effect. If you especially like the chunky feel then use MODE 2 or MODE 5.

Whichever mode is being used we can refer to points on the screen using a grid 0 to 1023 points high by 0 to 1279 points across. We move to a point using the command MOVE followed by the number of points across, a comma, and then the number of points up. This command:

```
MOVE 640,512
```

will move us to the centre of the screen:

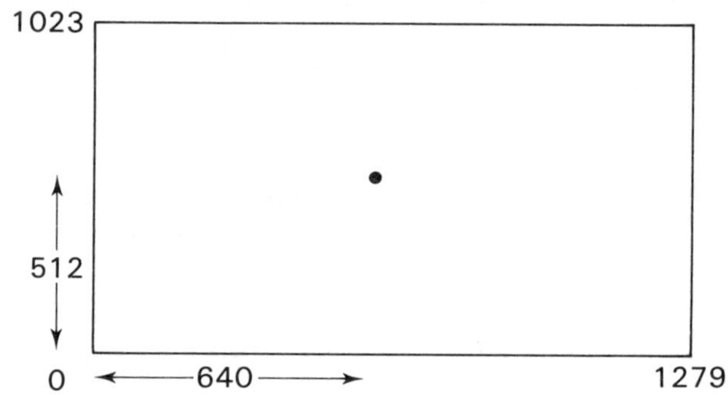

To draw a line we use the command DRAW, again followed by two numbers showing the position we wish to draw to. A line will then be drawn joining that spot to whatever point was previously moved to. Using this command after the MOVE command we just had:

```
DRAW 0,512
```

will draw a line from the centre to the left edge of the screen. Any further DRAW commands will join up to each other in a continuous chain.

We will be using movement up and down the vertical axis, from 0 to 1023, to represent the changing pitches of our sounds. Our pitch values can go up to 255. If we did a straight plot of pitch value to the screen we would only be using the bottom quarter of it. To make fuller use of the space available we can multiply each pitch value we want to plot by 4.

Moving across horizontally, from 0 to 1279, will represent the progression of the sound in time. We need to keep count of each horizontal point as we go across, then when we reach maximum, 1279, we clear the screen and start again with 0. We will use the variable X to keep count.

We start the program, then, by choosing our MODE and setting X equal to 0:

```
5 MODE 0
7 X=0
```

Once we have chosen the first LO value, as we did in line 10, we can MOVE to its equivalent point on the screen at the far left edge to start the plotting. Remember we are multiplying its value by 4 to make fuller use of the vertical range:

```
15 MOVE 0,LO*4
```

Then for each step we go through in the loop we make X one value bigger:

```
43 X=X+1
```

and draw to the pitch's equivalent point on the screen represented by 4 times the pitch value P:

```
47 DRAW X,P*4
```

The same commands need to be included in the down loop:

```
83 X=X+1
87 DRAW X,P*4
```

This will continue without any problem until X=1279. If we take no action at that point then the plotting will just continue into an invisible area off the right-hand side of the screen. To avoid that happening we need to check to see if the value of X has exceeded 1279. If it has then we can clear the screen, set X back to 0 again, and move to the current pitch position at the left of the screen ready to draw to the next point. All that is done by slipping in this extra statement between line 40 and line 50:

```
45 IF X>1279 THEN CLS:X=0:MOVE 0,P*4
```

Notice that we can include a number of different commands to be done after the THEN part of the statement by separating them with colons. These commands will only be carried out if X is greater than 1279, otherwise they will be ignored and the program will continue with the next line, line 50 in this case.

The same check will also need to be incorporated into the down loop:

```
85 IF X>1279 THEN CLS:X=0:MOVE 0,P*4
```

Here is the complete program with lines renumbered:

```
10 MODE 0
20 X=0
30 LO=RND(255)
40 MOVE 0,LO*4
50 HI=LO+RND(255-LO)
60 FOR P=LO TO HI
70 SOUND &11,-15,P,1
80 X=X+1
90 IF X>1279 THEN CLS:X=0:MOVE 0,P*4
100 DRAW X,P*4
110 NEXT P
120 LO=RND(HI)
130 FOR P=HI TO LO STEP -1
140 SOUND &11,-15,P,1
150 X=X+1
160 IF X>1279 THEN CLS:X=0:MOVE 0,P*4
170 DRAW X,P*4
180 NEXT P
190 GOTO 50
```

A variation is to omit the CLS command in lines 90 and 160 so that the screen is not cleared and subsequent mountains plot over the top of whatever was there before. The command will then look like this:

```
IF X>1279 THEN X=0:MOVE 0,P*4
```

and the resulting display will look something like this:

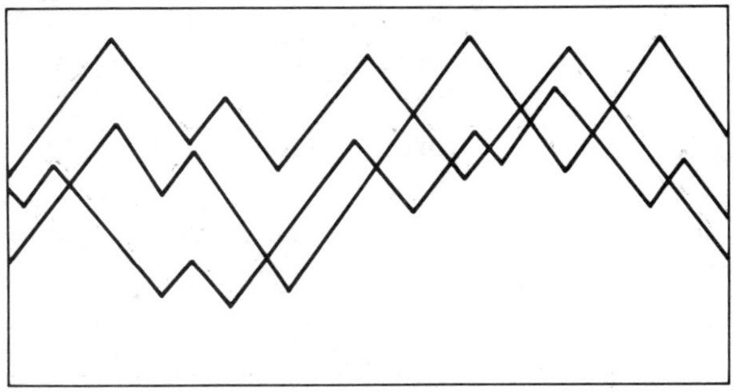

Scrolling

An alternative to plotting is to use the PRINT command. That way it is possible to make use of the screen's natural scrolling facility. Instead of plotting higher points when the sound goes higher we will print a star to the right, and then to the left when the sound goes lower, corresponding to the pitch arrangement on a piano keyboard, for example. There will be just one star on each line, and after printing the screen will automatically scroll up ready for the next line. It actually involves less alterations to the original sound-only program than the full plotting version we just developed.

We can print the star at the appropriate position on the line using the PRINT commands tabulation control. If TAB(N) is placed straight after a PRINT command, whatever needs to be printed will be positioned N places across.

If we use MODE 0 we have up to 80 columns available. As with the previous program we use the current value of P to work out how far across to go. If we divide the value of P by 3.2 then the maximum 255 will scale down to just below 80 and so fit within the column limit; the other values will adjust accordingly.

Going back to the sound-only version of the program, with its original numbering, we just need now to add these lines:

```
 5 MODE 0
45 PRINTTAB(P/3.2)"*"
85 PRINTTAB(P/3.2)"*"
```

Run in this form the program plots too fast to be of any real interest. To slow it down, so that we can more easily follow the shape of the sounds being generated, we could, say, just print a star on every eighth note. This will make it eight times slower. A simple way of identifying every eighth note is to see if the current value of P is an exact multiple of 8 and if so then print a star. This expression will do just that:

```
IF P MOD 8 = 0 THEN . . . etc.
```

The special function here, MOD (short for modulus), works out the remainder when P is divided by 8. If it is an exact multiple of 8 then the remainder will be 0. The command can be finished off by completing the action which needs to be taken in such a case:

```
45 IF P MOD 8 = 0 THEN PRINTTAB(P/3.2)"*"
85 IF P MOD 8 = 0 THEN PRINTTAB(P/3.2)"*"
```

Here is the renumbered program with scrolling commands incorporated:

```
 10 MODE 0
 20 LO=RND(255)
 30 HI=LO+RND(255-LO)
 40 FOR P=LO TO HI
 50 SOUND &11,-15,P,1
 60 IF P MOD 8 = 0 THEN PRINTTAB(P/3.2)"*"
 70 NEXT P
 80 LO=RND(HI)
 90 FOR P=HI TO LO STEP -1
100 SOUND &11,-15,P,1
110 IF P MOD 8 = 0 THEN PRINTTAB(P/3.2)"*"
120 NEXT P
130 GOTO 30
```

Glissandi in two parts

More interesting effects can be produced by using more than one sound channel. This little program makes two glissandi go simultaneously in opposite directions:

```
10 FOR P=0 TO 255
20 SOUND &11,-15,P,1
30 SOUND &12,-15,255-P,1
40 NEXT P
50 GOTO 10
```

The pitch of the first sound channel goes up from 0 to 255 as before. The pitch of the second channel needs to drop from 255 to 0. We cannot use a different loop to control that separately since these two things are to happen at the same time. All we need do is use the value 255−P for the pitch of the second channel. At the start of the loop when P is 0 this value will be 255, then as P increases the value of 255−P gets progressively less until it reaches 0 when P is at its maximum value of 255.

The effect can be represented by this diagram:

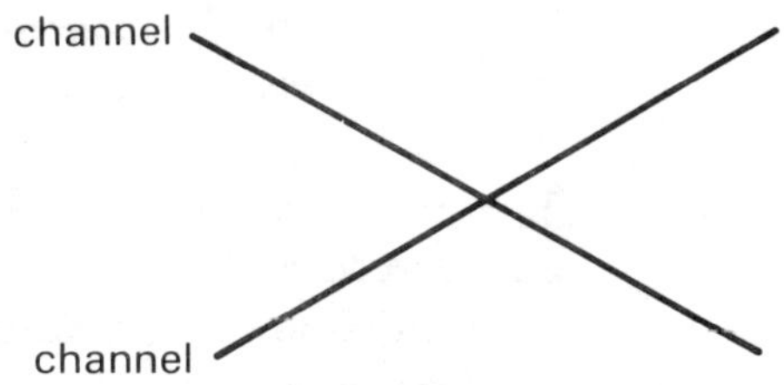

When continuously repeated the glissandi appear to link up at the ends and make a sequence of overlapping waves:

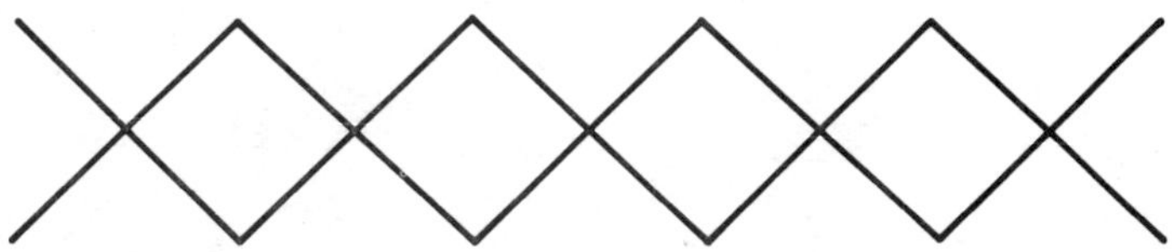

Many of the programs earlier in the chapter can be extended to work in three or more parts. It is worthwhile experimenting by adding extra lines and playing around with the loop limits.

5 Walking

random walks, beige music and fractal curves

Random walk

When selecting random pitches in previous chapters the choice of each pitch has been made independently. They may have been made to fall within certain limits but never in such a way that choosing a particular pitch influences the choice of a pitch which follows it. There is a full mathematical theory of events linked, or chained, in this way, when a particular outcome influences whatever follows. Such linked events, be they musical or otherwise, are known as **Markov Chains** after the Russian mathematician A. A. Markov who first investigated them. The idea came to him as he considered the arrangement of vowels and consonants in Pushkin's *Eugene Onegin*; the very same novel which inspired Tchaikovsky to write an opera with one of the most complicated plots ever devised.

The mathematics of Markov Chains is rather complicated, but there is a simplification we can use to good effect musically known as a **Random Walk**. We start by choosing our first note at random. For the next note we move to a neighbouring pitch, either one up or one down. It will produce a pattern something like this:

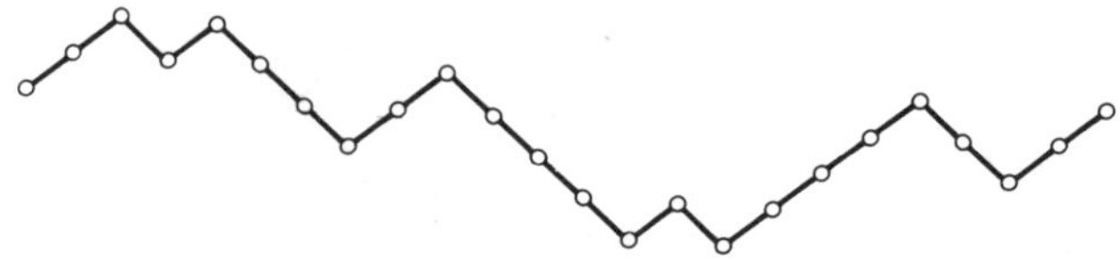

Notes wander up and down rather like a drunken man tottering backwards and forwards: hence a random walk. Another name for this type of movement is **Brownian Motion** after the Scottish botanist, Robert Brown, who in 1827 (the year Beethoven died) noticed that the individual are constantly busy doing their own random walks through space as they charge around bumping into each other. We are going to make some "molecular music".

First we choose a pitch at random:

```
10 P=RND(255)
```

Next we want to move up or down on to a neighbouring pitch value. We need to add one, or subtract one from the value of P. In other words we have to choose between two alternatives. The function RND(2) will produce a 1 or a 2. It can be used in an IF . . . THEN . . . ELSE statement to make the choice and change the value of P accordingly:

```
20 IF RND(2)=1 THEN P=P+1 ELSE P=P-1
```

If RND(2) gives a value of 1 then P is increased by 1. Otherwise (in other words when RND(2)=2), P will be reduced by 1.

Having moved on to a neighbouring pitch value, we want to hear the sound:

```
30 SOUND 1,-15,P,1
```

and then return to line 20 to keep the random walk going. Here is the program as it stands:

```
10 P=RND(255)
20 IF RND(2)=1 THEN P=P+1 ELSE P=P-1
30 SOUND 1,-15,P,1
40 GOTO 20
```

It produces a rather ghostly wail. In this form the notes are passing through neighbouring pitch values which, you will recall, are only one-eighth of a tone apart. To move the notes through semitone intervals and so move up and down a chromatic scale, we need to increase or decrease the pitch each time by 4 instead of 1, like this:

```
10 P=RND(255)
20 IF RND(2)=1 THEN P=P+4 ELSE P=P-4
```

```
30 SOUND 1,-15,P,2
40 GOTO 20
```

We have also made the note duration slightly longer. Represented in conventional notation we get an output sounding something like this:

which is rather like Rimsky Korsakov's *Flight of the Bumble Bee*.

Barriers

Usually whenever we are dealing with random walks it is necessary to take into account what happens when the pitch reaches an upper or lower limit. In this case 255 and 0 respectively.

We can have a random walk with **absorbing barriers**, which means that when a value reaches one of the limits it sticks.

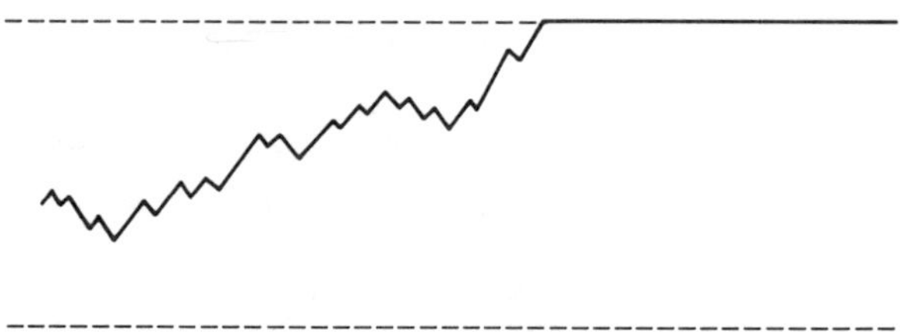

Alternatively a random walk with **reflecting barriers** means that when a value attempts to cross a limit it is reflected back into range. It will keep bouncing off the limit until the computer decides it has had enough and values start to move towards the opposite side again:

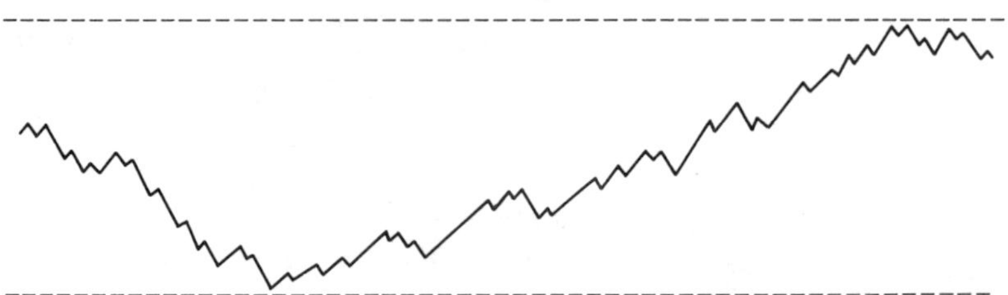

Whichever of these types of barriers is used it would normally be necessary to incorporate checks into a program to see if a pitch was over the limit, and then take appropriate action.

Because of the nature of the BBC computer's SOUND command a third option is possible: a random walk with **wrap-around barriers**. You will have discovered that when a pitch value goes above 255 it "wraps around" and re-emerges at the bottom end of the range. So 256 is heard as pitch value 0, 260 as pitch value 4, and so on. The same thing happens to values below 0 so that −1 is the same as 255, −2 as 254.

This effect means that we do not need to make any provision for recognizing barrier limits in the type of program we have been using so far. It keeps the program much neater. If, though, you do not like the way the sound may suddenly jump from one extreme to the other you can incorporate checks like this:

```
IF P>255 THEN P=255
IF P<0 THEN P=0
```

They can also be used as a way of reducing the width of the limits. This program will just wander between middle C and the C above:

```
10 P=RND(255)
20 IF RND(2)=1 THEN P=P+4 ELSE P=P-4
30 IF P>149 THEN P=149
40 IF P<101 THEN P=101
50 SOUND 1,-15,P,2
60 GOTO 20
```

Speeding things up

We can use the &1 prefix, as in Chapter 4, to make the changes occur as fast as possible. Reverting to the original pitch steps of plus and minus one gives us this result:

```
10 P=RND(255)
20 IF RND(2)=1 THEN P=P+1 ELSE P=P-1
30 SOUND &11,-15,P,1
40 GOTO 20
```

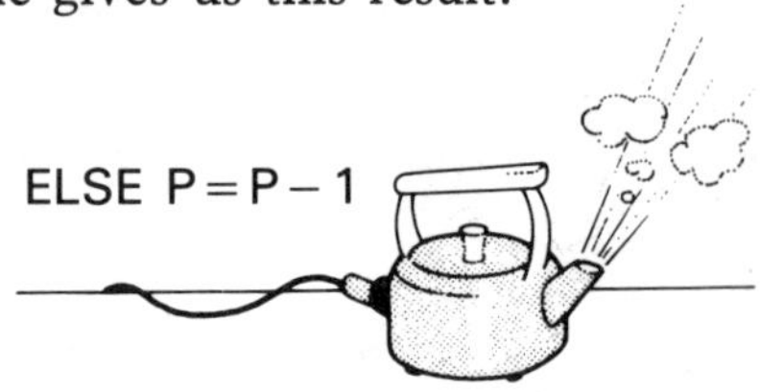

It sounds rather like a kettle on the boil. Indeed, since Brownian motion is a model of a natural process we would expect some of these sounds to have parallels in the natural world.

The overall contour of the sounds is the same as before, only now we have more detail:

Plotting the result

As with the glissandi in the previous chapter it is not too difficult to plot on screen what is happening. The same commands are added as were used before (see p.63):

```
10  MODE 0
20  X=0
30  P=RND(255)
40  MOVE 0,P*4
50  IF RND(2)=1 THEN P=P+1 ELSE P=P-1
60  X=X+1
70  IF X>1279 THEN X=0:MOVE 0,P*4
80  SOUND &11,-15,P,1
90  DRAW X,P*4
100 GOTO 50
```

Because of the way the plotting commands work the resulting picture is artificially compressed horizontally. Even though the plotting commands allow us to specify up to 1279 points across, only a half, or a quarter, of these are distinct, separate points, depending upon which mode is being used. In MODE 0, for example, positions 20 and 21 are actually the same point. In MODE 1, where the graphics resolution is not so detailed, positions 20, 21, 22 and 23 are the same. In modes 2 and 5, with lowest resolution, there are eight plotting values for each actual screen point. This means that in our program, stepping across one position at a time, which is controlled by line 60, will actually result in plotting on the same point twice. To separate the points we just need to change the amount added to X each time to 2 or 4, say:

```
60 X=X+4
```

This also has the effect of speeding up the plotting, since a line can move across the screen in a quarter of the time.

As the program stands, once plotting gets to the right edge of the screen it will go back to the left edge to continue without wiping out what is already there. This has the effect of drawing superimposed mountain outlines on the screen:

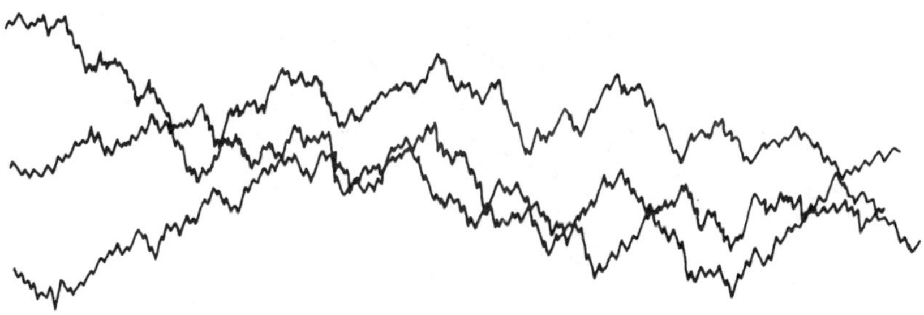

If you prefer to clear the screen each time, the command CLS can be added to line 70, as with the Mountains program in Chapter 4, but the extra time taken by the program to do this makes a click in the sound which can be distracting.

Fresh starts

A little more variety can be given to the sound by generating a sequence of undulating pitches, then starting afresh on a different source pitch for another sequence. We could, say, have sequences up to 500 steps long. We need to frame the main part of the program with a loop allowing up to 500 repetitions and then return to line 30 to choose a new value of P. Line 40 will also be adapted to MOVE to the new value of P at whatever value X happens to have at the time, rather than always starting at 0 on the far left of the screen:

```
10  MODE 0
20  X=0

30  P=RND(255)
40  MOVE X,P*4

45  FOR I=1 TO RND(500)
50  IF RND(2)=1 THEN P=P+1 ELSE P=P-1
60  X=X+4
70  IF X>1279 THEN X=0:MOVE 0,P*4
80  SOUND &11,-15,P,1
90  DRAW X,P*4
100 NEXT I

110 GOTO 30
```

The spaces between lines and brackets have been put in to help show the program structure. It will produce an output something like this:

Or if we let the program run a while to superimpose a number of outlines:

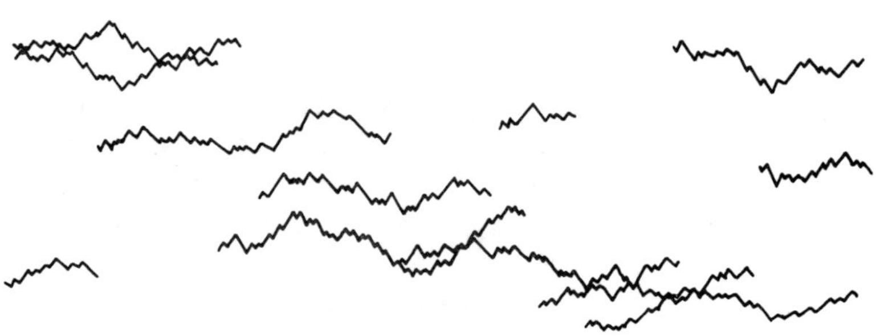

Three-part wailing

It is not too difficult to adapt the program to use all three sound channels and do random walks in three parts. We want them to move independently so we will need to use three different pitch variables P1, P2 and P3. We need to repeat every command involving P three times, substituting P1, P2 and P3 respectively. To draw three simultaneous lines on screen at the same time involves added complications, so for the time being we will return to the sound-only version of the program we had at the start. We get this result:

```
10  P1=RND(255)
20  P2=RND(255)
30  P3=RND(255)

40  FOR I=1 TO RND(500)
50  IF RND(2)=1 THEN P1=P1+1 ELSE P1=P1-1
60  IF RND(2)=1 THEN P2=P2+1 ELSE P2=P2-1
70  IF RND(2)=1 THEN P3=P3+1 ELSE P3=P3-1
80  SOUND &11,-15,P1,1
90  SOUND &12,-15,P2,1
100 SOUND &13,-15,P3,1
110 NEXT I

120 GOTO 10
```

You can make use of the ↑ and COPY keys to save re-typing every time the parts that are the same.

A rather jarring variation of this program is effected by having all three strands start on the same pitch and then go their own separate ways from there. It makes a series of pitches at closely similar frequencies cross backwards and forwards over each other. As they move in and out of tune, they generate beats; like a tuner tuning a piano but more intensely. Perhaps before running the program you should warn your neighbours.

To achieve this variation, we need to make the values of P2 and P3 at the start of the program the same as the value chosen for P1. Lines 10 to 30 will therefore be:

```
10 P1=RND(255)
20 P2=P1
30 P3=P1
```

The output will be something like this:

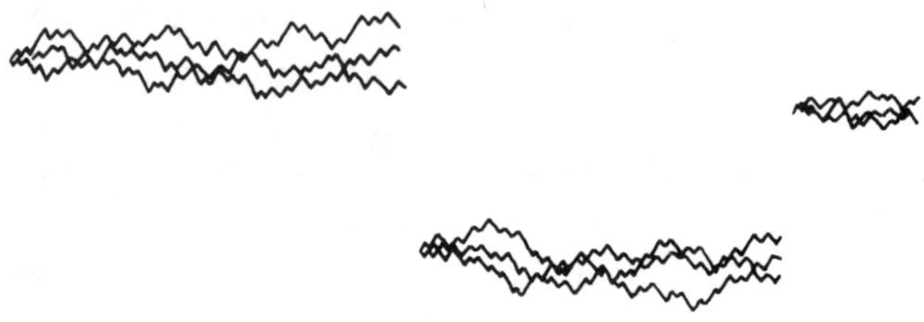

A channel array

Before trying to plot this output on the screen we will make a few modifications to the program to make the coding more efficient.

You will have noticed that many of the lines in this last program are almost identical except for the use of P1, P2 or P3. As we have done before, we can make use of a loop to save repeating the same statements many times. This time, however, since the actual name of a variable changes, as well as its values, we have to use a small **array**, which is simply a list of numbers referred to by one variable name. We will use an array to replace the three variables P1, P2 and P3; an obvious name for the array will therefore be P. P will always be followed by a number in brackets which identifies which position in the array, first, second or third, is being used at the time. The advantage of this is that another variable, I for example, can be used to refer to a position in the array. We would write P(I) in this case.

At the start of the program the BASIC language requires that the array is identified using a DIM statement which tells the program how big the array is going to be:

```
5  DIM P(3)
```

This is quite useful in helping the computer to spot mistakes. If you try to use a value which is not there, P(4) for example, the computer will remind you.

The values in the array are set at the beginning of the program as before:

```
10 P(1)=RND(255)
20 P(2)=P(1)
30 P(3)=P(1)
```

but now, when we need to change these values and use them in a SOUND statement we can use a loop which goes through each channel's pitch value in turn. Since it is the channel number which is changing we will use the letter C for the loop variable:

```
50 FOR C=1 TO 3
60 IF RND(2)=1 THEN P(C)=P(C)+1 ELSE P(C)=P(C)-1
```

Line 60 replaces the three previous lines 50, 60 and 70.

Next we need a SOUND statement. We can use P(C) for the pitch value, but also need to take into account the changing channel number in the first parameter of the SOUND statement. Instead of &11, &12 and &13 we can put &10+C. At the first step in the loop, when C=1, this value will be &10+1 which is &11 as required. Similarly on subsequent steps when C=2 and then 3 the values will become &12 and &13:

```
80 SOUND &10+C,-15,P(C),1
```

This replaces lines 80 to 100. We then close off the C-loop, giving us this result for the program so far:

```
5   DIM P(3)
10  P(1)=RND(255)
20  P(2)=P(1)
30  P(3)=P(1)

40  FOR I=1 TO RND(500)
50  FOR C=1 TO 3
60  IF RND(2)=1 THEN P(C)=P(C)+1 ELSE P(C)=P(C)-1
80  SOUND &10+C,-15,P(C),1
100 NEXT C
110 NEXT I

120 GOTO 10
```

Maps of Cornwall

Now, instead of having to add three different DRAW statements, just one will suffice, placed inside the C-loop:

```
DRAW X,P(C)*4
```

The complete program, with lines renumbered, and the same additional plotting commands incorporated as before, will look like this:

```
10  MODE 0
20  DIM P(3)
30  X=0

40  P(1)=RND(255)
50  P(2)=P(1)
60  P(3)=P(1)
70  MOVE X,P(1)*4

80  FOR I=1 TO RND(500)
90  FOR C=1 TO 3
100 IF RND(2)=1 THEN P(C)=P(C)+1 ELSE P(C)=P(C)-1
110 SOUND &10+C,-15,P(C),1
120 DRAW X,P(C)*4
130 NEXT C
140 X=X+4
150 IF X>1279 THEN X=0:MOVE 0,P*4
160 NEXT I

170 GOTO 40
```

Notice that lines 140 and 150 need to be done only once per step and so are put outside the channel loop.

Instead of drawing three separate strands this program keeps plotting from one pitch value to the pitch value of the next channel. This has the effect of filling up the gaps in between and so picks out the movement of the highest and lowest pitch values. The result ends up looking rather like a map of Cornwall:

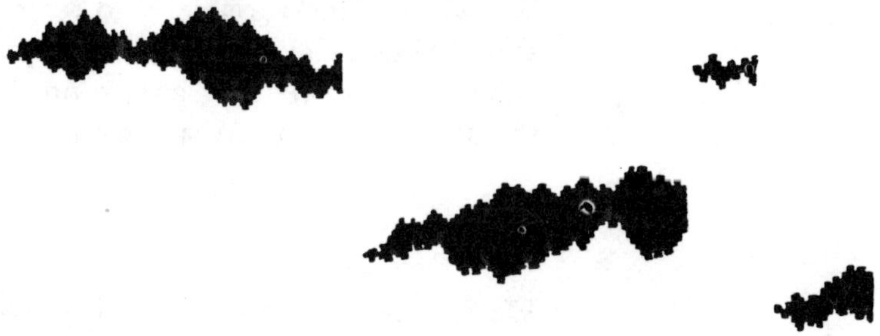

The visuals can be made more attractive by changing the colour at random each time a new source pitch is chosen. This command does the job:

```
65 GCOL 0,RND(8)
```

To get a wider spectrum of colours the mode could be changed at line 10:

```
10 MODE 2
```

This will produce a chunkier plot. Line 140 can also be changed to make it plot faster:

```
140 X=X+8
```

Stepping on scales

We will return to where we left off at p.70 when we were moving up and down the chromatic scale. It is not quite so straightforward to move up and down notes from the standard major scale (i.e. the white notes of the piano) since the gaps in between the notes change in size as they go up. We need to store in advance a set of values corresponding to the notes being used and then move up and down those values. Again we have to use an array. Since it is storing scale values we will call it SC. These 12 values cover a suitable range:

We will use the variable N to refer to the Nth note of the scale. Thus SC(1) is the first note of the scale and has the value 101, SC(2)=109, and so on. We first need to identify the array with a DIM statement:

```
10 DIM SC(12)
```

We can then use a loop which progresses through the twelve notes and reads in each scale value in turn from a DATA statement, like this:

```
20 FOR N=1 TO 12
30 READ SC(N)
40 NEXT N
50 DATA 101,109,117,121,129,137,145,149,157,165,
        169,177
```

We now have the 12 scale values stored in an array which we could represent like this:

SC() array

position number	1	2	3	4	5	6	7	8	9	10	11	12
scale value	101	109	117	121	129	137	145	149	157	165	169	177

To move up and down notes in the scale we just move up and down the position numbers and read off each position's corresponding scale value from the array. To begin we choose a note at random:

```
60 N=RND(12)
```

Then as before, move it up or down one:

```
70 IF RND(2)=1 THEN N=N+1 ELSE N=N-1
```

But when we come to the SOUND statement, instead of putting N straight into the pitch parameter position, we use it to get the required scale value from the SC array:

```
100 SOUND 1,-15,SC(N),4
```

With this version of the program we have to be careful about limits. Before, the pitch wrap-around effect took care of itself. Here, if N ends up greater than 12 or less than 0 it means that an attempt could be made to read from the 13th position in the SC array, for example, which does not exist. The program would stop and deliver a cursory error message. We need to incorporate these two lines to check the limits:

```
80 IF N> 12 THEN N=12
90 IF N< 1 THEN N=1
```

Instead of bringing the note back to stay on the limit at 12 or 0, we could make N jump back into the centre of the range, to 6 or 7, say. Or perhaps the note could be nudged back just inside the range, to 11 or to 2. It is worth experimenting with various alternatives. Here, then, is the program in full:

```
10  DIM SC(12)
20  FOR N=1 TO 12
30  READ SC(N)
40  NEXT N
50  DATA 101,109,117,121,129,137,145,149,157,165,
          169,177
60  N=RND(12)
70  IF RND(2)=1 THEN N=N+1 ELSE N=N-1
80  IF N> 12 THEN N=12
90  IF N< 1 THEN N=1
100 SOUND 1,-15,SC(N),4
110 GOTO 70
```

It will produce an output which in conventional notation would look something like this:

The rhythm can be livened up a little using the same technique as we used in Chapter 2. There are two possibilities: D for a quaver or D *2 for a crotchet duration:

```
100 SOUND 1,-15,SC(N),D*RND(2)
```

An initial value of D will need to be set at the beginning of the program to select a speed; say between 2 for a fast tempo and 5 for something a little slower:

```
5 D=3
```

A zero step

We can make use of a variant on the random walk idea to allow a note to be repeated in addition to the possibilities of moving up or down to an adjacent note. In other words, as well as moving through an interval of 1 or −1, we also have the possibility of an interval of 0.

The function RND(3) will generate three possible numbers: 1, 2 or 3. If we subtract the value of 2 from whatever number is generated then we will end up with −1, 0 or 1:

value of RND(3)	1	2	3
value of RND(3) − 2	−1	0	1

Without disturbing any program already in the computer you can verify this by typing in the single line:

```
1 PRINT RND(3)-2:GOTO 1
```

Run the program and stop it by pressing escape as usual. When you have satisfied yourself that it is doing what it is supposed to, remove the line by typing 1 and a RETURN.

Instead of needing to use the IF . . . THEN . . . ELSE statement we had before we can obtain the next value of N simply by changing line 70 to:

```
70 N=N+RND(3)-2
```

This has the effect of moving the value of N up or down by 1, or leaving it as it is when RND(3)=2 making RND(3)−2=0.

Now that we are using repeated notes we need to use an ENVELOPE so that they are heard distinctly and do not merge into one another (see p.23). This one will do:

```
7 ENVELOPE 1,1,0,0,0,0,0,0,60,–1,–1,–1,–1,126,100
```

and we will need to change the –15 in the SOUND statement to 1 as well:

```
100 SOUND 1,1,SC(N),4
```

With repeated notes a possibility, a sequence will be generated something like this:

Do you remember the monkeys and typewriters (p.36)? In theory there is a reasonable chance that this sequence could be generated:

. . . etc.

which you may recognize as a slightly disguised form of Beethoven's *Ode to Joy* from his ninth symphony.

As with our wailing sounds we could generate a random number of adjacent notes, say up to 30 of them, and then leap to a new starting note. Incorporating the extra loop to do this the program becomes:

```
5  D=3
7  ENVELOPE 1,1,0,0,0,0,0,0,60,–1,–1,–1,126,100
10 DIM SC(12)
20 FOR N=1 TO 12
30 READ SC(N)
40 NEXT N
50 DATA 101,109,117,121,129,137,145,149,157,165,
        169,177

60 N=RND(12)
65 FOR I=1 TO RND(30)
70 N=N+RND(3)–2
80 IF N>12 THEN N=12
```

```
90  IF N< 1 THEN N=1
100 SOUND 1,1,SC(N),D*RND(2)
110 NEXT I

120 GOTO 60
```

Beige music

Real tunes are not limited to simple movement only in steps; neither do they consist of unrelated pitches picked out of the blue. Whereas these alternatives represent the two extremes which we have encountered so far, the character of natural melodies lies somewhere in between.

Purely random sounds, as we discovered in Chapter 3, change so frequently that the consequent lack of perceivable pattern soon makes the result incomprehensible and boring. A type of random noise, familiar to electronic engineers, where any frequency is equally likely to occur, is known as **white noise**. Because of the relation between such noise and notes chosen at random, music generated in this way is often known as **white music**.

At the other extreme we have music generated from random walks which meanders around aimlessly. It is so relatively predictable that although tolerable in small doses, it also soon becomes boring. Because of the relationship between this music and Brownian motion some clever individual decided to coin the term **brown music**.

What would be useful is some sort of compromise between brown and white music which has a measure of predictable movement, but retains elements of random surprise. I suppose it should be called **beige music**!

We need to find some way of biasing the intervals between notes towards smaller values yet admitting the possibility of occasional larger leaps. In a sense we were doing this when we generated a short sequence of a random walk then allowed a new starting value to be chosen for another sequence. To force the bias we seek we could set up arrays of values and put complex checks into the program, but instead there is a fairly simple mathematical function we can use.

So far, we have used the random number generator RND(N) where the number inside the bracket, N, has always been greater than 1. If instead we use RND(1) then it gives us a decimal number between 0 and 1. The numbers will be evenly distributed within that range. Now if 1 is divided by a decimal value less than 1, it produces a number bigger than 1. For example, 1 divided by 0.2 is 5; dividing by 0.33 gives 3, dividing by 0.1 gives 10. This chart shows the result of dividing 1 by nine single digit decimal values with the result rounded down to the nearest whole number:

decimal value	0.9	0.8	0.7	0.6	0.5	0.4	0.3	0.2	0.1
1/decimal value	1	1	1	1	2	2	3	5	10

It is easy to see that we end up with many more 1s than other numbers, and higher numbers become progressively rarer. If we use 1/RND(1) to generate the random values we need, we discover that the larger a number is, the less likely it is to occur. We get mostly 1s, 2s slightly less often, 3s less often still, and so on, with numbers much above 10 occuring very rarely indeed.

It is possible to test this out using a simple one-line program as we did before:

```
1 PRINT 1/RND(1):GOTO 1
```

You will find that the values move up the screen quite quickly and we get numbers with many decimal places which we do not require. Type this straight in to the computer (without a line number):

```
@%=517
```

and put an extra semicolon at the end of the PRINT statement:

```
1 PRINT 1/RND(1);:GOTO 1
```

Now when you run the program again you will find the numbers arranged in a more civilized fashion and just to one decimal place. It is easy to see the bias. (Do not forget to remove the line by typing 1 when you have finished with it.)

For our purposes we will be generating intervals, or gap sizes, between notes. We want to limit ourselves to an interval of one octave, that is a gap of seven notes. Jumps bigger than this are rare in most melodies. We can incorporate a check into the program so that if a value is too big, it is ignored and another is chosen. This command will do the job:

```
REPEAT:G=1/RND(1):UNTIL G<8
```

In fact G will nearly always be less than 8 the first time and the choice will not need to be repeated. Only occasionally will G turn out to be too big making another choice necessary.

Having worked out the gap size, G, we then decide whether the movement is to be up or down. We can either use the IF . . . THEN . . . ELSE option, as we did at the beginning of the chapter, to decide whether G is added to or subtracted from the current note value N:

```
IF RND(2)=1 THEN N=N+G ELSE N=N-G
```

or else, if we allow the possibility of a note remaining unchanged which gives a different sort of melody, we can use RND(3)−2 again. The expression by itself will produce +1, 0 or −1, so if we multiply it by the value of G we will get +G, 0 or −G:

```
N=N+G*(RND(3)-2)
```

We can now incorporate these changes into our original scale stepping program (p.81) to get this result:

```
10 ENVELOPE 1,1,0,0,0,0,0,0,60,-1,-1,-1,126,100
20 D=4
30 DIM SC(12)
40 FOR N=1 TO 12
50 READ SC(N)
```

```
60  NEXT N
70  DATA 101,109,117,121,129,137,145,149,157,165,
         169,177
80  N=RND(12)
90  REPEAT:G=1/RND(1):UNTIL G<8
100 N=N+G*(RND)(3)-2)
110 IF N>12 THEN N=12
120 IF N< THEN N=1
130 SOUND 1,1,SC(N),D*RND(2)
140 GOTO 90
```

Even though this program produces reasonable melody lines over a short period of time, after a while the interest wains and it becomes boring again. The theory behind the structure of real melodies is much more complicated than the mere consideration of intervals between notes. Books have been written on this subject from centuries ago to the present day, and it has now become an important part of artificial intelligence research.

There are many different aspects of rhythmical and harmonic progression that need to be taken into account. In the next chapter a few more rules are introduced to generate reasonable melodies with a proper start and finish. For the moment, we can bear this in mind in making a slight adjustment to the limit checks in lines 110 and 120.

Now that we are using larger interval gaps there is a tendency to hit the limits at 1 and 12 more frequently. This means that notes can get stuck there and then receive artificial prominence. One way to avoid this is to jump back into the middle of the range, say to 6 or 7 as we suggested before, when a limit is crossed. These notes will still end up being artificially emphasized but not as much as the limit notes were before, when the melody may have repeatedly tried to break the bounds and each time be put back on the limit note.

One of the features of a "real" tune is the prominence of a key note. With a melody in the key of C, for example, the note C itself tends to occur more often than other notes, with G, a fifth above, running a close second. We can use this fact to bring the melody back to C (note number 8) when the upper limit is crossed, and to G (note number 5) when the lower limit is crossed. Thus, even though these notes are given extra prominence, it is more in keeping with the features of a natural melody. Lines 110 and 120 become:

```
110 IF N> 12 THEN N=8
120 IF N< 1 THEN N=5
```

Fractal curves

This biased interval change can be incorporated into the plotting programs from the earlier part of the chapter (see p.72, for example). The line which previously moved the value of P up or down by 1 went like this:

```
50 IF RND(2)=1 THEN P=P+1 ELSE P=P-1
```

It can be replaced by these two lines:

```
50 REPEAT:G=1/RND(1):UNTIL G< 10
55 IF RND(2)=1 THEN P=P+G ELSE P=P-G
```

or you can use the alternative for line 55 if 0 gaps are to be allowed:

```
55 P=P+G*(RND(3)-2)
```

which gives us in full:

```
10  MODE 0
20  X=0
30  P=RND(255)
40  MOVE 0,P*4
50  REPEAT:G=1/RND(1):UNTIL G< 10
55  P=P+G*(RND(3)-2)
60  X=X+1
70  IF X> 1279 THEN X=0:MOVE 0,P*4
80  SOUND &11,-15,P,1
90  DRAW X,P*4
100 GOTO 50
```

and produces plots looking like this:

There are many variations worth trying. You can vary the largest gap size by changing the value at the end of line 50. If you make it too big the picture soon shoots off the edge of the screen. You could compensate by putting in extra limit checks. Alternatively, you can make the screen wrap-around, like the sound, by changing line 90 to:

```
90 DRAW X,P*4 MOD 1024
```

Once you start playing with screen wrap-around you might as well go the whole way, delete line 70, and amend line 90 again to:

```
90 DRAW X MOD 1280,P*4 MOD 1024
```

which effectively does the same thing.

It is worth varying the scale by changing line 60 to:

```
60 X=X+4
```

for example, or even to X=X+8. You can tune the pitches and slow everything down by changing line 80 to:

```
80 SOUND 1,-15,P*4,3
```

in which case the sound and picture will end up slightly out of synchronization.

These plots are examples of types of curves, or "curves" with corners, that are called **fractals**. They have the property of being what is known as **self-similar**. This means that the overall shape of the curve has the same character as the individual bits of it. The French mathematician, Mandlebrot, noticed that coastlines and other natural forms have this property. The same coastline viewed from an atlas, or from a larger scale map, or from direct observation on the ground, tends to have the same characteristic bumpiness or jaggedness at whatever scale it is examined. In his book *Fractals: Form, Chance and Dimension* he uses fractal curves to try to create artificial landscapes and islands quite successfully. Exploiting this link between geography and music, the American composer Larry Austin transcribed the Canadian coastline to generate melody lines for one of his pieces. As long ago as the 1940s the Brazilian composer Villa-Lobos transcribed the New York city skyline for his orchestral debut there.

The sounds and patterns which we have been making are related to a particular type of naturally occuring noise known as **one-over-f** noise. The American, Richard Voss, and others have developed musical and graphic ideas from the same concepts.

More substitutions

As well as being used to determine gap sizes, the 1/RND(1) function can be put straight into a SOUND command to generate notes biased to a particular value. If we substitute into the simple random note program we started with in Chapter 3 we get:

```
10 ENVELOPE 1,1,0,0,0,0,0,0,60,-1,-1,-1,126,100
20 SOUND 1,1,1/RND(1),4
30 GOTO 20
```

This will give us a series of notes which are mainly at pitch value 1. We need to make use of an envelope since most of the notes are the same, and would otherwise be heard as a continuous duration.

We can add any value to the basic pitch to give an alternative root. The pitch wrap-around effect will mean that a rogue lower note will occasionally intrude, but that does not disturb the general effect. We can also multiply by 4 to tune the result to even semitones:

```
20 SOUND 1,1,1/RND(1)*4+32,4
```

I have used a similar technique to generate note material for part of an orchestral piece. The idea was to represent the flames in a lake of fire where there would be small flames flickering most of the time, with the occasional tongue of fire erupting from the surface. The results were transcribed to be played by conventional instruments. This sort of pattern was produced:

6 Melody rules

programming rules for computer-generated melodies

Airs

Over the centuries there have been many attempts to work out rules for composing melodies automatically. Before computers were available it could be done with the aid of dice. Samuel Pepys had sets of musical playing cards from which selections could be made in a specified sequence in order to compose tunes.

In the 1950s various groups of Americans experimented with Markov Chain methods (see Chapter 5) of analyzing and reconstructing melodies by computer. At the same time, a Russian engineer by the name of Zaripov analyzed Russian folk tunes to see how they were structured. After careful scrutiny of such popular numbers as *Don't knit me a red sweater, mum* and *A young Cossack strolls by the Don*, he worked out rules which could be made into a computer program and used to generate new tunes. He called these, "Ural Airs". To derive his rules he looked at phrase length, amount of repetition, shape of the melody, and so on. One of his observations was that long notes tend to be associated with larger intervals and short notes with smaller intervals, for example. Some of his new tunes were quite convincing.

More recently, in France, Pierre Barbaud has, in addition, programmed harmony rules into a computer. In a rather charming manner, to be expected from a romantic Frenchman, he makes use of girls' names to label the procedures inside his programs. One of his computer-composed creations enjoys the distinction of introducing the news on French Television every evening.

We are going to make use of just one or two rules to generate our own simple melodies on the BBC computer.

Rhythm

We begin by making a few decisions about the structure:

1. Each melody will be eight bars long
2. We will use four beats in a bar (for the time being)
3. A crotchet, i.e., one beat, will be the shortest note-length
4. Notes must fit squarely into a bar; in other words, there are no ties across bars
5. There will be no rests
6. The last bar will consist of one note only, a semibreve lasting for four beats

We must devise a means of generating a rhythm for each bar. The problem is rather like having a lego brick, from a child's construction set, with four "buttons" on it:

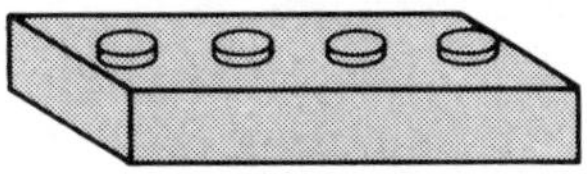

On top of this brick we can place any combination of one-, two- or three-size bricks, as long as they fit exactly without overlapping at the end. So, for example, we could put on a one-er, followed by another one-er:

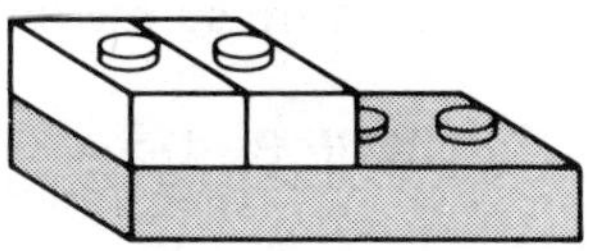

This leaves us with two gaps which could be filled with one two-er, or two more one-ers, but not with a three-er, which would hang over the end. Adding a two-er gives this result:

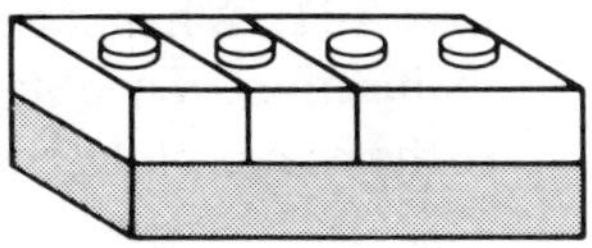

which is equivalent to the rhythm:

We will now attempt to express this reasoning in the form of a computer program. At the start, the number of beats, B, is set to 0. We choose each duration, D, at random to be 1, 2 or 3 and keep a running total of the number of beats covered, by updating the value of B each time:

```
20 B=0
40 D=RND(3)
70 B=B+D
```

This has to be continuously repeated until the number of beats reaches four. We can put it inside a REPEAT . . . UNTIL loop:

```
20 B=0
30 REPEAT
40 D=RND(3)
70 B=B+D
80 UNTIL B=4
```

There is a slight complication we need to watch for. If, say, a duration of 2 is followed by a duration of 3, B will end up equal to 5 and there will be too many beats in the bar. We need to add a check to spot amounts which overlap at the end and chop the duration down to fit into the space available. In other words, the duration must become the difference between the bar length, 4, and the number of beats used up so far, which is B:

```
50 IF B+D>4 THEN D=4-B
```

The SOUND command to produce the note using the value of D will then be placed straight after the line where D's value was fixed. For now, just to demonstrate this rhythm part of the program, we will use a constant pitch value, a C at 101. When D has a value of 1 it represents a crotchet duration. To obtain a reasonable note length we will multiply the value of D by a fixed amount; 6 will do:

```
60 SOUND 1,1,101,D*6
```

To hear the notes distinctly we must make sure that an envelope has been defined:

```
5 ENVELOPE 1,1,0,0,0,0,0,0,60,-1,-1,-1,126,100
```

So far we have generated just one bar of notes. To complete the whole melody we repeat the bar-section seven times, using a loop, and add a single semibreve (duration 4*6) for the final note:

```
  5 ENVELOPE 1,1,0,0,0,0,0,0,60,-1,-1,-1,126,100
 10 FOR BAR=1 TO 7
 20 B=0
 30 REPEAT
 40 D=RND(3)
 50 IF B+D>4 THEN D=4-B
 60 SOUND 1,1,101,D*6
 70 B=B+D
 80 UNTIL B=4
 90 NEXT BAR
100 SOUND 1,1,101,24
```

To convince yourself that you are achieving the desired result, adding these lines will print out the duration values as the program goes along:

```
65 PRINT D;
85 PRINT
110 PRINT 4
```

This is a typical rhythm pattern generated by the program, in normal music notation:

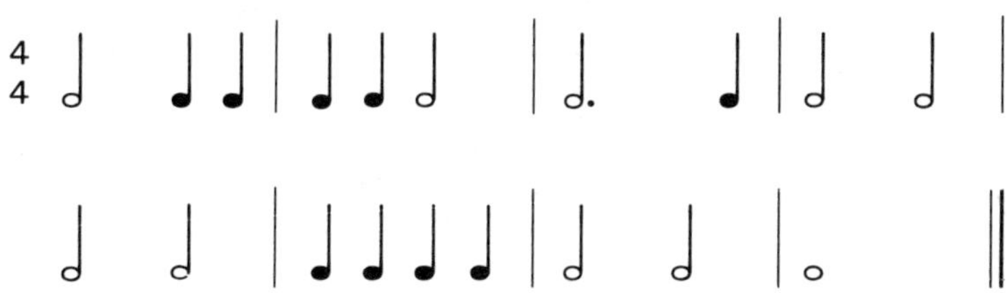

Beats and tempo

As it stands the program will only produce rhythms with four beats in a bar, in other words in 4/4 time. It is a simple matter to adapt it to generate rhythms with any number of beats in a bar. It will then be able to generate waltz rhythms in 3/4, or even curious Bulgarian rhythms in 5/4 time.

We will use the variable NB to stand for the number of beats in a bar. It will need to be set at the beginning:

```
7 NB=3
```

Then, whenever we used 4 to represent the number of beats in a bar in the original program, we can replace it with NB. It gives this result:

```
  7 NB=3
 10 FOR BAR=1 TO 7
 20 B=0
 30 REPEAT
 40 D=RND(3)
 50 IF B+D>NB THEN D=NB-B
 60 SOUND 1,1,101,D*6
 70 B=B+D
 80 UNTIL B=NB
 90 NEXT BAR
100 SOUND 1,1,101,NB*6
```

Notice that in the last line we have made the duration equal to the total number of beats in a bar times 6, to match line 60.

Three beats to a bar generates a rhythm like this:

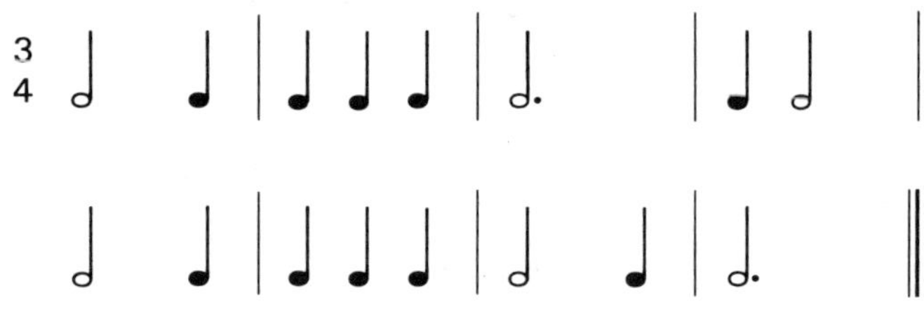

For a more exotic flavour setting NB equal to 5 will produce a typically Bulgarian rhythm like this:

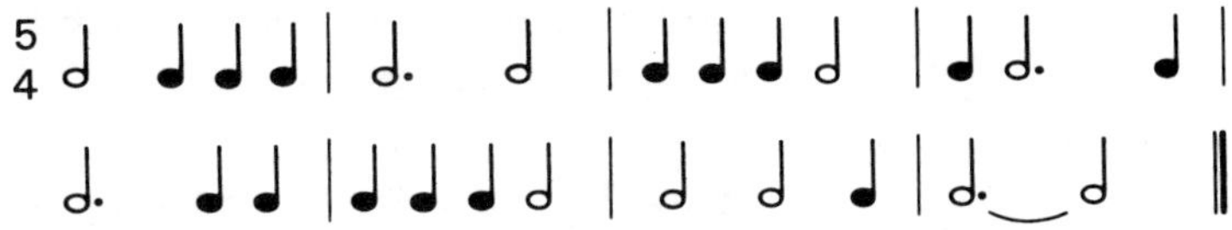

Shortening the bar length to 2 will produce simpler rhythms. For the sort of melodies we are aiming to produce, bar lengths of 2, 3 or 4 are most suitable. If we want one of these values to be chosen at random each time the program is run, we can use the line:

```
7 NB=1+RND(3)
```

It is not difficult to make the tempo variable so that we can produce fast and slow rhythms. We need to change the constant amount by which D is multiplied in line 60. We have used a value of 6 so far. A suitable range of values is 2 to 11. If we replace this number by the variable T, it can be chosen at random at the beginning of the program:

```
8 T=1+RND(10)
    :
60 SOUND 1,1,101,D*T
    :
100 SOUND 1,1,101,NB*T
```

Melody movement

Having sorted out the rhythm we can now add the rules which generate the note pitches. We will use the same program as we used to generate **beige music** in Chapter 5. This gives us a bias towards smaller intervals between notes and allows us to step up and down the equivalent of the white notes on the piano.

This time we will use a slight modification to deal with the limits. Before, when a note value hit a limit, we either made it stay there, or else jumped back to a fixed value inside the range. This time, we will use **reflecting** barriers, so that if a note value goes outside of range it is reflected back by the same amount that it overshot. In other words, the direction of the interval is changed.

With an interval gap of G, these two lines will check and adjust the note generated:

```
IF N>12 THEN N=N-2*G
IF N<1 THEN N=N+2*G
```

If adding G to N makes it exceed the limit of 12, then taking G from N once cancels the effect by bringing N back to its old value; twice, and the direction of the interval is changed. This is the same as if G had been subtracted instead of added in the first place:

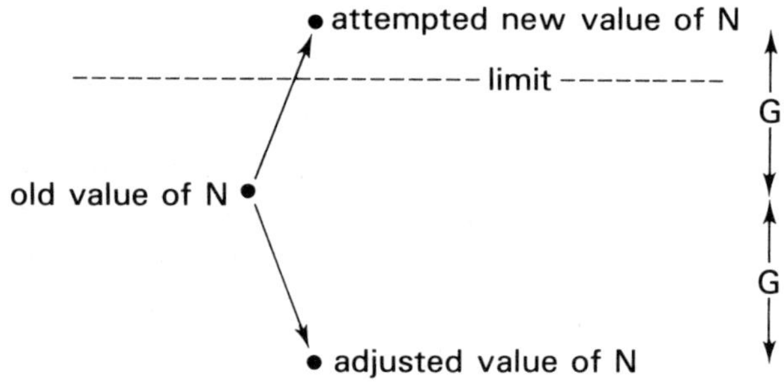

Similarly, at the lower limit, adding 2*G will bring an out-of-limit note back into range.

We have to take a little care to tidy up the intervals being generated. As we discovered in the last chapter, when we use the expression:

```
G = 1/RND(1)
```

then G becomes a number followed by several decimal places. It could be 5.437928 . . ., for example. Since we are measuring a precise gap size, the value of G should be an **integer**, that is to say, an exact whole number. We can convert the value to an integer by using the BASIC function INT around the expression so that it looks like this:

```
G = INT(1/RND(1))
```

This will chop off any decimal part leaving just the whole number behind. It also has the added bonus of rounding down numbers between 1 and 2 to 1. This gives a gap size of

1 an even greater chance of occurring and adds to a more convincing melodic result.

We must be careful not to generate intervals so large that they might be reflected right back over the barrier at thc opposite limit—so the largest value of G must be 6.

We will use the version of the program which only gives up-and-down-steps of G and does not allow for repeated notes where G=0. In other words, we make use of the line:

```
IF RND(2)=1 THEN N=N+G ELSE N=N-G
```

Merging the programs

We now have the task of merging these two programs for rhythm and pitch selection. We begin with the routine definition of the envelope, and the scale array:

```
10 ENVELOPE 1,1,0,0,0,0,0,0,60,-1,-1,-1,126,100
20 DIM SC(12)
30 FOR N=1 TO 12
40 READ SC(N)
50 NEXT N
60 DATA 101,109,117,121,129,137,145,149,157,165,
        169,177
```

Before the melody begins, we will select the number of beats in a bar, the tempo, and the starting pitch:

```
70 NB=1+RND(3)
80 T=1+RND(10)
90 N=RND(12)
```

Unlike the note duration the pitch selected does not depend upon a note's position in the melody as a whole. For this reason the duration program will form the basis of the combined program, with the pitch selection commands slotted in appropriately. The bar loop and rhythm selection will come next:

```
100 FOR BAR=1 TO 7
110 B=0
120 REPEAT
```

```
130 D=RND(3)
140 IF B+D>NB THEN D=NB-B
```

Then we put in the statements to choose and check the note pitch:

```
150 REPEAT:G=INT(1/RND(1)):UNTIL G<7
160 IF RND(2)=1 THEN N=N+G ELSE N=N-G
170 IF N>12 THEN N=N-2*G
180 IF N<1 THEN N=N+2*G
```

Everything is now ready for the SOUND statement:

```
190 SOUND 1,1,SC(N),D*T
```

followed by the balancing statements of the rhythm loops:

```
200 B=B+D
210 UNTIL B=NB
220 NEXT BAR
```

To choose the pitch of the last note we will need to put in the four-note selection statements, the same as lines 150 to 180, all over again. To avoid this additional labour it is easier to incorporate the last bar into the main bar loop, so that it goes from 1 to 8:

```
100 FOR BAR=1 TO 8
```

Then we need to add an extra line after line 130 which makes D equal to the number of beats in a bar if the loop has reached bar 8:

```
135 IF BAR=8 THEN D=NB
```

The completed program now looks like this:

```
10 ENVELOPE 1,1,0,0,0,0,0,0,60,-1,-1,-1,126,100
20 DIM SC(12)
30 FOR N=1 TO 12
40 READ SC(N)
50 NEXT N
60 DATA 101,109,117,121,129,137,145,149,157,165,
        169,177
```

```
70 NB=1+RND(3)
80 T=1+RND(10)
90 N=RND(12)
100 FOR BAR=1 TO 8
110 B=0
120 REPEAT
130 D=RND(3)
135 IF BAR=8 THEN D=NB
140 IF B+D>NB THEN D=NB-B
150 REPEAT:G=INT(1/RND(1)):UNTIL G<7
160 IF RND(2)=1 THEN N=N+G ELSE N=N-G
170 IF N>12 THEN N=N-2*G
180 IF N<1 THEN N=N+2*G
190 SOUND 1,1,SC(N),D*T
200 B=B+D
210 UNTIL B=NB
220 NEXT BAR
```

If you prefer the more mellow tone of notes an octave lower you could define pitches in the data statement of line 60 using the values for notes one octave down. More simply, 48 can be subtracted from the pitch values in the SOUND statement:

```
190 SOUND 1,1,SC(N)-48,D*T
```

This program produces modal melodies characteristic of folk songs. It uses the same notes as a major scale, equivalent to the white notes on a piano, but they will not necessarily fall within the key of C. A tune may finish on any note, or other notes may have particular prominence. This modal flavour sometimes gives a tune an unfinished, hanging-in-the-air feel, just as with some folk songs. Here are a couple of examples, in normal music notation, of the sort of melodies the program will produce:

Displaying graphics: pitch

It would be useful to be able to display a musical score on the screen to help follow the progress of the melody. To display a neat score in conventional notation requires some rather involved programming which, although fairly routine, can be long and tedious to work out. However, we can plot quite a convincing representation of the sound just by adding one or two extra lines.

Without going into a graphics mode we can print text symbols at appropriate positions on the screen using the PRINTTAB facility which we came across in Chapter 4. This allows us to place text at a specified position from 0 to 39 columns counting across the screen and from 0 to 23 lines counting down. Notice that TAB counts down from the top of the screen whereas normal graphics commands count up from the bottom. As the tune progresses, we can move across the screen bar by bar, and beat by beat, plotting the letter O to represent the note, at a vertical position which corresponds to its pitch.

First we want to clear the screen ready for plotting. We can put the command in at line 95 before the first bar is tackled:

```
95 CLS
```

The PRINTTAB command will be slipped in after the SOUND statement.

For **horizontal** position we can move from 0 to 39. Since there are eight bars which can contain up to four beats, we need to be able to accommodate 32 beats. Using one beat per position allows the tune to fit comfortably on to the screen. Multiplying the current bar number by 4 and adding the current beat value will give the right number of columns to plot across. So, for example, a note on the third beat of bar 5 will be plotted at 5*4+3 (that is 23) columns across. The first beat of bar 6 will be at 6*4+1 (that is 25) and so on.

For **vertical** position we want the highest note value of 12 to be near the top, and the lowest note value of 1 to be near the bottom of the screen. If the position is worked out by subtracting the note number, N, from 20, then the highest value will be plotted 8 lines down, and the lowest at 19 lines down. That seems to give a reasonable spread across the central part of the screen. The printing command will thus be:

```
195 PRINTTAB(BAR*4+B,20-N)"O"
```

It will produce an output looking something like this:

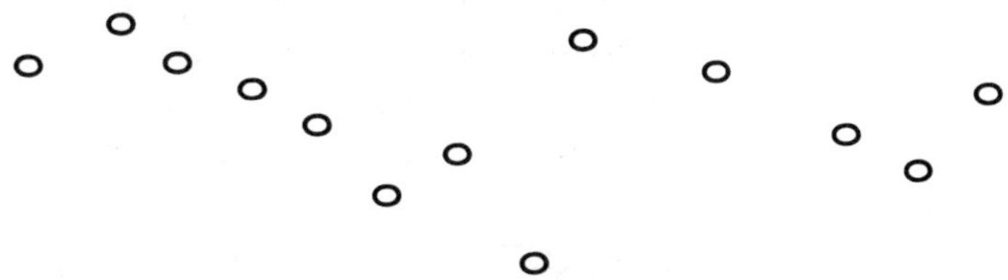

When the program finishes the cursor ends up remaining wherever the last note happened to be. It can be rather confusing having to type new instructions into the middle of the display. To move the cursor to the bottom, where we expect it to be, add this line:

```
230 PRINTTAB(0,23)
```

Co-ordinating picture and sound

You will notice that the notes plotted on screen tend to march ahead of the notes being heard. This happens as the notes queue up in the sound buffer patiently waiting their turn, whilst the previous note completes its required length. Meanwhile, the rest of the program proceeds apace cycling through the plotting commands as fast as it can. Only when the sound buffer is full, does the program slow down to the same speed at which the notes can be sounded. It means that the note heard is always five notes, that is a buffer's length, behind what appears on the screen.

To a musician who is used to reading scores it can be quite useful to plot a few notes ahead and thereby be able to anticipate what is coming next, but to most other observers it becomes an annoying distraction. For them it makes far more sense to have a note plotted on screen at the same time as it is heard.

We need to slow the program down to work at the same speed as the notes are sounded. This can be done by putting in a delay after the SOUND and PRINT statements to force the computer to wait the full length of the note before carrying on.

There is a clock built into the BBC computer which counts in regular steps of one-hundredth of a second. Its value is constantly registered in a variable called TIME. If TIME is set to zero at a given moment, it will immediately start counting up again from there, and its value can be checked to find out how much time has elapsed.

The SOUND statement has a duration set to D*T. This is measured in twentieths of a second. For an equivalent TIME duration this value must be multiplied by 5. After setting TIME equal to 0, a dummy loop is repeated until the TIME value reaches D*T*5 with these commands:

```
TIME=0
REPEAT
UNTIL TIME>D*T*5
```

Since these lines have to be inserted into the program after the PRINT command in line 195, we will put them into one continuous statement separated by colons, like this:

```
197 TIME=0:REPEAT:UNTIL TIME>D*T*5
```

Now, when the program is run, sound and graphics should match.

Adding colours

A good effect is produced by making the notes plot in different colours. It is possible to associate each of the seven notes of the scale with its own colour, so that every C is red, every D green, and so on.

Composers and scientists in the past have had some interesting ideas about the colour associations of musical notes. Newton arbitrarily derived his seven colours of the spectrum by analogy with a musical scale. The Russian composer Scriabin had some very exotic ideas about musical colour associations, designing and writing for a colour organ in the process. Although some musical educators seem to have used colour quite successfully in their work, others vigorously dispute its significance. However, whether it is useful, meaningful or not, colour makes our program prettier to look at.

With the computer in Mode 7, as it is when you switch on, colour can be obtained by printing a column of invisible code characters down the left hand side of the screen. Each code makes anything else printed on that line appear in one particular colour. If we start with C as red, then this chart shows the colour which each note will be, and the control code required to produce it:

number	note	colour	code
1	C	red	129
2	D	green	130
3	E	yellow	131
4	F	blue	132
5	G	magenta	133
6	A	cyan	134
7	B	white	135 or 128
8	C	red	129
9	D	green	130
10	E	yellow	131
11	F	blue	132
12	G	magenta	133

Conveniently, in MODE 7 there are seven colours available which means that there is a different one for each note of the scale.

To print the necessary codes we can use a loop which takes the note value N from 1 to 12. For the first seven values adding the value of N to 128 will produce the required code. On reaching note 8, when we return to C again, we want the note once more to be red, with a code of 129. To derive the number we need we can again make use of the MOD function (see p.66) and add on N MOD 7. When N is 8, then 8 MOD 7 will be added, which is 1, to give code 129.

The invisible code is placed on the screen using the function CHR$ (which stands for CHaracteR) inside a PRINT statement. Since the codes need to be plotted at an equivalent number of lines down to the notes themselves, an equivalent TAB position of 20 − N is used. The necessary statements therefore become:

```
FOR N=1 TO 12
PRINTTAB(0,20-N)CHR$(128+N MOD 7)
NEXT N
```

These lines could go in as 96, 97 and 98, but instead we will use another very useful programming technique.

Procedures

The program is now becoming quite lengthy. Trying to insert new lines between the old ones can be complicated. To keep the program manageable it is desirable to make use of **procedures**.

In its simplest form a procedure is just a mini-program which is written to do a particular, specialist job. It can be given a name, and then whenever the job is required to be done in the main program, the procedure can be called by its name. This makes programs much easier to follow. A procedure is particularly useful when the same job needs to be done a number of times but at different places in the program.

The job under consideration at the moment is to print the colour codes on to the screen. A suitable name for the procedure would therefore be **colours**. The procedure definition begins with a DEFPROC command followed by the name we have decided to use:

```
DEFPROCcolours
```

Notice that there must not be a space between them. Using lower case letters for the procedure's name helps to identify it more clearly.

The lines of the procedure then follow, the same as were listed above, the procedure finishing with the line:

```
ENDPROC
```

(N.B. ENDPROC can be abbreviated to just E., which can be a useful time saver. When the program is listed it will automatically reappear in its full form.)

The procedure definition can be tacked on to the end of the program, after formally completing the main program with an END command:

```
240 END
250 DEFPROCcolours
260 FOR N=1 TO 12
270 PRINTTAB(0,20-N)CHR$(128+N MOD 7)
280 NEXT N
290 ENDPROC
```

In order to use the procedure, at the appropriate place in the main program we insert the call:

```
97 PROCcolours
```

It needs to come after the CLS command and before the BAR loop.

Here is the amended program in full which will produce multi-coloured rainbow melodies:

```
10 ENVELOPE 1,1,0,0,0,0,0,0,60,-1,-1,-1,126,100
20 DIM SC(12)
30 FOR N=1 TO 12
40 READ SC(N)
50 NEXT N
60 DATA 101,109,117,121,129,137,145,149,157,165,
        169,177
70 NB=1+RND(3)
80 T=1+RND(10)
90 N=RND(12)
95 CLS
97 PROCcolours
```

```
100 FOR BAR=1 TO 8
110 B=0
120 REPEAT
130 D=RND(3)
135 IF BAR=8 THEN D=NB
140 IF B+D>NB THEN D=NB-B
150 REPEAT:G=INT(1/RND(1)):UNTIL G<7
160 IF RND(2)=1 THEN N=N+G ELSE N=N-G
170 IF N>12 THEN N=N-2*G
180 IF N<1 THEN N=N+2*G
190 SOUND 1,1,SC(N)-48,D*T
195 PRINTTAB(BAR*4+B,20-N)"0"
197 TIME=0:REPEAT:UNTIL TIME>D*T*5
200 B=B+D
210 UNTIL B=NB
220 NEXT BAR
230 PRINTTAB(0,23)
240 END
250 DEFPROCcolours
260 FOR N=1 TO 12
270 PRINTTAB(0,20-N)CHR$(128+N MOD 7)
280 NEXT N
290 ENDPROC
```

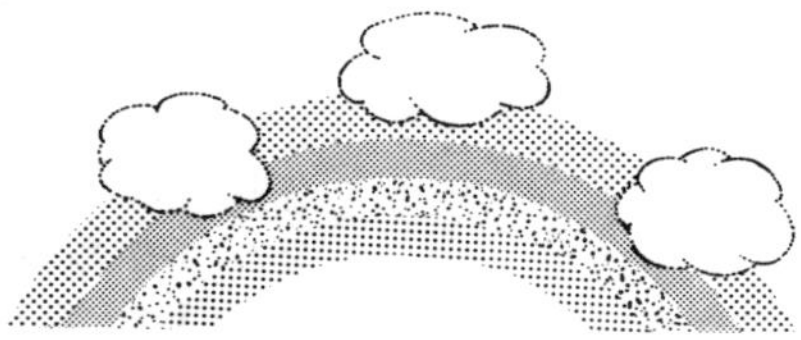

Plotting time values

With some melodies it can be quite difficult to follow exactly what the rhythm is doing. It would help if the screen display could give some idea of the notes' durations. To display something like conventional notation with crotchets and minims, as explained before, would require a considerable amount of additional programming. We can achieve a more simple improvement by making the PRINT statement at line 195 print the current value of D, rather than 0:

```
195 PRINTTAB(BAR*4+B,20-N);D
```

The semicolon before D is used to make sure that it is printed without leading spaces.

It would also help us follow the rhythm if the bars were more clearly separated. In the program's present form each bar has four spaces reserved for it. If a tune ends up in 2- or 3-time it only uses the first two or three spaces. This leaves a gap before the next bar starts and helps to keep them separate. In 4-time this does not happen.

If we make each bar five spaces apart then bars in 4-time will be better separated. There is just enough room on the screen to do this, but the bars must count from 0 to 7 rather than 1 to 8 in order to use all the available space. Rather than changing the BAR loop itself, which would involve changing other lines, we can substitute (BAR − 1) for BAR in the TAB position instruction. Adding an extra 1 at the end of the expression shifts everything over one space to the right as a final modification:

```
195 PRINTTAB((BAR − 1)*5 + B + 1,20 − N);D
```

It is also useful to have the time-signature printed on the screen before the melody begins. This can be plotted at the top, say three lines down. It will be the value of NB with 4 printed below it and needs to be inserted into the program between the CLS command and the BAR loop:

```
98 PRINTTAB(0,3);NB';4
```

The apostrophe after NB has the effect of starting a new line.

These changes in the program will produce an output something like this:

```
3
4

   1
2   2            3
      1             3
        2                  3
            2           2
          1              1

              1
```

Adding a stave

If five stave-lines are printed on to the screen, corresponding to the conventional musical stave, it makes it possible to see precisely which note-pitches are being played. This is simply a matter of printing five lines of dashes on alternate lines from 9 down (where the Fs appear on note 11) to 17 down (where the Es appear on note 3).

These lines will do the job:

```
FOR J=9 TO 17 STEP 2
FOR I=1 to 39
PRINTTAB(I,J);"-";
NEXT I
NEXT J
```

As we did with the colour codes, we will incorporate the statements into a procedure, this time called PROCstaves. It can be called at line 96 and the definition tacked on to the end of the program:

```
96 PROCstaves

300 DEFPROCstaves
310 FOR J=9 TO 17 STEP 2
320 FOR I=1 TO 39
330 PRINTTAB(I,J);"-";
340 NEXT I
350 NEXT J
360 ENDPROC
```

Lines 90 to 100 are becoming cluttered, so it is worth renumbering. (Remember that to renumber automatically you just have to type RENUMBER followed by RETURN.) The program becomes:

```
 10 ENVELOPE 1,1,0,0,0,0,0,0,60,-1,-1,-1,126,100
 20 DIM SC(12)
 30 FOR N=1 TO 12
 40 READ SC(N)
 50 NEXT N
 60 DATA 101,109,117,121,129,137,145,149,157,165,
         169,177
 70 NB=1+RND(3)
 80 T=1+RND(10)
 90 N=RND(12)
100 CLS: PRINTTAB(0,3);NB';4
110 PROCstaves
120 PROCcolours
```

```
130 FOR BAR=1 TO 8
140 B=0
150 REPEAT
160 D=RND(3)
170 IF BAR=8 THEN D=NB
180 IF B+D>NB THEN D=NB-B
190 REPEAT:G=INT(1/RND(1)):UNTIL G<7
200 IF RND(2)=1 THEN N=N+G ELSE N=N-G
210 IF N>12 THEN N=N-2*G
220 IF N<1 THEN N=N+2*G
230 SOUND 1,1,SC(N)-48,D*T
240 PRINTTAB((BAR-1)*5+B+1,20-N);D
250 TIME=0:REPEAT:UNTIL TIME>D*T*5
260 B=B+D
270 UNTIL B=NB
280 NEXT BAR
290 PRINTTAB(0,23)
300 END
310 DEFPROCcolours
320 FOR N=1 TO 12
330 PRINTTAB(0,20-N)CHR$(128+N MOD 7)
340 NEXT N
350 ENDPROC
360 DEFPROCstaves
370 FOR J=9 TO 17 STEP 2
380 FOR I=1 TO 39
390 PRINTTAB(I,J);"-";
400 NEXT I
410 NEXT J
420 ENDPROC
```

It will produce an output looking something like this:

```
4
4

  1
---1---1------------------------4--
     2                        1
------------------------------3------
2      1                   2
---------2-------------------------
             1          2
-----------2---2------1------------
                  3
----------------1------------------
```

Now that staves are present, you could try reverting to 0s again in the PRINT statement, at line 195, to see how they look. Notice that when a middle C occurs below the bottom of the stave it does not have a line through it as it would in conventional notation. If you find the free-floating Cs disturbing, it is not too difficult to add an extra check and then frame any note 1 generated with dashes on either side.

Repeating a melody

The program plays through the melody it has composed once only. It would be useful to have the option of repeating the melody for further hearings. Simply to go back to the beginning again with a GOTO instruction, or putting the program into a loop, as we did before, will not work. This is because random choices are being used which will be different each time round; the tune itself is not stored in the computer. It is an ephemeral creation consumed by time; like a sandcastle, a cream gateau, or indeed a musical performance. In a sense, to make a tune repeatable departs from the point of the program, but it is possible to achieve.

We could store the notes of the tune as they are generated, then go back and read them out of the memory for a repeat performance, but there is an easier way. It makes use of a programming possibility with the RND function, to reproduce the same random number sequence if required. Effectively, a tune is recomposed as the same decisions which put it together are made over again.

If the random number generator is called with a negative value, in a dummy statement, like this:

```
A = RND(-24798)
```

then any random numbers produced after it will always follow the same sequence. The negative number, −24798 in this case, can be called the seed of the sequence. A seed value can be generated at random near the beginning of the program:

```
65 X = -RND(1000000)
```

(this will produce a million different possibilities) and then the value used in a dummy call:

```
85 A = RND(X)
```

When we want to repeat a melody, we can send the program back to the dummy call, which will make it produce an identical random sequence. If we want a different melody we send the program back to the earlier command to choose a new seed.

On reaching the end of a melody we can make the program wait for a response from the user to determine which of the options is to be taken. We could, say, require the user to press the space bar to repeat the melody, and press any other key for a new one. We can use the GET command. This makes the computer wait for the user to press a key and then takes the key's code value. Pressing the space bar will give a code value of 32. We can check to see if this was the value registered. If it was, the program will jump to line 85 to repeat the tune with the same seed. If any other value was registered then the program will jump further back to line 65 to generate a new seed for a different tune:

```
300 IF GET=32 THEN 85 ELSE 65
```

If a particularly good tune appears which you want to be able to generate at a later date, you can stop the program with ESCAPE and get the computer to PRINT the current value of X:

```
PRINT X                              (no line number)
```

The next time you run the program, whatever the value of X it can be substituted as a fixed value in line 85. Like this, for example:

```
85 A=RND(-34728)
```

and the same sequence as before will be generated.

Adding a title

A final touch can be added to the program by making it generate and display appropriate titles for the melodies. Not to be outdone by Barbaud, we will use girls' names, preceded by a conjunction and followed by an action verb. We can store a set of words in the computer and choose from them at random. To make each title match the character of a particular melody, we can use the tempo value to choose from a list of verbs. These will be appropriately scaled from fast and active, down to slow and passive actions. The set of words to be used for the titles will need to be stored in three-string arrays which have to be DIMensioned at the beginning of the program. We will call them CJ$, NAME$ and VERB$. There are 11, 13 and 15 words respectively in each category:

```
5 DIM CJ$(11),NAME$(13),VERB$(15)
```

A procedure will be used to load the words into their arrays. Loops, READ and DATA statements are used in the same way as they were used for reading in the SC array values, but this time we are dealing with words instead of numbers as data.

```
430 DEFPROCreadwords
440 FOR I=1 to 11:READ CJ$(I):NEXT
450 DATA So,But,When,As,If,Where,And,Though,How,
         Why,
460 FOR I=1 to 13:READ NAME$(I):NEXT
470 DATA Alison,Andree,Caroline,Hannah,Heidi,Jenny,
         Joanne
480 DATA Laura,Libby,Natasha,Nichola,Rachel,Stephanie
490 FOR I=1 TO 15:READ VERB$(I):NEXT
500 DATA runs,laughs,rides,dances,comes,smiles,walks,
         sings
510 DATA moves,departs,sighs,frowns,weeps,rests,sleeps
520 ENDPROC
```

Notice that we have included an empty space as one of the "conjunction" words which gives the possibility of a "conjunction" being omitted altogether. The verbs have been arranged in rough sequence from active to passive.

The procedure must be called near the beginning of the program. Just after the scale array has been defined will be a suitable place:

63 PROCreadwords

The title itself can be positioned in the centre at the bottom of the screen, at TAB position (10,23), say. Words are chosen at random from the CJ$ and NAME$ arrays just by indicating a random position in the array. The word chosen from the VERB$ array will depend directly on the value of T. If T is 1, the tempo is fast and the first word in the array, "runs", will be used. If T is 14, the tempo is slower and the 14th word in the array, "rests", will be used. So the instruction for printing the title will appear like this:

```
PRINTTAB(10,23)CJ$(RND(11))" "NAME$(RND(13))" "
VERB$(T)
```

Note the space between the words.

As the program stands, the value of T goes from 2 to 11 (see p.97). If T is 1, the tempo is too fast for the tune to be heard. Similarly, if T is much greater than 11 the tune becomes tediously slow. To make full use of the range of words we can use a different variable, V, to choose the verb, and then calculate the value of T from that. If we make V a random number between 1 and 15, and use this expression to work out T:

```
T=(3+V)/2
```

then T will vary between 2 and 9, which is a more reasonable range. We will need to change line 80 in the program, which works out the value of T, to:

```
80 V=RND(15):T=(3+V)/2
```

And the title printing line will then be:

```
105 PRINTTAB(10,23)CJ$(RND(11))" "NAME$(RND(13))" "
VERB$(V)
```

It will give us titles like:

When Libby Smiles
or *As Jenny Dances*
or *Heidi Sings*

The amended program complete, with some juggling of the line numbers, now looks like this:

```
 10 DIM CJ$(11),NAME$(13),VERB$(15)
 20 ENVELOPE 1,1,0,0,0,0,0,0,60,-1,-1,-1,126,100
 30 DIM SC(12)
 40 FOR N=1 TO 12
 50 READ SC(N)
 60 NEXT N
 70 DATA 101,109,117,121,129,137,145,149,157,165,
        169,177
 80 PROCreadwords
 90 X=-RND(1000000)
100 NB=1+RND(3)
110 T=1+RND(10)
120 A=RND(X)
130 N=RND(12)
140 CLS:PRINTTAB(0,3);NB';4
150 PRINTTAB(10,23)CJ$(RND(11))" "NAME$(RND(13))" "
        VERB$(V)
160 PROCstaves
170 PROCcolours
180 FOR BAR=1 TO 8
190 B=0
200 REPEAT
210 D=RND(3)
220 IF BAR=8 THEN D=NB
230 IF B+D>NB THEN D=NB-B
240 REPEAT:G=INT(1/RND(1)):UNTIL G<7
250 IF RND(2)=1 THEN N=N+G ELSE N=N-G
260 IF N>12 THEN N=N-2*G
270 IF N<1 THEN N=N+2*G
280 SOUND 1,1,SC(N)-48,D*T
290 PRINTTAB((BAR-1)*5+B+1,20-N);D
300 TIME=0:REPEAT:UNTIL TIME>D*T*5
310 B=B+D
320 UNTIL B=NB
330 NEXT BAR
340 PRINTTAB(0,23)
350 IF GET=32 THEN 120 ELSE 90
360 DEFPROCcolours
370 FOR N=1 TO 12
380 PRINTTAB(0,20-N)CHR$(128+N MOD 7)
390 NEXT N
400 ENDPROC
410 DEFPROCstaves
```

```
420 FOR J=9 TO 17 STEP 2
430 FOR I=1 TO 39
440 PRINTTAB(I,J);"-";
450 NEXT I
460 NEXT J
470 ENDPROC
480 DEFPROCreadwords
490 FOR I=1 TO 11:READ CJ$(I):NEXT
500 DATA So,But,When,As,If,Where,And,Though,How,
         Why,
510 FOR I=1 TO 13:READ NAME$(I):NEXT
520 DATA Alison,Andree,Caroline,Hannah,Heidi,Jenny,
         Joanne
530 DATA Laura,Libby,Natasha,Nichola,Rachel,Stephanie
540 FOR I=1 TO 15:READ VERB$(I):NEXT
550 DATA runs,laughs,rides,dances,comes,smiles,walks,
         sings
560 DATA moves,departs,sighs,frowns,weeps,rests,sleeps
570 ENDPROC
```

Even though many of the melodies thrown up by the program are not particularly interesting, some little gems occasionally emerge. Here are a couple more examples, with the titles that accompanied them:

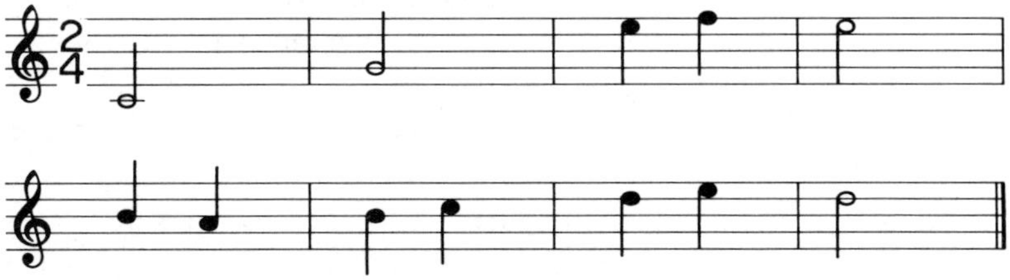

So Joanne sighs

Natasha smiles

Expanding the program

There are a number of ways in which the program could be adapted.

To identify the beat more clearly, another channel could be used to produce a ping at the beginning of each bar. For example,

```
183 SOUND 2,1,200,T
186 SOUND 2,0,0,(NB-1)*T
```

This does tend to intrude and spoil the sound and other solutions are preferable.

One of the reasons that the pulse is often unclear is that in 3-time there is a tendency to generate a 1–2 rhythmic pattern: a crotchet followed by a minim. This is not a common pattern in most natural melodies. It would improve the result if a check were incorporated into the program to avoid it.

Another possibility for extending the program is to generate longer melodies, with each group of eight bars forming a phrase. Using the random number seed option, a phrase could be made to repeat itself, then a new phrase produced, then the original phrase made to repeat again, for example. This idea is developed in Chapter 14.

It is a simple matter to change the vocabulary for the titles by using different word data. You could also change the categories, to generate titles consisting of an adjective followed by a noun, for example. Linking the adjective to the tempo you could generate odd titles like *Fast Blancmange*, or *Tired Raindrops*.

If you prefer the cosy security of tunes which finish on C, in a proper major key, then you can specify a C as the final note and generate the tune backwards using the same rules. It will be necessary to store the note and duration values as they are generated in an array first. When the composition of the melody has been completed, the array can then be read the right way round to sound the notes and display them.

7 Aural training

Computers in music education

A useful and developing application of computers is in music education, particularly in aural training. With the help of a computer it is possible to work through routine tests and training sessions where the computer plays sounds and checks the user's responses. This cannot be done with a book—and without a computer there needs to be a tutor or teacher to play the sounds and check the answers, which means the operation can be very tedious for both teacher and pupil alike.

Computer-assisted aural training has been available in the United States for a number of years. Before small personal computers were available, institutions such as Dartmouth College used terminals connected to a large computer with special sound synthesizers attached.

A number of specific aural training programs and packages have appeared for use with the BBC computer, and others are under development. In this chapter we will show how we can develop a program to test one elementary musical skill: interval recognitiion.

In earlier chapters we explained how an interval is the gap in pitch between two notes. By developing the skill of being able to recognize the intervals between notes instantly, it becomes easier to write down the notes of a melody, for example. Singers also need to be able to hear intervals in their heads, in order to sing from music at sight.

Interval names

Each interval has a name. In order to explain them, we will take C as our reference note and count up in semitone steps to each note above it. This chart shows the names the intervals have:

note	number of semitone steps above C	name of interval
C	0	unison
Db	1	minor second
D	2	major second
Eb	3	minor third
E	4	major third
F	5	perfect fourth
F♯	6	augmented fourth
G	7	perfect fifth
Ab	8	minor sixth
A	9	major sixth
Bb	10	minor seventh
B	11	major seventh
C	12	octave

An interval is named by counting up the white notes, or letter names, from C, including the top and bottom notes. So from C to F is four notes (C, D, E and F) and is called a fourth. If the interval turns out to be 2, 3, 6 or 7 notes apart, it is known as a major second, third, sixth or seventh respectively. Should the higher note be a black note, which just falls short of its equivalent white note (for example C to E♭), then it is called a minor third, second, sixth or seventh.

Fourths and fifths are different. An exact number of white notes is called a perfect fourth or fifth. The interval just bigger than a fourth, to F# in our case, is called an augmented fourth. If F# had been called G♭ (they are the same note) then the interval would be known as a diminished fifth. When this interval is heard out of the blue, and the notes are not seen written down, there is no way of telling whether F# or G♭ was intended. Either name will do to describe this strange interval of 6 semitones.

If you are not very familiar with music theory then the naming system may seem rather curious but there are sound historical and theoretical reasons for its use.

Generating simple intervals

With this type of training application, most of the program is taken up with printing the instructions on to the screen. The actual sound-making statements are quite simple. We begin by defining an appropriate envelope, and make sure we are in MODE 7 which gives the best text display (though MODE 1 or 4 would do almost as well):

```
10 ENVELOPE 1,1,0,0,0,0,0,0,126,-60,-1,-1,126,115
20 MODE 7
```

Next we can display a title, using the TAB command to put it at an appropriate position on the screen:

```
30 PRINTTAB(0,10)"Interval Recognition"
```

Whenever a message or instruction is displayed on the screen it is necessary to hold the program up until the user is ready to continue. We could put in a delay which makes the program pause for a short time before displaying the next item, but it is much better to make the computer wait for a response from the user. We can use the GET command in a dummy statement. Then when the user presses any key the program will continue. A prompt on the screen will explain this:

```
40 PRINTTAB(0,23)"Press any key to continue"
50 A=GET
```

We now want to display a list of intervals from which the user can make a choice:

```
60  CLS
70  PRINTTAB(0,3)"Choose intervals from this list"
80  PRINTTAB(0,6)"1 minor second"
90  PRINT"2 major second"
100 PRINT"3 minor third"
110 PRINT"4 major third"
120 PRINT"5 perfect fourth"
130 PRINT"6 augmented fourth / diminished fifth"
140 PRINT"7 perfect fifth"
150 PRINT"8 minor sixth"
160 PRINT"9 major sixth"
170 PRINT"10 minor seventh"
180 PRINT"11 major seventh"
190 PRINT"12 octave"
```

Notice that after the PRINTTAB in line 80 the screen cursor automatically goes down to the following line, so further TAB commands are not required.

We will fix the pitch of the lower note, L, at 81 for now (that is a G). The program will then choose an interval value, I, at random:

```
200 L=81
210 I=RND(12)
```

The value of I is used to calculate the higher note, H. Its value must be multiplied by 4 to make them into semitone steps (as in previous chapters, see p.11). This is then added to the lower note:

```
220 H=L+I*4
```

The two notes can now be played. As before we will use a dummy GET statement so that the user can press a key when ready. We will put the SOUND statements into a procedure called PROCplay:

```
230 PRINT'''"Press any key when ready"
240 A=GET
250 PROCplay
```

The PROCplay procedure just contains the two SOUND statements required to play the lower note followed by the higher note. A duration value of 20 is reasonable:

```
400 DEFPROCplay
410 SOUND 1,1,L,20
420 SOUND 1,1,H,20
430 ENDPROC
```

Once the notes have been played the program waits for the user to type in an answer identifying which interval he or she thought it was.

We make use of an INPUT statement. As part of this statement we can incorporate a message which is printed on the screen to show the user that a response is expected. The number the user types in will be stored in the variable A:

```
260 INPUT"Answer: ",A
```

We can then compare the response, A, with the actual interval generated, I. If they are the same then the answer is correct, if not the answer is wrong. To program this, it is again much clearer to use procedures which show what action to take in each case:

```
270 IF A=I THEN PROCright ELSE PROCwrong
```

If the answer is correct then we can print the good news on the screen. The PROCright procedure will be:

```
440 DEFPROCright
450 PRINT"That is correct"
460 ENDPROC
```

IF the answer is not correct then it is not much use to the user to be given a bald "WRONG!" message. It makes more sense to give the correct answer and play the interval again. The PROCwrong procedure will look like this:

```
470 DEFPROCwrong
480 PRINT"No. That was wrong"
```

```
490 PRINT''It was number '';I;''. Listen again.''
500 FOR I=1 TO 4000:NEXT
510 PROCplay
520 FOR I=1 TO 4000:NEXT
530 ENDPROC
```

After the answer has been tested, and the appropriate answer given, the program cycles back to the beginning ready for another interval:

```
280 PRINT''Press any key to continue''
290 A=GET
300 GOTO 60
```

Here, then, is the complete program so far:

```
10  ENVELOPE 1,1,0,0,0,0,0,0,126,-60,-1,-1,126,115
20  MODE 7
30  PRINTTAB(0,10)''Interval Recognition''
40  PRINTTAB(0,23)''Press any key to continue''
50  A=GET

60  CLS
70  PRINTTAB(0,3)''Choose intervals from this list''
80  PRINTTAB(0,6)''1 minor second''
90  PRINT''2 major second''
100 PRINT''3 minor third''
110 PRINT''4 major third''
120 PRINT''5 perfect fourth''
130 PRINT''6 augmented fourth / diminished fifth''
140 PRINT''7 perfect fifth''
150 PRINT''8 minor sixth''
160 PRINT''9 major sixth''
170 PRINT''10 minor seventh''
180 PRINT''11 major seventh''
190 PRINT''12 octave''
200 L=81
210 I=RND(12)
220 H=L+I*4
230 PRINT' ' ''Press any key when ready''
240 A=GET
250 PROCplay
260 INPUT''Answer: '',A
270 IF A=I THEN PROCright ELSE PROCwrong
```

```
280 PRINT''Press any key to continue''
290 A=GET
300 GOTO 60

400 DEFPROCplay
410 SOUND 1,1,L,20
420 SOUND 1,1,H,20
430 ENDPROC

440 DEFPROCright
450 PRINT''That is correct''
460 ENDPROC

470 DEFPROCwrong
480 PRINT''No. That was wrong''
490 PRINT''It was number '';I;''. Listen again.''
500 FOR I=1 TO 4000:NEXT
510 PROCplay
520 FOR I=1 TO 4000:NEXT
530 ENDPROC
```

Keeping a score

We can put in additional lines to keep count of the number of correct and incorrect answers. It will then be possible to print a running score of the total as the test proceeds. We will use NC for the number of correct answers and NW for the number of wrong answers. They must both be set to 0 at the start:

```
15 NC=0:NW=0
```

We can keep track of the number of correct and incorrect answers by putting in lines to increase the value of NC or NW at the beginning of the appropriate procedure. Each time the PROCright procedure is called NC will be increased by 1, and each time PROCwrong is called NW will be increased by 1:

```
445 NC=NC+1

475 NW=NW+1
```

At the end of each cycle the current score can be displayed. The total number of intervals attempted will be NC+NW:

```
265 PRINT''Your score is '';NC;'' out of '';NC+NW'
```

Changing the range and sequence

The program we have just developed plays the intervals in their simplest form, that is rising from a fixed lower note. We can make the tests a little more difficult by varying the way in which the intervals are played.

First, we can change the **starting note**, L. As the program stands it is always the same. It soon becomes easy to recognize intervals which are always rising from the same starting note. It is more difficult to pick out intervals occuring in any part of the audible range. We will change the program to make the lower note vary over three octaves (36 notes) from low C, with pitch value 5. We just need to alter line 200:

```
200 L=RND(36)*4+1
```

Second, we can change the interval's **direction** by making it fall instead of rise. For some reason, falling intervals often seem more difficult to identify. To generate falling intervals we just change the order of the SOUND statements in the PROCplay procedure:

```
400 DEFPROCplay
410 SOUND 1,1,H,20
420 SOUND 1,1,L,20
430 ENDPROC
```

Third, for an even trickier test we can make the notes sound **simultaneously** by playing them on different channels:

```
400 DEFPROCplay
410 SOUND 1,1,L,20
420 SOUND 2,1,H,20
430 ENDPROC
```

User-selected alternatives

Making the changes just suggested produces a crop of different programs. It would be useful to be able to build all the possibilities into one program and allow the user to select the alternatives required. Again, most of the program is taken up with statements to display the instructions.

We will use variables to store which of the alternatives have been selected. Each variable can take the value 1 or 2. The letters R, S and D will be used:

R for the range: limited or wide
S for separate or simultaneous notes
D for interval direction: up or down

Since a single digit response is required we will use a GET statement to obtain each value. GET by itself will not return the value of a number pressed, but will return an ASCII code which is different (see Chapter 9 for more detail). We need to use instead the command GET$ which will read in a symbol as it is printed on the keyboard. Using the function VAL (for VALue) will produce the actual numerical value of the symbol. This sounds complicated but it just means that instead of putting:

```
A=GET
```

we must use:

```
A=VAL(GET$)
```

to obtain what we want.

When using GET there is a greater chance of the user pressing a wrong key by mistake. (Using the INPUT command the user sees what was typed appear on the screen and has a chance to delete and correct it before pressing RETURN.) For this reason it is a good idea to incorporate an input trap into the program which will spot if any stray key has been pressed and make the user try again. Since there will be three different responses to check, it makes sense to package the appropriate program lines into a procedure. It can be called PROCget1or2:

```
DEFPROCget1or2
REPEAT
PRINT''You must press 1 or 2: '';
A=VAL(GET$)
UNTIL A=1 OR A=2
ENDPROC
```

This procedure leaves the variable A holding the value of whatever key was pressed.

The lines to display the options on screen and elicit the user's preferences will go at the beginning of the program. It will be necessary to renumber the lines of the program we had originally. The screen is cleared before each option is presented:

```
70  CLS
80  PRINTTAB(0,5)''Do you want''
90  PRINT' ''1 limited range (easy), or''
100 PRINT''2 full range (difficult)''
110 PROCget1or2
120 R=A
130 CLS
140 PRINTTAB(0,5)''Do you want''
150 PRINT' ''1 separate notes, or''
160 PRINT''2 simultaneous notes''
170 PROCget1or2
180 S=A
190 IF S=2 THEN D=1:GOTO 260
200 CLS
210 PRINTTAB(0,5)''Do you want''
220 PRINT' ''1 rising intervals, or''
230 PRINT''2 falling intervals''
240 PROCget1or2
250 D=A
260 CLS
```

Notice in line 190, that if simultaneous notes are selected, then it does not make sense to ask for a rising or falling interval. The program will jump past the next choice. D must nevertheless be given some value, it makes no difference which it is. Setting it to equal 1 will do.

The values which have been given to R, S and D are then used in the rest of the program to control the way the notes are played.

First, the value of the lower note is chosen. IF R=1 then L must be set to the constant value, 81, as we had in the original version of the program. Otherwise, where R=2, it can be chosen at random from a wider range, as explained in the previous section. It can be done by this statement:

```
IF R=1 THEN L=81 ELSE L=RND(36)*4+1
```

Second, we use the value of S in the PROCplay procedure to determine whether the notes play consecutively or simultaneously. This is easy. S is simply substituted for the channel number in the second SOUND statement:

```
SOUND 1,1,L,20
SOUND S,1,H,20
```

When S=1 the two channel numbers are the same. The second statement must wait for the first sound to finish before its own sound can be made. If S=2 the channel numbers are different and they will both sound off together.

Third, we have to decide which way round the notes appear; low or high first. We could use an IF . . . THEN command which tested the value of D and accordingly chose from two different sets of sound statements. A more interesting technique is to replace the pitch values L and H with these expressions:

```
H*(D-1)+L*(2-D)
L*(D-1)+H*(2-D)
```

When D is 1 the first half of each statement will equal 0 and so disappear, leaving just L in the first line and H in the second. When D=2 the second half of each statement will disappear leaving H in the first line and L in the second.

These last two adjustments will make the SOUND statements in the PROCplay procedure look like this:

```
SOUND 1,1,H*(D-1)+L*(2-D),20
SOUND S,1,L*(D-1)+H*(2-D),20
```

Incorporating these changes into the renumbered program we get this result:

```
10  ENVELOPE 1,1,0,0,0,0,0,0,126,-60,-1,-1,126,115
20  NC=0:NW=0
30  MODE 7
40  PRINTTAB(0,10)"Interval Recognition"
50  PRINTTAB(0,23)"Press any key to continue"
60  A=GET

70  CLS
80  PRINTTAB(0,5)"Do you want"
90  PRINT' "1 limited range (easy), or"
100 PRINT"2 full range (difficult)"
110 PROCget1or2
120 R=A
130 CLS
140 PRINTTAB(0,5)"Do you want"
150 PRINT' "1 separate notes, or"
160 PRINT"2 simultaneous notes"
170 PROCget1or2
180 S=A
190 IF S=2 THEN D=1:GOTO 260
200 CLS
210 PRINTTAB(0,5)"Do you want"
220 PRINT' "1 rising intervals, or"
230 PRINT"2 falling intervals"
240 PROCget1or2
250 D=A

260 CLS
270 PRINTTAB(0,3)"Choose intervals from this list"
280 PRINTTAB(0,6)"1 minor second"
290 PRINT"2 major second"
300 PRINT"3 minor third"
310 PRINT"4 major third"
320 PRINT"5 perfect fourth"
330 PRINT"6 augmented fourth/diminished fifth"
340 PRINT"7 perfect fifth"
350 PRINT"8 minor sixth"
360 PRINT"9 major sixth"
370 PRINT"10 minor seventh"
```

```
380 PRINT"11 major seventh"
390 PRINT"12 octave"
400 IF R=1 THEN L=81 ELSE L=RND(36)*4+1
410 I=RND(12)
420 H=L+I*4
430 PRINT'''Press any key when ready"
440 A=GET
450 PROCplay
460 INPUT"Answer: ",A
470 IF A=I THEN PROCright ELSE PROCwrong
480 PRINT"Your score is ";NC;"out of ";NC+NW'

490 PRINT"Press any key to continue"
500 A=GET
510 GOTO 260

520 DEFPROCplay
530 SOUND 1,1,H*(D-1)+L*(2-D),20
540 SOUND S,1,L*(D-1)+H*(2-D),20
550 ENDPROC

560 DEFPROCright
575 NC=NC+1
580 PRINT"That is correct"
590 ENDPROC

600 DEFPROCwrong
610 NW=NW+1
620 PRINT"No. That was wrong"
630 PRINT"It was number ";I:". Listen again."
640 FOR I=1 TO 4000:NEXT
650 PROCplay
660 FOR I=1 TO 4000:NEXT
670 ENDPROC

680 DEFPROCget1or2
690 REPEAT
700 PRINT"You must press 1 or 2: ";
710 A=VAL(GET$)
720 UNTIL A=1 OR A=2
730 ENDPROC
```

Ways of extending the program

There are a number of ways in which the program could be extended or adapted.

It might be desirable to play each interval twice, which can be done by repeating the PROCplay instruction in line 450:

```
450 PROCplay:PROCplay
```

As with the other alternatives an additional question could be supplied at the beginning of the program inviting the user to type in the number of times he wanted each interval to be played.

The test can be made more challenging for musical experts by incorporating compound intervals, that is, intervals larger than an octave. It can be done simply by changing line 410, which chooses the interval, to:

```
410 I=12+RND(12)
```

The menu of interval names from which the answers are taken will then need to be interpreted to mean an octave plus the interval name. Again this could be built in as another option in the choices at the start of the program. If C, say, could equal 1 for simple intervals and 2 for compound intervals, then line 410 would become:

```
410 I=(C-1)*12+RND(12)
```

In the same way that we used an input trap for illegal responses in the PROCget1or2 procedure, a check could be incorporated to spot out-of-range values in the answers themselves. If a number was put in less than 1 or greater than 12, the user would be asked to type in the answer again keeping it within range.

The program could be adapted for use specifically as a training rather than testing program. Even as it stands it is suitable for training, providing the user does not mind getting wrong answers to start with. This can be rather demoralizing for a beginner.

A simple means of printing staves and notes, as was used in Chapter 6, could be incorporated. It would help to demonstrate what an interval looked like when written down, and would also give some visual representation of its size.

A really useful interval recognition training program would suggest tunes from whose opening notes particular intervals may be identified and remembered. It is the way in which interval recognition is often taught. (The alternative is to step up the scale mentally from the lower note to the higher one counting the notes in between. It is unreliable and not to be recommended.)

Each music teacher tends to have their own favourite list of tunes. Here are some suggestions:

minor 2nd	up and down	*Jaws Theme* *Sailor's Hornpipe* (see Chapter 2)
major 2nd	up	*Frère Jacques*
	down	*Yesterday* (Beatles)
	up and down	*Strangers in the Night*
minor 3rd	up	*Greensleeves*
	down	*Hey Jude* (Beatles), *Oranges and Lemons*
major 3rd	up	*And did those feet . . . (Jerusalem)*
	down	opening of Beethoven's 5th
	up and down	*Come to the cook-house door* (Bugle call)
perfect 4th	up and down	*The British Grenadiers (Some talk of Alexander . . .)* opening of Mozart's *Eine Kleine Nachtmusic*
augmented 4th	up	*Maria (West Side Story)*
perfect 5th	up	*Baa Baa Black Sheep*
minor 6th	up and down	Theme from *Love Story*
major 6th	up	*Dashing through the Snow . . . (Jingle Bells)*
minor 7th	up	*There's a place for us (West Side Story)*
major 7th	up (almost)	*Bali Hi (South Pacific)* (1st and 3rd notes, tricky one this)
octave	up and down	*The Lonely Goatherd (Sound of Music)*

Other ideas for aural training programs

Many of the programs in other chapters have potential for "dressing up" as programs for specific aural training or music educational use.

The Etchamus program (Chapter 10), and other programs with visual representation of sounds are good ways of developing pitch recognition and awareness of pitch movement. The rhythms generated at the beginning of Chapter 6, and some of the rhythmic patterns in the noise chapter (Chapter 11) could be combined with a visual display and form a useful demonstration. The program structure could be changed so that, for example, instead of selecting a chosen rhythm from a list, the computer chooses a rhythm to play and then the user has to say which one it was. Rhythm, and especially rhythmic notation, has tended to be a rather neglected area, as far as developing musical literacy is concerned.

8 Envelopes

shaping notes to change their sound quality

What is an envelope?

A single note played by any instrument will not keep a steady volume level all the way through. It starts from silence, builds up to a peak and dies away again. We could represent this basic shape with a diagram like this:

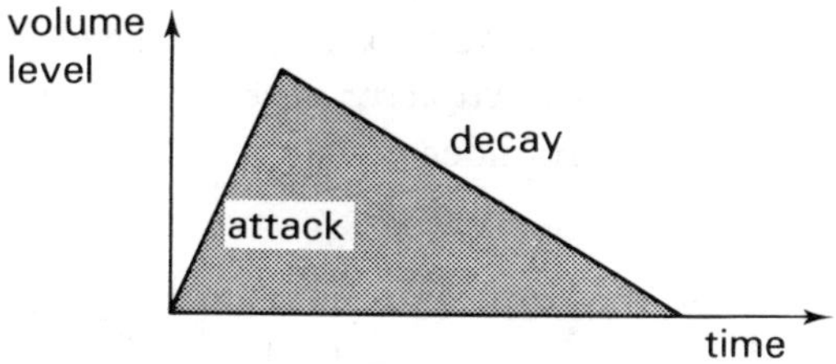

The part of the sound where the note builds up in volume is known as the **attack**. The part where it dies away is the **decay**. A natural sound would not normally have such a simple shape as the one above. Its volume would have a more complicated outine which grows and decays in a rather wobbly fashion, more like this:

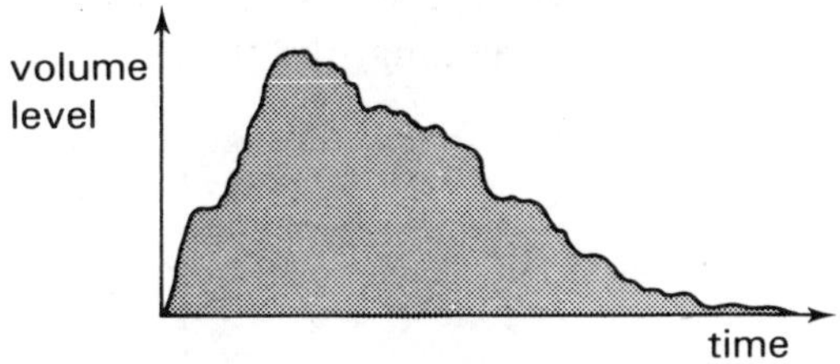

An outline of this sort, which describes the way a sound builds up and dies away, is known as its **envelope**. It is very important in giving sounds their particular, individual character. The notes of different instruments will always have different envelope shapes.

A piano note, as with the sound of any hit percussion instrument, rises to a peak very quickly. Its volume will then drop steeply at first, but gradually level out to linger for some time. It could be represented like this:

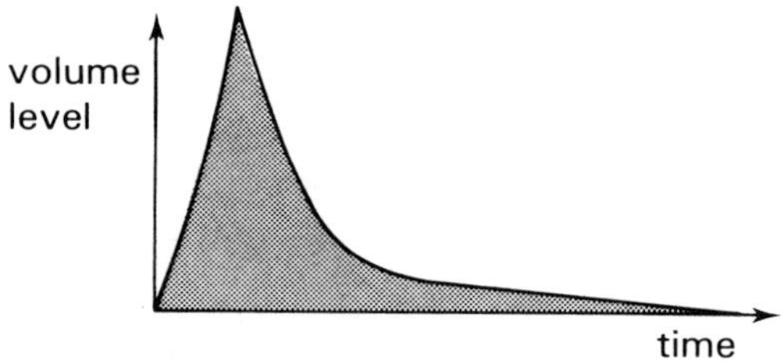

On the other hand, a string sound, such as a violin, builds up to a peak more slowly as the player catches the string with the bow. The sound level is then sustained as the bow is drawn across the string, forcing it to vibrate. It has a much rounder envelope:

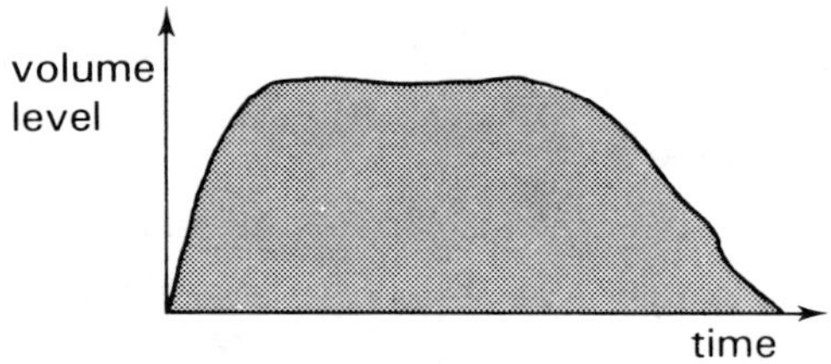

Notes from brass instruments, such as the trumpet, have their own characteristic shape. They tend to overblow a little at the beginning, due to the slight explosive effect of tonguing, then settle down on to a lower level as the note is sustained, something like this:

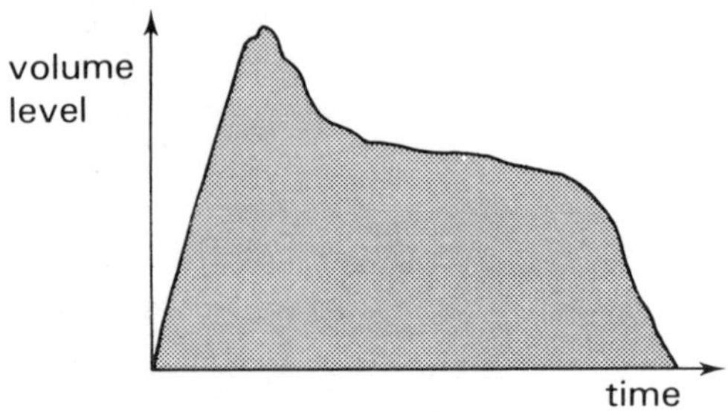

Synthesizer envelopes: the ADSR shape

If a synthesizer is to copy a natural envelope shape there must be some compromise. Simple synthesizers only have controls for attack and decay, just sufficient to achieve the two-stage envelope we saw at the start of this chapter: they are rather limiting. To obtain something closer to the more complex envelopes of natural musical instruments, a four-stage shape is often used:

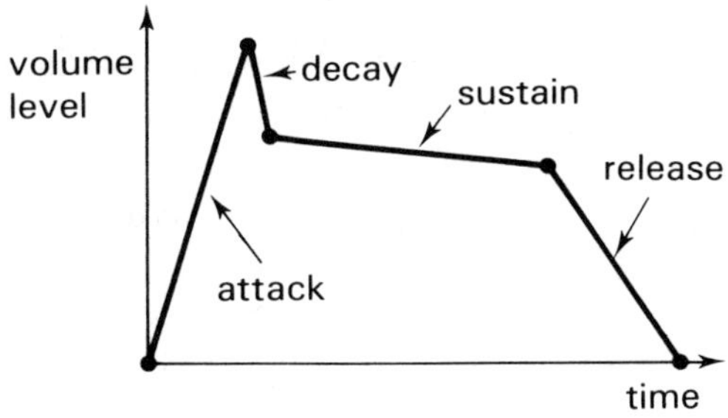

This consists of four sections: Attack, Decay, Sustain and Release. For that reason it is known as an ADSR envelope.

The **attack** portion of the envelope is how it begins, as was explained above.

The **decay** portion is where the sound first begins to die away.

The **sustain** portion is where the sound subsequently holds its level for the rest of the note's duration.

The **release** portion is where the sound dies away after the duration has been completed. On a piano this would be when the key is released. On a wind instrument it would be when the player stops blowing.

With this four-part envelope a much better approximation to real envelopes can be achieved. A piano-like sound, for example, will have a steep decay and gentle sustain, with the release part interrupting to cut it off when the note's duration is complete; as if the piano key had been released and the damper had fallen back on to the string:

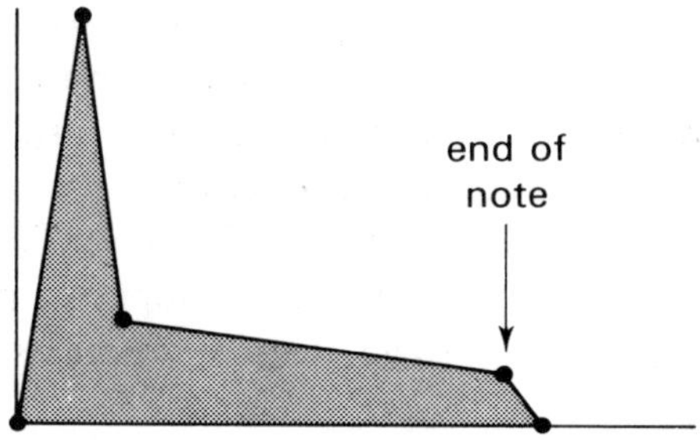

Similarly, the shape of the first ADSR envelope above can be used to obtain a brass-like sound.

On an older, conventional synthesizer, the ADSR levels would be controlled with knobs. On a computer synthesizer, their levels can be set as numbers in a program.

The ENVELOPE statement

The instruction for specifying an envelope on the BBC computer sound synthesizer is the word ENVELOPE followed by 14 numbers, or parameters. It helps to think of them in three groups: a group of 2, followed by two groups of 6. A typical ENVELOPE command might look like this:

```
10 ENVELOPE 1,1,
            0,0,0,0,0,0,
            126,-5,-1,-1,126,120
```

We have put the values on three different lines for clarity. When you type them in, keep them all on one continuous line.

The first parameter is the envelope number. It is possible to have up to 16 different envelopes, but you would not normally need more than four. Most of the time just one will do.

The second parameter is the size of the time unit being used to define the envelope, in hundredths of a second. Each time unit is known as a **step**. It will nearly always be 1, but can be usefully increased for particular effects.

The next six values allow the pitch of a note to be modified to produce more complicated sounds. They control what is known as the **pitch envelope**, and are considered on p.148. Often these values are not needed and can all be set to 0. That is how we will leave them for the time being.

The remaining six values are used to define volume envelopes with shapes like those described in the last section. This is often known as the **amplitude envelope**. We will look at this part first.

The amplitude envelope

It is useful to use letters to refer to the six parameters in the amplitude part of the ENVELOPE statement. The first four of these are used to set ADSR slopes, like those explained on p.137, and so can simply be called A, D, S and R for Attack, Decay, Sustain and Release. The remaining two of the six set the actual volume levels to which the attack, and then the decay slopes are directed. They can be called AT for Attack Target, and DT for Decay Target.

Positioned in the ENVELOPE statement, they appear like this:

```
ENVELOPE 1,1,
         0,0,0,0,0,0
         A,D,S,R,AT,DT
```

This diagram shows how they relate to the envelope shape:

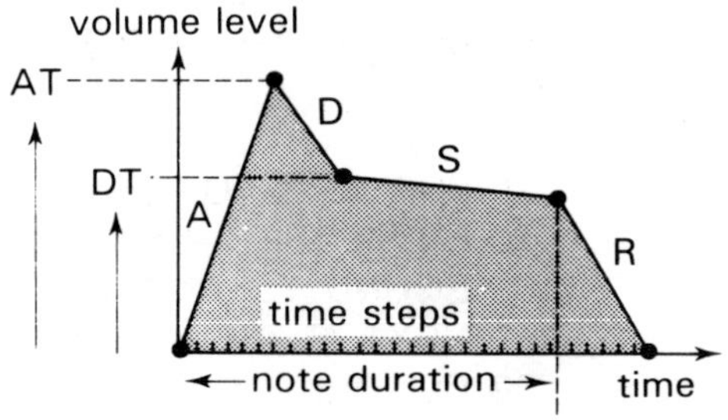

We will now see what range of values these parameters can take, and what effects they will have.

Attack

A, the attack slope value, will be a number between 1 and 126. It represents how many volume units the sound rises for each time step of the envelope.

If it is set to a low number, it will rise slowly. That will produce a soft attack where the sound gradually builds up to its maximum volume. This is characteristic of a violin or cello sound, for example.

If A is set to a high number it will produce a sharp attack where the sound reaches its maximum volume almost immediately. This is characteristic of percussion instruments. Most familiar sounds have a fairly sharp attack, so this will nearly always be set high unless an unusual effect is desired.

You should notice that there is little or no difference in the effect produce by different numbers, when the value of A is high. A value of 50 sounds much the same as a value of 100. On the other hand, differences in low values are much more noticeable. An attack slope value of 1 will make the sound build up fairly slowly. Increase it to 2, and the sound will build up twice as fast, which is quite an appreciable difference.

If the slope level is very small, and the envelope is being used on a short note, the note may actually complete its duration and stop before the attack reaches its target level.

This program demonstrates some of these effects by stepping through all possible attack values in sequence. The other parameters are given fixed values for the time being; they will be explained later. Pitches are selected at random:

attack

```
10 FOR A=1 TO 126
20 ENVELOPE 1,1,0,0,0,0,0,0,A,-1,-1,-1,126,10
30 SOUND 1,1,RND(12)*4+50,20
40 NEXT A
50 GOTO 10
```

Notice that once it gets past the first few notes, the sound quality changes very little.

The attack part of a sound is nearly always much steeper than the decay. Very soft attacks are unusual with natural sounds, but may be used for particular effects.

One such effect is a piano sound played backwards, familiar to those who have experimented with tape recorders. The note envelopes are all reversed. The attacks become decays, and what were the decays become attacks. The notes appear to build up gradually to maximum volume, then immediately drop down ready for the next note to begin. It produces a strange sort of whooping effect:

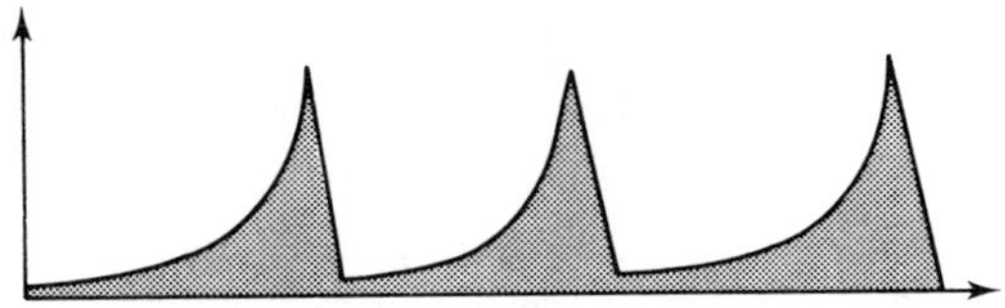

A way of programming this effect is shown on p.146 after the decay parameter has been explained.

Experts on old performance techniques suggest that early instruments like viols were played to produce the same sort of scooping sound. Some "authentic" performances of Bach and Handel deliberately cultivate the effect which can sound quite odd to modern ears.

Attack target

The **attack target** is the last-but-one number. It must also be between 1 and 126. It gives the maximum volume level which the attack slope will aim for. Effectively, it sets the general volume level and will nearly always be equal to the maximum value of 126.

When using SOUND statements without envelopes before, the volume level was specified as a number between 0 and −15. This attack target parameter is really equivalent to that, but instead of having just 15 degrees of loudness, there are 126. The comments made in Chapter 2 about the scale of volume levels also applies in this case. There is a much more significant difference in loudness between 120 and 126, say, than between 20 and 26.

In order to regulate the volume of a sequence of notes when using an envelope, to make them gradually louder for example, it is necessary to redefine the whole envelope before each note is sounded. This is demonstrated in later chapters; the disappearing steam train effect, for instance, in Chapter 11.

We mentioned before that if you attempt to sound a short note with a low A value, to get a soft attack, you may discover that it does not reach the specified AT value before the note's duration is up. If that happens, and another note follows, the second note will begin at the volume level where the first note left off. It will continue to complete the rest of the attack slope until the AT value is reached. This can be annoying, since it usually results in an unintentional effect. This program demonstrates what happens:

attack

```
10 ENVELOPE 1,1,0,0,0,0,0,0,1,-1,-1,-1,126,100
20 SOUND 1,1,RND(255),20
30 GOTO 10
```

attack target

Experiment with different duration values at the end of line 20. Taking the duration up to 30 will make the notes long enough to sound singly. Reducing it to 4 will result in seven different pitches for each attack period!

We would not normally require attacks longer than those obtained setting A to 1, but it is sometimes desirable for particular effects. It can be done by increasing the size of the time step unit, the second parameter of the ENVELOPE statement. Changing it from 1 to 2, for example, effectively stretches a whole envelope to twice its length, and accordingly halves all the slopes. Examples of this occur later.

Decay and sustain

The decay slope, sustain slope and decay target are used to define the shape of the rest of the envelope. Since D and S represent slopes which go down, as opposed to the attack slope which goes up, they are expressed as negative numbers. They would normally be set to a figure like −1, though their full available range is 0 to −126.

The comments made about attack slope values equally apply here. There is a much more significant difference between lower values than between high ones. −2 gives a decay twice as steep as −1. It would not normally be necessary to use any value beyond −10, say, apart from −126 itself for an immediate cut-off effect.

We can juggle with the relative values of D and S to obtain different shaped slopes. Setting D to −2, followed by −1 for S will produce a concave slope like this, where the sound starts to die away quickly then levels off to linger for a while:

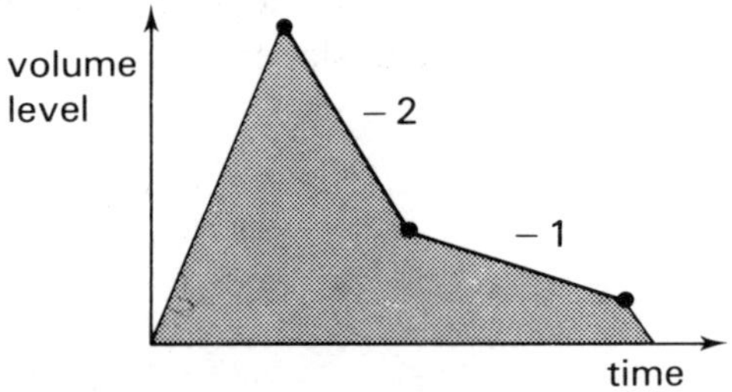

The reverse situation, setting D to −1, followed by −2 for S, will produce a convex slope where the sound fades gently at first then suddenly starts to die away faster:

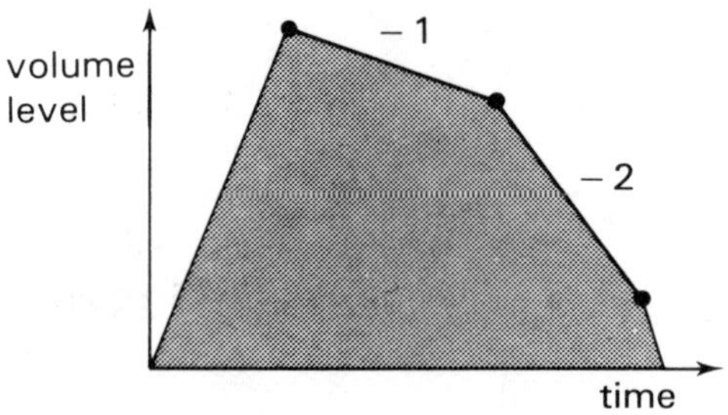

The value of DT, the decay target volume level, is set so that once the decay slope reaches that value, it changes to the sustain slope. In the concave example above it would need to be reasonably low, say at 70. In the convex example it would be higher, say at 110.

The appropriate ENVELOPE statements would be:

For the concave slopes: decay | decay target

```
ENVELOPE 1,1,0,0,0,0,0,0,126,-2,-1,-1,126,70
```

sustain

and for the convex slope:

decay target

decay

ENVELOPE 1,1,0,0,0,0,0,0,126,–1,–2,–1,126,110

sustain

D and S can also be set equal to 0, which means they may not change at all.

Sometimes there may be more than one way of defining the same envelope. In this example, the attack is followed by a single slope:

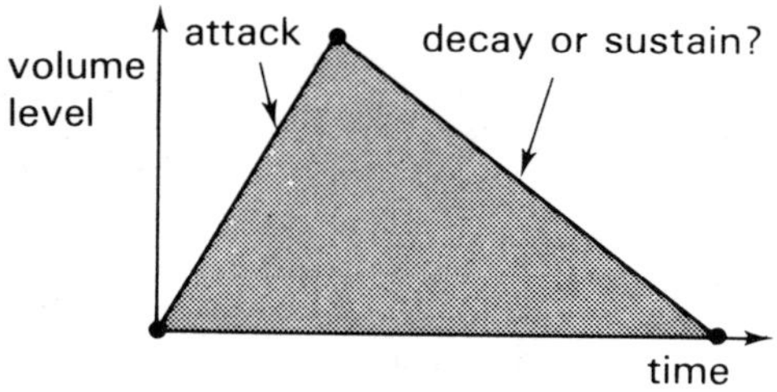

It can be defined as a simple decay with no sustain:

decay   sustain

ENVELOPE 1,1,0,0,0,0,0,0,30,–1,0,0,126,0

or as a sustain with no initial decay, in which case the attack target, AT, will equal the decay target, DT:

decay   sustain

ENVELOPE 1,1,0,0,0,0,0,0,30,0,–1,0,126,126

AT = DT

Many different envelopes are used throughout this book. Examine them to see what values for A, D, S, R, AT and DT have been used. Experiment by changing their values, and try different envelopes in different programs.

Honky-tonk piano and reversed piano

We can get a piano-like envelope (see p.137–8) by making D fairly steep, and S more gentle. We end up with an envelope like this:

```
10 ENVELOPE 1,1,0,0,0,0,0,0,60,-10,-1,-1,126,100
20 SOUND 1,1,RND(24)*4,4
30 GOTO 20
```

Of course, this is still a long way from a real piano sound. We are rather limited by the fixed square-waves of the computer's sound generator. Nevertheless, there are other possibilities to liven up the sound.

Any piano note is actually produced by the vibration of up to three different strings which, even on the best pianos, may be very slightly out of tune. When they are badly out of tune they produce the familiar honky-tonk sound. We can double up our piano sound on channel 2, at a pitch which is 1 step higher, and therefore slightly out of tune with channel 1:

```
20 P=RND(24)*4
30 SOUND 1,1,P,2
40 SOUND 2,1,P+1,2
```

In addition, a piano note will contain a hint of pitches one octave higher and beyond. We can make the third channel play notes one octave above, that is 48 pitch steps higher:

```
50 SOUND 3,1,P+48,2
```

We have used a duration value of 2 here since shorter sounds tend to be more convincing. The ear does not have time to register the inconsistencies before the next note is upon it. Putting these bits together, and making use of the 1/RND(1) function we came across in Chapter 5 to choose the pitches, the honky-tonk piano program becomes:

```
10 ENVELOPE 1,1,0,0,0,0,0,0,60,-10,-1,-1,126,100
20 P=INT(1/RND(1))*4
30 SOUND 1,1,P,2
40 SOUND 2,1,P+1,2
50 SOUND 3,1,P+48,2
60 GOTO 20
```

We can also define an envelope to get the **reverse piano** effect we described on p.141. A slow attack, with A=2, will need to be followed with a sharp decay, where D=−126. DT will equal 0. S and R can take any value since in this case they do not get used:

attack decay

```
10 ENVELOPE 1,1,0,0,0,0,0,0,2,-126,0,0,126,0
20 SOUND 1,1,RND(24)*4,20
30 GOTO 20
```

For an effect closer to the seventeenth-century technique of bowing string instruments, which was also mentioned before, the decay slope should be set less steeply: −3 is a reasonable value.

Release

The release portion of the envelope determines what happens to a note once its full duration has been completed. Very often it will die away almost immediately with a value of say, −10. Alternatively, it may linger for a while, dying away gently like a bell sound, in which case it would have a value of −1.

The release phase will only come into effect and be heard if a note is followed by a rest. Since most of the music we have been making has produced continuous, uninterrupted sequences of notes, the release portion would never be heard, except perhaps at the very end of a sequence. Here, for example, it is only heard after the seventh note, the last in the group, has sounded:

release

```
10 ENVELOPE 1,1,0,0,0,0,0,0,60,-1,0,-1,126,100
20 FOR I=1 TO 7
30 SOUND 1,1,RND(255),6
40 NEXT I
```

If R is set to 0, then when a note completes its duration it will continue to sound at whatever volume level it reached at the end of the sustain period. Unless stopped, it will carry on for ever. To demonstrate this, change the ENVELOPE definition in the program above to:

```
                                    release
                                          ↘
10 ENVELOPE 1,1,0,0,0,0,0,0,60,-1,-1,0,126,100
```

Pressing ESCAPE will stop the sound.

It is important to realize that when one note follows straight after another, it always begins at the volume with which the previous note ended, as we found when considering attacks. For example, if an envelope is defined with this shape:

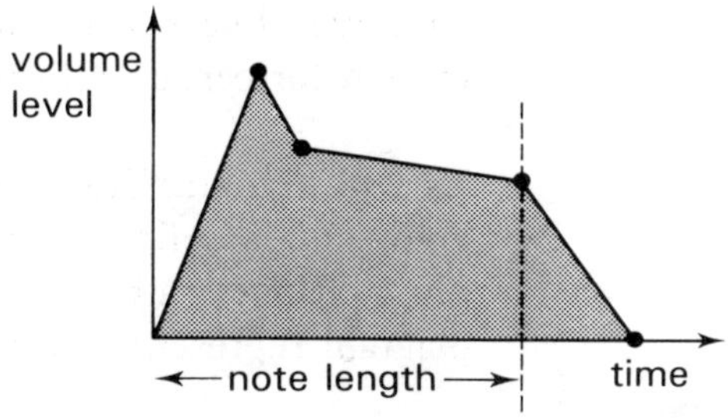

Then used with a sequence of short notes where the envelopes joined up, it would produce an effect like this:

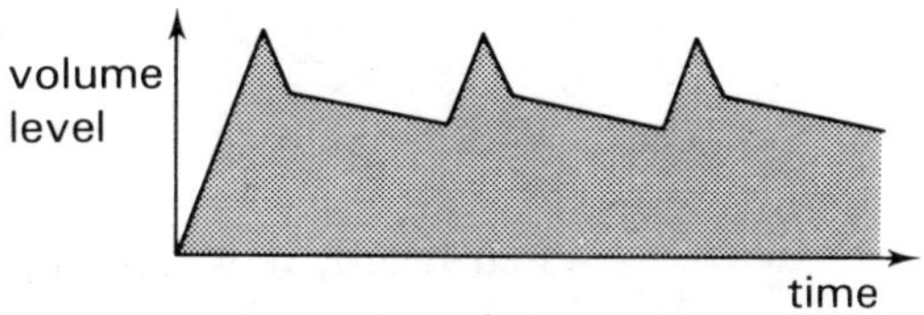

In practical terms, when a sharp attack is being used it usually makes no audible difference. Sometimes it means that the first note in a sequence sounds slightly different to the ones which follow.

It is also possible to give negative values to the attack slope, A, and positive values to the decay slope, D. Oddly-shaped wheezing sounds may then be produced, when the chaining effect of the envelopes is taken into account:

```
                                 attack ↘   ↙ decay
10 ENVELOPE 1,1,0,0,0,0,0,0,-2,2,-2,-2,0,126
20 SOUND 1,1,RND(255),RND(30)
30 GOTO 20
```

The pitch envelope

We will now consider the middle group of six values which have so far been occupied by 0s. Whereas the last six values are used to change the **volume** of the sound, the middle six are used to modify the **pitch** of the sound. This is known as the **pitch envelope**.

With an ordinary melody it can be used to make the pitch wobble, and so produce a vibrato. Used more adventurously it can produce a wide range of sound effects. The pitch envelope operates quite independently of the amplitude envelope. They do not normally need to be co-ordinated, though for certain effects it can be useful, as we shall see.

As with the amplitude envelope, a pattern of slopes, or gradients, is defined, but this time they are slopes which set pitch changes rather than volume changes. For example, this diagram represents a pitch envelope:

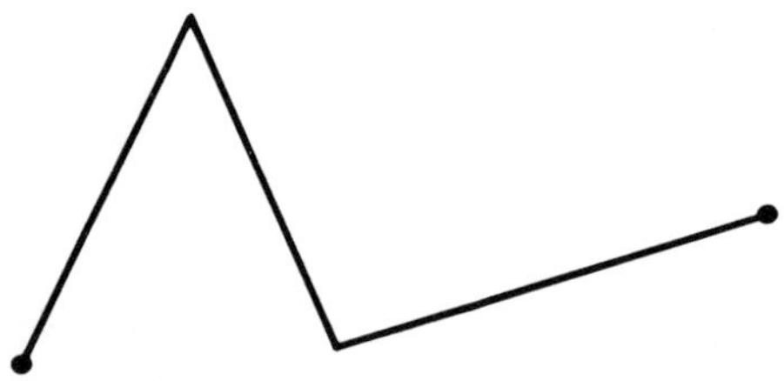

When heard, it would appear to make a sound which rises steeply from a base pitch to a peak, falls steeply back again, and then rises slowly once more. In fact, pitch envelopes like this are similar to some of the glissandi shapes produced in Chapter 4.

There is a major difference between the pitch envelope and the amplitude envelope in the way they spread over the duration of a note. The amplitude envelope extends the whole length of a note, whereas the pitch envelope has a fixed length, and normally keeps repeating itself until the note length set by the SOUND statement is completed. The previous example pitch envelope shape, when repeated throughout a note's duration, would produce an effect like this:

The base pitch from which the envelope starts is the value set in the SOUND statement used to make the note. If the base pitch is high, and the pitch envelope tries to go above the maximum pitch value of 255, then the wrap-around effect mentioned before comes into play. Sounds will reappear at 0 pitch to complete the pitch envelope from there.

For the purposes of defining a pitch envelope, the shape can be split into three segments. Our earlier example could be measured up like this:

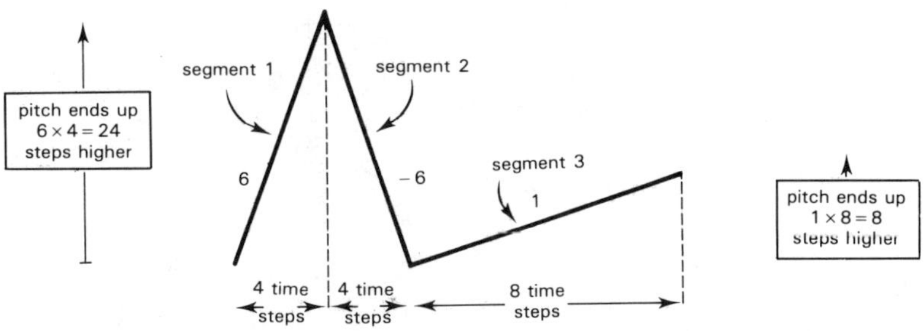

For each of the segments we need to specify:

(1) how long it lasts (how many time steps)
(2) the slope or gradient (the pitch change per step)

In the above example we can give the first segment a length of 4 steps and make the gradient fairly steep with a value of 6. This means that the pitch will rise by a total of 24 pitch steps in that segment. Segment 2 will have the same length as segment 1, and an equivalent descending gradient of −6 to bring the pitch back to 0. Segment 3 will be longer, at 8 time steps, and with a gentler gradient of 1. These six values are not put into the ENVELOPE statement in segment order, but are grouped so that the three gradients come first, followed by the three segment length values. In our example they will end up like this:

6, −6, 1, 4, 4, 8

Here they are incorporated into a complete ENVELOPE statement:

gradients

```
10 ENVELOPE 1,1,6,−6,1,4,4,8,60,−1,−1,−1,126,0
20 SOUND 1,1,RND,20
30 GOTO 20
```

segment lengths

The other lines have been included to demonstrate what this pitch envelope will sound like.

Two-segment pitch envelopes

The last example produced quite a complicated vibrato effect. Very often we will only need two segments to get the effect we are after in a pitch envelope. For example, a more straightforward vibrato has this shape:

This only needs two segments to specify its shape: a rise of 1 pitch step for 1 time step in the first, and a fall of 1 pitch step for 1 time step in the second. The redundant spaces reserved for the third segment in the ENVELOPE statement can be occupied by 0s. The six values of the pitch envelope will then be:

1, −1, 0, 1, 1, 0

Here it is incorporated into a small program to demonstrate the effect:

```
              pitch envelope
10 ENVELOPE 1,1,1,-1,0,1,1,0,30,-1,0,0,126,0
20 SOUND 1,1,RND(24)*4,20
30 GOTO 20
```

This produces quite a fast, almost buzzing vibrato. A more natural vibrato would be slower. In other words, the time segments should be longer. The problem is, if the segment lengths are increased by making them equal to a larger number of time steps, then the pitch will also rise through an equivalent number of pitch steps, even with the gradient still at 1. That is not the effect we wanted.

Another way to increase the segment lengths is to change the value of the time unit, T. This is the second number in the ENVELOPE statement's parameter list, which we identified on p.138. Up to now it has always been equal to 1. Increasing its value to 2 will effectively stretch the envelope to twice its length, halving all the slope values in the process. It not only affects the pitch envelope, but also the amplitude part of the envelope, having a general mellowing effect all round. Setting T equal to 5 or 6 produces a vibrato closer to the sound of a soprano voice. For example:

```
          [T]
10 ENVELOPE 1,5,1,-1,0,1,1,0,30,-1,0,0,126,0
20 SOUND 1,1,RND(25)*4+120,20
30 GOTO 20
```

Other values are also worth trying out.

Returning to the envelope we had before, where T=1, we can see what happens when we increase the segment lengths:

```
10 ENVELOPE 1,1,1,-1,0,27,27,0,30,-1,0,-1,126,0
20 SOUND 1,1,RND(200),20
30 GOTO 20
                                 segment
                                 lengths
```

This produces a sequence of wobbly, up-and-down glissando sounds, not unlike the wolf-whistles we encountered in Chapter 4. If we make the note duration longer in the SOUND statement, and change the amplitude part of the ENVELOPE so that the sound is always at maximum volume, we get a wailing siren:

```
10 ENVELOPE 1,1,1,–1,0,27,27,0,126,0,0,–126,126,0
20 SOUND 1,1,RND(200),200
30 GOTO 20
```

amplitude envelope

Changing the segment lengths, 27 in the example above, varies the depth and speed of the siren. We can also change the amplitude envelope to make the siren appear to come closer and then move away:

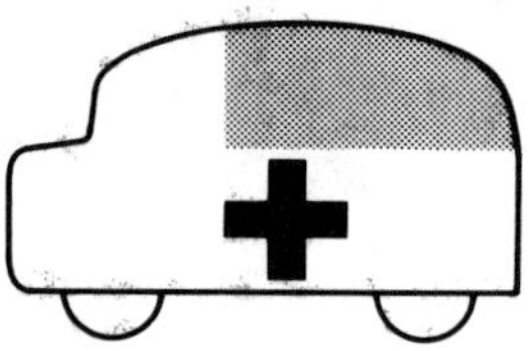

```
10 ENVELOPE 1,1,1,–1,0,24,24,0,1,–1,0,0,126,10
20 SOUND 1,1,RND(200),100
30 GOTO 20
```

One-segment pitch envelope, and other effects

We can slim the pitch envelope down even further to just one segment, for example to give just the rising part of a glissando:

```
10 ENVELOPE 1,1,1,0,0,25,0,0,126,0,0,–126,126,0
20 SOUND 1,1,RND(200),RND(100)
30 GOTO 20
```

If we increase the gradient to 4, it means that the pitch steps come in regular semitones. With the time step, T, set to 1 this is heard as a continuous glissando. Increasing T to a higher value, say 8 for example, has the effect of making each pitch step heard as a distinct note. This will produce a sequence of rising chromatic scales:

```
10 ENVELOPE 1,8,4,0,0,25,0,0,126,0,0,–126,126,0
20 SOUND 1,1,RND(200),RND(200)
30 GOTO 20
```

By changing line 20, we can introduce notes on other channels as well, to produce parallel staircases of ascending scales:

```
10 ENVELOPE 1,8,4,0,0,25,0,0,126,0,0,–126,126,0
20 SOUND RND(3),1,RND(200),RND(200)
30 GOTO 20
```

By making use of the other segments of the pitch envelope,

set to different gradients and lengths, overlapping cascades of scale patterns can be produced:

```
10 ENVELOPE 1,8,4,-7,15,25,27,6,126,0,0,-126,126,0
20 SOUND RND(3),1,RND(200),RND(100)
30 GOTO 20
```

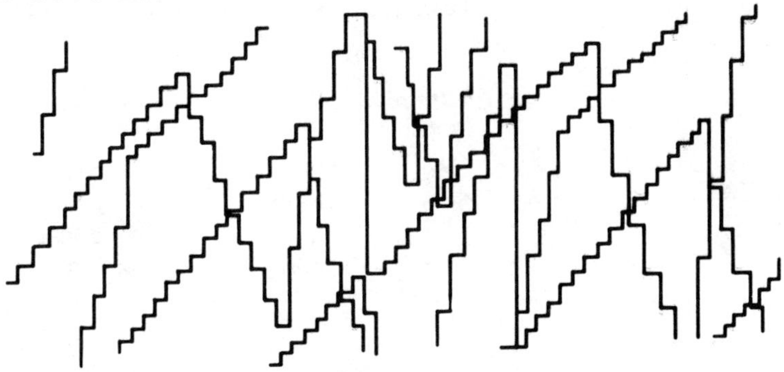

With complex pitch envelopes notes can be set to continue endlessly by making the SOUND statement's duration equal to 255:

```
10 ENVELOPE 1,4,47,-100,12,107,89,34,126,0,0,0,
            126,0
20 SOUND 1,1,RND,255
```

The effect of the envelope produces a rich and constantly changing sound. In such a case, you can continue listing, editing or even run a completely different program whilst the sound goes on regardless. Pressing ESCAPE will stop it.

Returning to a two-segment pitch envelope again, we can get an interesting sound using a short time step and a large pitch change gradient:

```
10 ENVELOPE 1,1,57,-57,0,1,1,0,126,-1,-1,-1,126,0
20 SOUND 1,1,RND(255),RND(30)
30 GOTO 20
```

This produces a trilling effect, where a variety of additional pitches may be heard. It sounds almost like a shimmering chord. Using different pitch gradient values will produce a range of similar sounds.

It is worth experimenting with different values and combinations to get various shades of effects between the limits which have been described. This chart gives a rough summary. Low values usually imply single digit numbers, say 1 to 9. High values can mean anything above 10 (or below −10). If required, pitch gradients can be between −128 and 127, and segment lengths between 0 and 255.

time step length	pitch gradient value	segment length	effect
1 to 5	low	short	vibrato
5+	high	long	cascades and scales
1 or 2	high	short	shimmering effect
1 or 2	low	long	wolf-whistles & sirens

Using a pitch envelope without auto-repeat

It is possible to make the pitch envelope operate so that it does not repeat itself automatically as it has been doing so far. Used in this way, the envelope will only affect the beginning of a note. It will produce a squelch, or twiddle at the start of each note, but the remainder of the note's duration will continue at a steady pitch. For example, the first pitch envelope we had on p.148, when used without auto-repeat, will produce a note with this pitch contour:

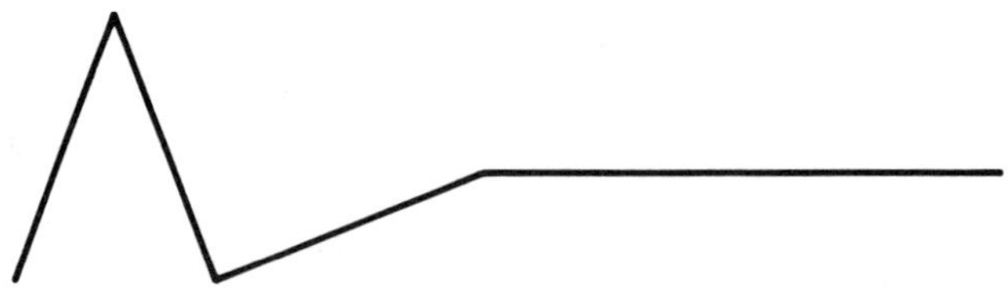

The method for cancelling the auto-repeat in the ENVELOPE statement is rather clumsy. The instruction has two possibilities: auto-repeat on, or auto-repeat off. Rather than waste space on an extra parameter just for that, one of the other parameters, T, has been made to double-up and do an extra job in addition to specifying the size of the envelope's time step.

Usually, T will have a value between 0 and 127. Setting this to a value greater than 127 is the means of telling the computer not to auto-repeat. It needs to become 128 + whatever the time step length is.

To specify a length of 1, which we have been using most of the time, and also cancel the auto-repeat, we would make T equal to 129.

This example ENVELOPE instructs the computer not to auto-repeat, using the pitch envelope shape drawn above, and lengthening the time step value to 2:

```
10 ENVELOPE 1,130,6,-6,1,4,4,8,60,-1,-1,-1,126,0
20 SOUND 1,1,RND,20
30 GOTO 20
```

You should be able to hear the wriggle at the beginning of each note, which then settles down on to a constant pitch. This is actually a characteristic of natural instrumental sounds which are often slightly distorted at the beginning, though not usually to quite the same extent as in this example! The effect would normally be kept more subtle by setting low gradient and segment length values.

Summary

This list summarizes the form of the ENVELOPE statement.

ENVELOPE N,T,G1,G2,G3,L1,L2,L3,A,D,S,R,AT,DT

	parameter	range	meaning
	N	normally 1 to 4 (but can go to 16)	envelope number
	T	0 to 127 or 128 to 255	size of the time step unit in hundredths of a second. Usually 1. Values above 128 stop the pitch envelope auto-repeating
pitch envelope	G1 G2 G3	−128 to 127	gradient of each segment of the pitch envelope. Low values for subtle effects, high for wild effects
pitch envelope	L1 L2 L3	0 to 255	Length of each segment of the pitch envelope. Usually quite a low value

(list continued overleaf)

(list continued)

amplitude envelope	A	−127 to 127	attack slope value	1: gentle slope ±127 = sharp slope
	D	−127 to 127	immediate decay slope value	
	S	−127 to 0	sustain slope value	
	R	−127 to 0	release slope value	
	AT	0 to 126	attack target value equivalent to overall volume level	
	DT	0 to 126	decay target value	

You can swap around and try out various combinations of different parts of the example envelopes that have been given in the chapter. Alternative envelopes can also be substituted in many of the programs throughout the book.

In other chapters we have explored the possibilities of random control and variation. It is interesting to try and make all of the envelope parameters work at random, producing a writhing mixture of sound. It is important to use sensible limits, or long, boring silences will intervene.

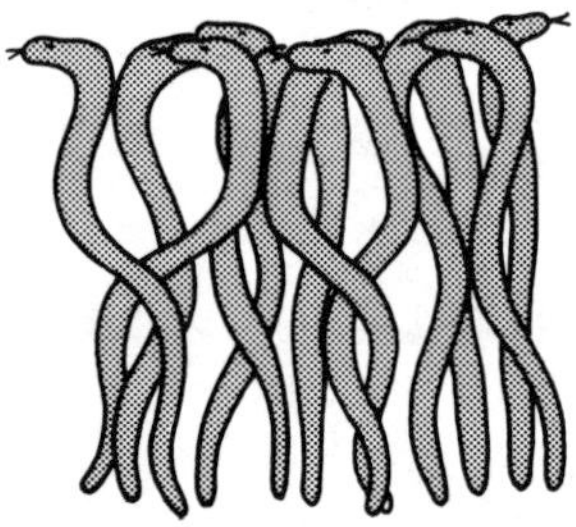

```
10 ENVELOPE 1,RND(20),RND,RND,RND,RND(100),
            RND(100),RND(100),RND(126),−RND(8),
            RND(2)−2,−1,126,RND(70)+50
20 SOUND RND(3),1,RND,RND(100)
30 GOTO 20
```

Notice that if RND is used by itself, without any number following in brackets, then the program automatically adjusts the value produced to fit within the permitted limits for that parameter, on the wrap-around principal.

In this program the computer will define a different envelope each time it is run. If you want to be able to recall a particular envelope that sounds good, the parameter values must be worked out first and then substituted into the ENVELOPE statement. The values can then be displayed on the screen, like this:

```
10  ON ERROR GOTO 20
20  T=RND(20)
30  G1=RND(255):G2=RND(255):G3=RND(255)
```

```
40 L1=RND(255):L2=RND(255):L3=RND(255)
50 A=RND(126):D=-RND(8):S=RND(2)-2
60 DT=RND(70)+50
70 ENVELOPE 1,T,G1,G2,G3,L1,L2,L3,A,D,S,-1,126,DT
80 CLS
90 PRINTTAB(0,10)"ENVELOPE 1,";T","
100 PRINTTAB(10,12);G1",";G2",";G3",";L1",";L2","
    ;L3","
110 PRINTTAB(10,14);A",";D",";S",-1,126",";DT
120 SOUND RND(3),1,RND,RND(100)
130 GOTO 120
```

When typing these lines in, do not add line 10 until last, after you have checked for typing errors in the rest of the program. The instruction in line 10 means that each time you press ESCAPE a new envelope will be defined. It also means that if you have made an error when typing in the program, the usual error checking procedure will not work. You will need to use BREAK to stop the program, and then type OLD to recover it if you need to.

A further alternative is to generate a few envelopes at random which can sound together on different channels.

```
10 ON ERROR GOTO 20
20 ENVELOPE RND(4),RND(20),RND,RND,RND,RND(100),
            RND(100),RND(100),RND(126),-RND(8),
            RND(2)-2,-1,126,RND(70)+50
30 SOUND RND(3),RND(4),RND,RND(100)
40 GOTO 20
```

The first time this is run, it will define just one envelope (unless some are already stored in the computer from previous programs). Press ESCAPE a few times to define a few different envelopes to start off with. Press ESCAPE again each time you want to change the sound.

An aural illusion — the endless glissando

You are probably familiar with the well-known optical illusion, or impossible object, of an endless staircase which appears to go inexorably onwards and upwards:

The graphic artist, Escher, used the illusion as the basis of a number of his etchings. It also works with a waterfall, for example. It is possible to produce a similar aural illusion which confuses the ears into thinking that they are hearing an endlessly descending (or ascending) glissando. It is a good example of how the pitch and amplitude parts of the envelope may be linked.

Sounds which are consistently one or two octaves apart tend to blend into each other and be heard as a single note. This forms the basis of the illusion.

We can generate a falling glissando which starts inaudibly at a high pitch, and then slowly increases in volume. After it has descended one octave a second glissando joins in, following the same pattern, whilst the first continues to get louder. As these two continue, others join in one by one, always one octave apart. Meanwhile, the original glissando, after peaking in volume in the middle of its range, proceeds to die away slowly as it drops through lower pitches. The other glissandi follow suit. Once a glissando reaches the bottom of its range, it reappears inaudibly at the top of its range and so continues the process indefinitely. The ear does not register the subtle entry and departure of the individual components, but just hears the whole sound as one constantly descending glissando which apparently has no start or end. It keeps moving down like the never-ending staircase.

On a large, sophisticated computer music system this effect can be produced convincingly. It is possible to produce, say, ten simultaneous glissandi all very carefully controlled in pitch and volume. At least two computer music composers have used the device to good effect in their compositions, the Frenchman Jean Claude Risset and the American, Lejaren Hiller.

On our little BBC machine the best we can hope for is a rough approximation to the effect, but we can nevertheless achieve quite a reasonable result.

With three sound channels available, the effect we are after can be represented by this diagram:

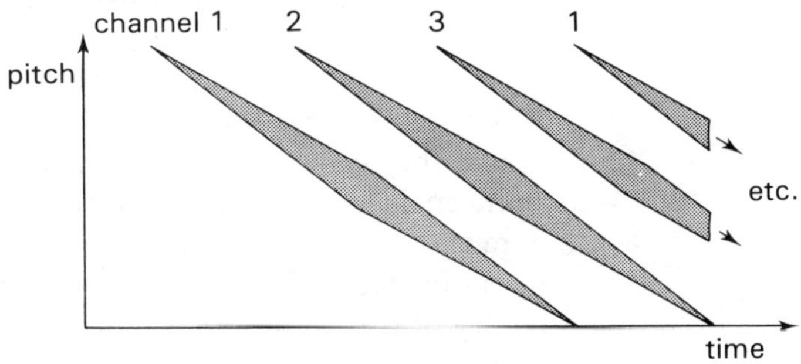

The thickness of the line represents the volume of the sound. We want each glissando to last for the maximum duration of a note, that is 254 steps of one twentieth of a second, which is a little over 10 seconds.

First we consider the pitch envelope. We need just one segment, with a slope of −1, and lasting for the maximum note duration of 254 steps. To make the envelope time steps, measured in hundredths of a second, match up to the duration value in the SOUND statement, measured in twentieths of a second, the step size T must be set to 5. The beginning of the ENVELOPE statement will then look like this:

```
10 ENVELOPE 1,5,-1,0,0,254,0,0, . . .
```

The amplitude envelope will need to rise smoothly from 0 to the maximum volume of 126 in its centre, and then fall back again to 0:

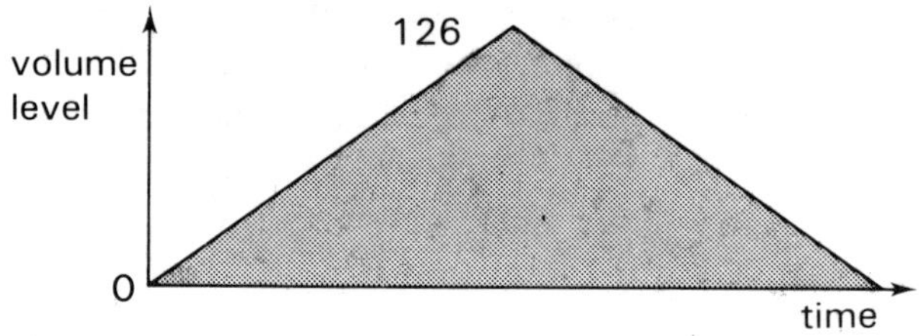

It only requires values of 1 and −1 for the attack and decay slopes respectively. Rising to the maximum attack target of 126 and falling back to a decay target of 0 makes the complete ENVELOPE statement look like this:

```
10 ENVELOPE 1,5,−1,0,0,254,0,0,1,−1,0,0,126,0
```

The starting pitch set in the SOUND statement will be given its maximum value of 255.

The second and third channel entries need to be delayed so that they come in exactly one octave after the preceding channel. In fact, it makes better use of the available pitch range if they are made to appear at two-octave intervals. It can be done by giving the channels dummy, silent notes to play at the beginning. To bring the second channel in on the 96th time step, and make it two octaves above the first, we can give its dummy note a duration value of 95. Similarly, the third channel's dummy note will have a duration of 96+95, which is 191. The complete program then becomes:

```
10 ENVELOPE 1,5,−1,0,0,254,0,0,1,−1,0,0,126,0
20 SOUND 3,0,0,191
30 SOUND 2,0,0,95
40 SOUND 1,1,255,254
50 SOUND 2,1,255,254
60 SOUND 3,1,255,254
70 GOTO 40
```

To change the direction of the glissando to up instead of down just change the pitch gradient value, the third parameter in the ENVELOPE statement, from −1 to 1. It is not even necessary to change the pitch value in the SOUND statements as the automatic wrap-around takes care of the limits. The program will work with any pitch values in the SOUND statement, as long as they are the same for all three channels, though producing slightly different effects. It is worth experimenting with them. You can also see what happens when you change the step and segment sizes in the pitch envelope.

The overall effect is not as good as it might be due to the doubtful tuning of the higher pitches, and the fact that the square waves produced by the BBC computer do not blend as well as pure sine waves would. It nevertheless demonstrates some of the flexibility and usefulness of the ENVELOPE command.

9 Organizing the keyboard

turning the keyboard into an organ

A silly organ for the fumble-fingered

We have seen that the simple form of the sound statement is:

```
10 SOUND 1,-15,pitch,4
```

This will produce a brief note at the loudest volume on channel 1 at whatever pitch we specify as the third parameter in the command. Instead of a pitch value we can put in the command GET, like this:

```
10 SOUND 1,-15,GET,4
```

On running this one-line program, when the computer reaches the command GET it will wait until a key on the keyboard is pressed. Each key will deliver a different number between 0 and 255 to the computer. This is known as its ASCII code. Thus the actual pitch sounded will depend on the key that is pressed after the program has been run.

To keep the process going continually we can make it into an endless loop. Each time the computer has played one note it will always be ready waiting for another key to be pressed:

```
10 SOUND 1,-15,GET,4
20 GOTO 10
```

Use ESCAPE to stop it running if you need to. After running it for a while and trying out the effect of pressing various different keys, a few points are evident.

First, we notice that the layout of the keyboard does not seem to correspond to a natural sequence of pitches. However, if you press a few numbers in sequence, 1, 2, 3, . . . etc., or press some letters in alphabetical order, you can hear that they proceed in regular steps. Holding down CTRL or SHIFT at the same time as pressing other keys will give a further range of notes.

CTRL	produces lowest notes
SHIFT	produces notes in the middle range
no CTRL or SHIFT	produces higher notes

Second, you will hear that the differences between neighbouring notes are very small. This is one eighth of a tone, the gap between consecutive pitch values, as was explained when the SOUND statement was introduced (Chapter 2). To make the pitches come in semitones, to which our ears are more attuned, the values must all be multiples of 4:

```
10 SOUND 1,-15,GET*4,4
```

Because of the "wrap-around" effect of pitch values, numbers which end up larger than 255 are automatically cut down to size. Thus 256 and 512 are the same as 0, 260 and 516 are the same as 4, and so on.

Third, if you press a few keys in rapid succession some notes will continue to play on even after you have stopped. This is because the keyboard has a buffer. The sound generator cannot use the next value which the keyboard tries to give it until it has played the full length of its current note. The next value, and the next, queue up in the buffer to wait their turn until the sound generator is ready. If we reduce the duration, say from 4 to 2, the note length is closer to the time taken to GET the values from the keyboard and the effect is not so great:

```
10 SOUND 1,-15,GET*4,2
```

Now you have to press the keys very rapidly indeed to "beat the buffer". You could reduce the duration to 1 but then the notes sound very spikey.

These two program lines can be combined into a rather neat one-line program. When BBC BASIC abbreviations are incorporated it becomes:

```
1 SO.1,-15,GET*4,2:G.1
```

which is about the shortest program there is which does something reasonably interesting.

An improved organ for the fumble-fingered

As it stands our brief program always produces notes of the same length. It would be much better if notes would continue to sound when a key is held down and then stop when it is released. The BBC computer has an automatic repeat on each key, useful for doing a line of dashes for example. A short time delay is built in to avoid making unintentional repeats. This time delay rather messes up the musical timing. If a key is held down there is a hiccup before the note sustains. Fortunately we can use a special "effects" (FX) command to remove the time delay:

```
*FX11,1
```

A similar command is used to shorten the time interval between the repeats on the key:

```
*FX12,1
```

We also want to make the note duration in the SOUND command as short as possible. Even a duration of 1 is long enough to block the buffer and spoil the timing.

There is an alternative version of the SOUND command available for us to use. If we put &1 in front of the channel number, making it &11 in this case, then as soon as the program reaches this line it will change the sound specification on that channel right away, interrupting whatever duration the previous note may have required. Thus the program cycles as quickly as possible and is always ready to GET the next key value.

Incorporating these changes the "disorgan" becomes:

```
10 *FX11,1
20 *FX12,1
30 SOUND &11,-15,GET*4,1
40 GOTO 30
```

If you use ESCAPE to interrupt and stop the program, and then try listing it, you will find your command appears on the screen looking something like this:

```
LLLLLLLLLIIIIIISSSSSSSSTTTTTTTT
```

This is because the repeat delay is still switched off! Another FX command will put things back to normal:

```
*FX12,0
```

But unless your fingers move at lightening speed you will have a problem typing it in. If you've already run the program and are stuck with an insoluble keyboard stutter your only solution is to press BREAK and type OLD to get the program back.

To make the program put things back to normal when it stops we need to add the FX command at the end:

```
10 *FX11,1
20 *FX12,1
30 SOUND &11,-15,GET*4,1
40 GOTO 30
50 *FX12,0
```

We still need an additional line. If the program is interrupted with ESCAPE it will jump out of the loop at line 30 or 40 and never get to line 50. One way round this is to use the command:

```
ON ERROR GOTO
```

at the beginning. When ESCAPE is pressed the program acts as if an error is registered and will jump to whatever line number is indicated.

Our short, completed "dis-organ" program now looks like this:

```
 5 ON ERROR GOTO 50
10 *FX11,1
20 *FX12,1
30 SOUND &11,-15,GET*4,1
40 GOTO 30
50 *FX12,0
```

If you omit line 20 the time gap between repeats remains at its original setting and gives the sound a tremulo effect. By changing the number after *FX12 in line 20 the rate of tremulo can be altered. Values between 5 and 10 work quite well:

```
*FX12,5  gives a fast tremulo
*FX12,10 gives a slow tremulo
```

Good keyboard players may wonder what is the point of this program. We will develop it to fit a conventional keyboard layout in the next section, but before we leave this one behind you will see that it is possible to have quite a bit of fun with it as it stands. It is also worth noting that a keyboard which makes sounds pitched in sequence for each letter of the alphabet could be useful to blind people, or for teaching young children the alphabet.

Some composers have made use of the letter names of notes to construct themes based on words. Schumann's first published composition was based on a theme with the notes A B E G G, the letters of a girl's name. The fact that only the first seven letters of the alphabet are available can be rather limiting. Germans have two extra letters to play with. They use H instead of our B, their B is our B♭, and they use S for our E♭. Hence BACH was able to incorporate notes corresponding to his name into some compositions. Dimitri Shostakovitch used his initial and the first three letters of the German spelling of his surname, DSCH, as a form of musical signature in many of his compositions. The contemporary composer Messiaen has worked out a way of linking each letter of the alphabet with a musical note so that he can use any group of words to construct themes. Even in the eleventh century the musician Guido d'Arezzo, who invented the music notation we still use today, devised a system of linking five notes to the five vowels. He used it as an instant method for setting the church liturgy to music. It is a curious coincidence that the surname of Charles Babbage, generally acknowledged to be the "father" of the computer, happens to consist entirely of musical letters. (Equally curious is the fact that Babbage had an almost pathological hatred of automatic musical instruments like barrel organs.)

With the computer keyboard functioning as an organ every letter has a note equivalent and we are not subject to the same limitations as Schumann. (Because the name of another girl he admired did not contain any musically useful letters he had to use the name of the town where she lived, ASCH, instead as the basis for one of his major works, *Carnival.*) Try typing your own name, or any other words, and listen to the tunes which result.

In order to play real tunes, if you are not a keyboard player, then you might just as well pick out notes on an unconventional keyboard as on a conventional one. And if you are a keyboard player, just try picking out a recognizable tune with this program. It is quite a challenging, but none-the-less useful, musical exercise to try it, and to remember which pitch corresponds to each key or letter.

Here are a few tunes in "dis-organ" notation to get you started. A dash, —, after a letter indicates that the note should be sustained:

Good King Wenceslas

T T T V T T O – Q O Q S T – T –

Twinkle, Twinkle, Little Star

M M T T V V T – R R Q Q O O M –

The Entertainer

J K L T – L T – L T –

J K L T – L T – L T –

J K L T – L T – L T –

T V X – T V X – T V T X T V X –

T V W X T V X – S V – T –

Q O N Q T X – V T Q V –

T V W X T V X – S V – T –

T V T X T V X – S V – T –

A musical keyboard for the nimble-fingered

We will now turn the computer keyboard into a model of a piano or organ keyboard. It is best to use the top two rows of keys for this. (That is the two rows below the red function keys.) The bottom two rows do not give as many notes and are not positioned well in relation to each other. On the other hand the top row of keys (numbers and symbols) extends further and fits squarely between the keys of the second row. They can happily take over the function of "black keys" on the piano. The second row of keys (QWERTY . . . etc.) will be the white keys.

We will design the keyboard to go from a low C on the far left (TAB key) up to a high D on the far right (↓key). The design of a conventional keyboard where black notes come in alternate groups of 2 and 3 will make keys 3,7,0 and ← redundant. ESCAPE will retain its usual function of allowing us to jump out of the program. This diagram shows how the notes will match the keys:

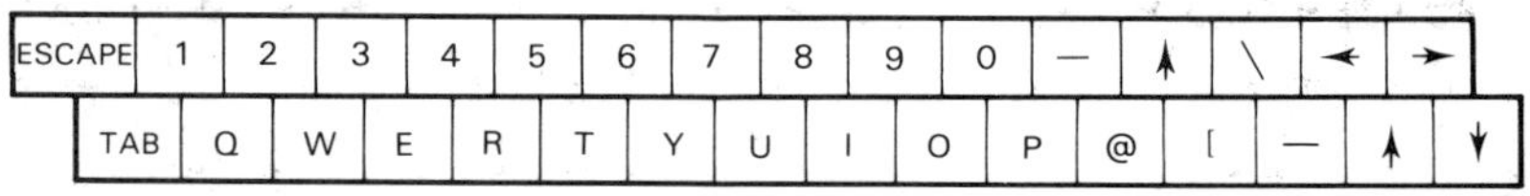

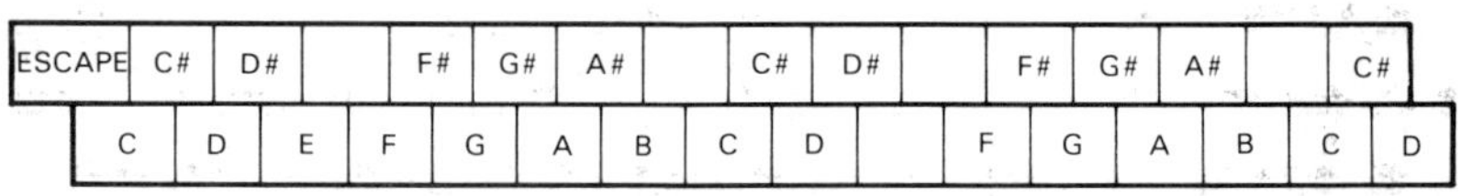

We have seen how each key will return an ASCII code, a number between 0 and 255, to the computer. What we need to do is find a way of changing each key's ASCII code into the required pitch number to sound the appropriate note on the keyboard. This chart lists the ASCII code for each key in ascending note sequence:

number	note	key	ASCII code
1	C	TAB	9
2	C#/D♭	1	49
3	D	Q	81

(continued)

(chart continued)

number	note	key	ASCII code
4	D# /E♭	2	50
5	E	W	87
6	F	E	69
7	F# /G♭	4	52
8	G	R	82
9	G# /A♭	5	53
10	A	T	84
11	A# /B♭	6	54
12	B	Y	89
13	C	U	85
14	C# /D♭	8	56
15	D	I	73
16	D# /E♭	9	57
17	E	O	79
18	F	P	80
19	F# /G♭	–	45
20	G	@	64
21	G# /A♭	^	94
22	A	[	91
23	A# /B♭	\	92
24	B	_	95
25	C		
26	C# /D♭		
27	D		

(N.B. This assumes CAPS LOCK is on.)

Special provision must be made for the last three keys, ↑, → and ↓, which are used to position the cursor for editing and will not normally return ASCII codes. A special FX command is available, *FX4,1 , which will change the normal function of these arrow keys to make them return ASCII codes instead and so complete our keyboard. Putting the command at the beginning of the program will make the keys return the values 139, 137 and 138 respectively, so the last three lines of the chart will be:

25	C	↑	139
26	C# /D♭	→	137
27	D	↓	138

We can get this information into the computer by setting up an array which will allow any ASCII code to be looked up in order to find the corresponding note number.

The array will have as many elements as the largest ASCII code to be encountered, that is 139. We will call the array N, reserving space for it at the start of the program with a DIM statement:

```
DIM N(139)
```

The best way to get the information into the array is to put the 27 ASCII codes into ascending note order as they are in the chart above. Using a loop the program then reads in the ASCII value, A, for each note in turn, goes to the Ath position in the N array and puts in the note number to which it corresponds, which will be the current value of I:

```
60 FOR I=1 TO 27
70 READ A
80 N(A)=I
90 NEXT I
100 DATA 9,49,81,50,87,69,52,82,53,84,54,89,85,56,
         73,57,79,80,45,64,94,91,92,95,139,137,138
```

As it stands this only reads the **note numbers** into the array. What we really require for making sounds are the **pitch values** understood by the SOUND statement. Multiplying each note number by four will give us the required semitone steps (as we did with GET *4 before). Also adding 1 will make the pitch values start at 5 for low C and then proceed 9 . . 13 . . 17 . . etc. in semitone steps as in the original note/pitch-value list in Chapter 2. A simple change to line 80 will give us the right values in the N array:

```
80 N(A) = I*4+1
```

When first defined the N array will have all its entries equal to 0. So, after reading in the 27 note-producing ASCII code values, all the remaining ASCII code positions in the array will give pitch values of 0. This is quite useful as it gives us a means of checking to see if any other stray key on the computer keyboard has been pressed, in which case the program can be instructed to ignore it:

```
110 P=N(GET)
120 IF P=0 THEN 110
```

Line 110 gets an ASCII value from the keyboard, looks up the pitch value in that position in the N array and assigns it to P. If line 120 were omitted then P would be able to assume the value 0 with the result that whenever a non music-making key was pressed the lowest note, with pitch value 0, would be heard. This can be irritating as it is easy to make frequent slips, especially with the 3, 7, 0 and → keys.

We now put all these parts together:
- —the "housekeeping" effects commands
- —error checking and declarations
- —setting up of the ASCII code pitch equivalents table
- —the repeated reading of the keyboard, as in the disorgan program

To give us the following result:

10 *FX4,1	set edit keys (←,↑,→,↓) to give ASCII values
20 DIM N(139)	declare note value array; all elements are initially 0
30 ON ERROR GOTO 150	make arrangements to put things back to normal when the program stops
40 *FX11,1	removes key auto-repeat delay
50 *FX12,1	shortens auto repeat gap to minimum
60 FOR I=1 TO 27 70 READ A 80 N(A)=I*4+1 90 NEXT I 100 DATA 9,49,81,50, 87,69,52,82,53,84, 54,89,85,56,73,57, 79,80,45,64,94,91, 92,95,139,137, 138	sets up pitch equivalents of ASCII values
110 P=N(GET)	gets ASCII value from keyboard and converts to its pitch value
120 IF P=0 THEN 110	checks for a wrong note
130 SOUND &11,−15,P,1	makes the sound at the required pitch
140 GOTO 110	goes back ready to read the next key pressed

150 *FX12,0	puts auto repeat delay and gap back to normal
160 *FX4,0	puts editing keys back to normal

Tuning and timbres

It is possible to tune the keyboard organ by changing the value added in line 80. This can be useful if the computer is being used to play with other instruments for example. If the computer is flat, adding 2 or 3 will sharpen it a little. If it is sharp, subtracting 1 or 2 will flatten it. Changing the line to:

```
80 N(A)=I*4+5
```

will raise the whole keyboard by a semitone.

The sound is much more interesting if an appropriate envelope is used rather than just the maximum volume of −15. A suitable envelope is:

```
5 ENVELOPE 1,1,0,0,0,0,0,0,126,-8,-4,-1,126,100
```

Remember that the SOUND statement must also be changed so that it becomes:

```
130 SOUND &11,1,P,1
```

You can experiment with different envelopes (see Chapter 8).

doubling

The sound may be made richer still by doubling up at the octave, or double octave, on another channel. Adding this line:

```
135 SOUND &12,1,P+96,1
```

will make channel 2 play the same notes two octaves above and produce a pleasing bell-like effect. This is best with short, fast notes.

Alternatively, if the second channel plays equivalent notes just one pitch step above, i.e., just slightly out of tune, it produces an interesting chorus effect:

```
135 SOUND &12,1,P+1,1
```

This is effective on longer, sustained notes.

Incorporating some of these changes and re-numbering produces this version of the program:

```
 10 REM ORGAN
 20 ENVELOPE 1,1,0,0,0,0,0,0,126,-8,-4,-1,126,100
 30 *FX4,1
 40 DIM P(139)
 50 ON ERROR GOTO 180
 60 *FX11,1
 70 *FX12,1
 80 FOR I=1 TO 27
 90 READ N
100 P(N)=I*4+1
110 NEXT I
120 DATA 9,49,81,50,87,69,52,82,53,84,54,89,85,56,73,
         57,79,80,45,64,94,91,92,95,139,137,138
130 N=P(GET)
140 IF N=0 THEN 130
150 SOUND &11,1,N,1
160 SOUND &12,1,N+96,1
170 GOTO 130
180 *FX12,0
190 *FX4,0
```

You will find the keyboard much easier to play if you put small stickers over the redundant keys on the top row: 3, 7, 0 and ←. This helps to clarify the pattern of "black notes", matching the arrangement of a piano keyboard.

Here are some tunes to play on the BEEBORGAN with their key-symbol equivalents:

The Entertainer (sensible version this time)

While Shepherds Watched Their Flocks

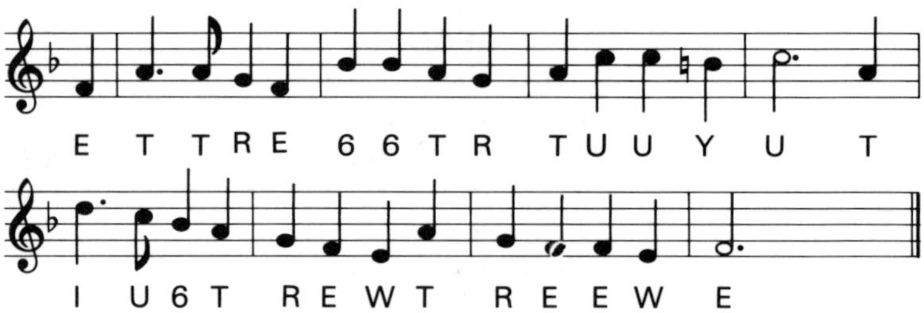

Many folk-songs and other similar tunes can be played just on the "black" notes, in our case the numbered keys. This is because they only use notes from the pentatonic scale (see Chapter 12). *Amazing Grace* is a good example:

Amazing Grace

Stops

Real organs usually have controls called **stops** which can be drawn or pressed to get a different sound. This program can be adapted so that pressing a particular key on the keyboard will be recognized by the program as a signal to change the sound specification. One way to do this would be to redefine the envelope whenever the appropriate key is pressed. But since we have already used "doubling up" as a method of changing the sound quality we will stay with that. It is similar to the way a real organ works and gives quite an effective result. If we make the amount added at line 160 into a variable, say K, then by changing the value of K, making it 1, 48 or 96 for example, we can change the type of sound produced:

```
160 SOUND &12,1,N+K,1
```

We now need a way of recognizing other keys as "stops". We already have a loop to check whether a non-music key has been pressed at lines 130 to 140. Rather than putting another check inside this one, which will hold things up when a music key is being pressed and may cause an unacceptable delay, we can instruct the program to perform an additional check for "stop" keys only after it recognizes a non-music key.

To make the amendment easier and to keep the program manageable we will put these checks into a procedure called PROCstopcheck, so line 140 now becomes:

```
140 IF N=0 THEN PROCstopcheck:GOTO 130
```

The procedure will then simply change the value of K as it recognizes a particular key. We will use the bottom row of keys (Z, X and C) as our stops.

```
200 END
210 DEFPROCstopcheck
220 IF GET$="Z" THEN K=96
230 IF GET$="X" THEN K=48
240 IF GET$="C" THEN K=1
250 ENDPROC
```

Now, when the program is run, pressing Z will produce more penetrating vibraphone-like sounds, pressing C will produce a gentler "chorus" effect and pressing X will be a less-pronounced octave doubling somewhere in between the two. K must also be given an initial value at the start of the program. The half-way value of 48 will do:

```
5 K=48
```

As a further extension the keys at the other end of the bottom row could perhaps be used to define envelope changes. Lines of this form could be added:

```
245 IF GET$="/" THEN E=1
```

In this case the variable E would be used to select from a set of envelopes which would have to be defined at the start of the program.

Notice that each envelope stop could combine with each "doubling" stop to produce a different sound. So if you have four doubling stops and three envelope stops there will be a total of 3*4 combinations, that is twelve different possible timbres.

Toccata

This program is monophonic, i.e., it can only produce one note at a time, not chords. It would only appear to be suitable for picking out small tunes. However, one of the most famous pieces of organ music, the *Toccata in D minor* by J. S. Bach, is actually monophonic for much of its duration. With a few modifications it can be played quite convincingly on this keyboard. In some places where two strands of notes alternate rapidly between each other an effect which sounds like two separate voices can be produced even though there is only really a single thread.

In case any purists may think that this is unwarranted interference with Bach's music it should be pointed out that Bach arranged much of his own, and other people's, music for quite different combinations of voices and instruments. He was also active in the scientific musical research of his time, making important contributions to developments in keyboard temperament and organ design.

Here then for the adventurous is an arrangement of Bach's *Toccata in D minor* for BBC Computer organ:

Toccata in D Minor

J. S. Bach
arranged for BBC Computer
by Kevin Jones

X
C
Z
X
C
X
Fast
C
Very Slow
Z

10 Etchamus

using the arrow keys to move the sound around

Moving sounds up and down

Another way of controlling sounds from the keyboard is to use the arrow-editing keys to "push" the sound in various directions. We will use them as an alternative to twisting control knobs as, for example, on hi-fi equipment or a synthesizer. The two aspects of a sound we can control easily are its pitch and volume. We will design the program so that pressing a right-arrow → will increase the volume, a left-arrow ← will decrease it, an up arrow ↑ will raise the pitch, and a down arrow ↓ will lower it.

First we need to use the special FX command to change the editing role of the arrow keys to make them deliver ASCII codes instead, as with the organ program (Chapter 9). We use *FX4,1.

(Notice that when you stop the program the arrow keys will continue to cease functioning as editing keys. The command *FX4,0 will revert them to normal if you want to edit with them.)

Next we can set starting values for volume (V) and pitch (P). Since we are going to be able to move them up or down, values somewhere in the middle of their range will be appropriate.

```
10 *FX4,1
20 V=8
30 P=130
```

Now we have to test to see if a key has been pressed. We can use GET (as with the ORGAN program) or INKEY. GET will wait indefinitely until a key has been pressed. INKEY, on the other hand, will only wait for a length of time specified in brackets after the command, and then continue with the program. If we use INKEY(0), the program will merely check to see if a key has been pressed and then continue, without waiting, to the next instruction in the program. We will use the variable K to hold whatever value may have been put in.

```
40 K=INKEY(0)
```

We then need to check the ASCII codes to see which key has been pressed to make the appropriate adjustments to pitch and volume. The ASCII codes produced by the arrow keys are shown here:

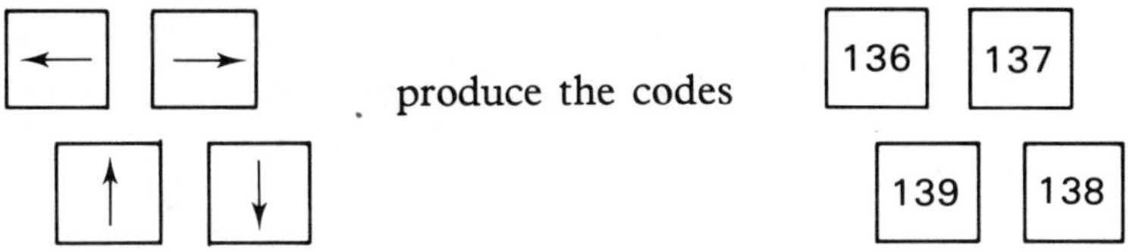

If the left arrow has been pressed, code 136 will have been produced and we need to reduce the volume V by subtracting 1 from its value. If the right arrow has been pressed we must increase the volume by adding 1 to V. Similarly, if the up or down arrow has been pressed, the pitch value P must be raised or lowered accordingly. These four lines carry out the required checks and alterations:

```
50 IF K=136 THEN V=V-1
60 IF K=137 THEN V=V+1
70 IF K=138 THEN P=P-1
80 IF K=139 THEN P=P+1
```

(If you are not familiar with programming in BASIC do not be confused by the fact that the equals symbol **=** is doing two different jobs here. When we say K=136 it means **is the same as**; the technical term is **equivalence**. When we say V=V-1 it means **becomes**, or in full **V takes on a new value which is one less than its old value**; the technical term is **assignment**.)

If any other key, or no key, is pressed, these lines are ignored and no changes are made.

We can now get the program to play the sound at current pitch and volume levels:

```
90 SOUND 1,-V,P,1
```

and instruct it to return to check the keys again in an endless loop:

```
100 GOTO 40
```

If you have attempted to run the program as it stands, you will see that if you hold one of the keys down continuously, say the ↑ key, the pitch will keep rising until it hits the maximum value (255) when it will jump at once to 0 and start climbing again. This is the "wrap-around" effect at work. Any number greater than 255 becomes that number minus 256. So 256 is 0, 257 is 1, and so on. This is not too distracting as far as pitch is concerned, but it tends to do strange things to the volume. This happens because the volume values move in fewer steps and quickly approach one of the limits. In addition, other values of V can be used to do different jobs; identifying an envelope, for example, which in this case is not defined. As a result keeping one of the volume control arrows depressed will produce a very messy sound rather like a bad telephone connection.

To avoid this we need to incorporate checks each time the value of V or P has changed, to make sure it has not passed the permitted limit, and bring it back into line if it has. These lines could all be put in a bunch after checking the values of K. Alternatively each check can be placed after the appropriate change where the limit may have been passed. This makes the logic of the program easier to follow. These lines will alternate with the lines to check the value of K, and so have been numbered to fit in between them:

```
55 IF V<0 THEN V=0
65 IF V>15 THEN V=15
75 IF P<0 THEN P=0
85 IF P>255 THEN P=255
```

The complete program so far, then, looks like this:

```
10  *FX4,1
20  V=8
30  P=130
40  K=INKEY(0)
50  IF K=136 THEN V=V-1
55  IF V<0 THEN V=0
60  IF K=137 THEN V=V+1
65  IF V>15 THEN V=15
70  IF K=138 THEN P=P-1
75  IF P<0 THEN P=0
80  IF K=139 THEN P=P+1
85  IF P>255 THEN P=255
90  SOUND 1,-V,P,1
100 GOTO 40
```

Varying the pitch movement

As it stands, running the program will cause a sound to be emitted continuously. Pressing the arrow keys will change the pitch or volume, but the sound will continue indefinitely until the program is killed by pressing ESCAPE. If we change line 40 to:

```
40 K=GET
```

then the program will wait until a key has been pressed. In other words, a sound will only be produced whilst an arrow key is held down.

With this version of the program it can sound better to make the pitch move up or down in larger steps, such as semitones. To do this we simply change the amount taken from or added to P in lines 70 and 80. Semitone steps will be produced by making this amount equal to 4:

```
70 IF K=138 THEN P=P-4
80 IF K=139 THEN P=P+4
```

Reverting to the original INKEY version of the program, another interesting possibility is to make the actual pitches represented in the SOUND statement vary at random within a particular range. We can change line 90 to something like this:

```
90 SOUND 1,-V,P+RND(20),1
```

When the program is run, a band of pitches will be produced which can be moved up or down with the arrow keys.

Plotting the movement on screen

It is much easier to follow what is happening to the sound if some sort of representation of its movement can be plotted on the computer screen. It makes an interesting audio-visual link-up, and only minor modifications need to be made to the program. A simple drawing statement, which uses the current values of V and P to work out the points to plot to, can make a line move around the screen following the changes in pitch and volume. When volume increases we will make the line move to the right; when pitch increases we will make the line move up.

As we saw in Chapter 4, the screen is considered to be divided up into a grid 1280 steps across (0 to 1279) by 1024 steps up (0 to 1023). A statement like DRAW 627,251 will draw a line from whichever point was last specified, to the point 627 steps across and 251 steps up. The numbers 627 and 251 are known as the point's co-ordinates.

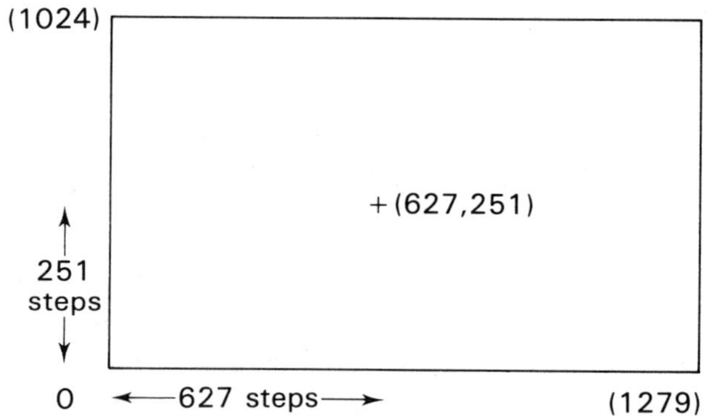

We want to make the first co-ordinate (across) depend on the value of V, and the second co-ordinate (up) depend on the value of P. If we used a statement like:

```
DRAW V,P
```

then all the plotting would be done in a tiny rectangle, 15 steps across by 255 steps up, in the bottom left-hand corner of the screen. In order to make full use of the screen we can multiply each value of V by 85. This will make its largest possible value 85*15 (which is 1275) and take it up to the far right edge. The value of P can be multiplied by 4, making its largest value 255*4 (which is 1020) and so use all of the availablc hcight on the screen.

To make the program draw the appropriate lines we add the statement:

```
95 DRAW V*85,P*4
```

At the beginning we need to tell the program where to start the plotting. Since V and P have starting values of 8 and 30 respectively, the co-ordinates of the starting point will be 8*85 and 130*4, which are 680 and 520 respectively. This starting point is specified using the command MOVE at the beginning of the program:

```
35 MOVE 680,520
```

Finally, before doing any plotting, we must specify a graphics mode for the machine to operate in. Any mode except 7 will do. Since we do not require colours, MODE 4 is appropriate. MODE 5 will draw thicker lines, but the chunky letters may be annoying when a program is interrupted to make adjustments:

```
5 MODE 4
```

You will notice when you run the program that pitch changes make neat little steps up or down, but volume changes are reflected in much more violent sweeps from side to side. This is because there are only 16 volume steps to cover the whole range. To make the distances match up on the screen we must reduce the quantity by which V is changed when an arrow key is pressed to a fractional amount less than one. A fifth, or 0.2 works quite well:

```
50 IF K=136 THEN V=V-0.2
60 IF K=137 THEN V=V+0.2
```

Try the program out with the modifications suggested before: with GET or INKEY, and with P by itself or P+RND(20) in the SOUND statement.

Here is the completed version of the musical etch-a-sketch program, with the lines renumbered:

```
 10 MODE 4
 20 *FX4,1
 30 V=8
 40 P=130
 50 MOVE 680,520
 60 K=INKEY(0)
 70 IF K=136 THEN V=V-0.2
 80 IF V<0 THEN V=0
 90 IF K=137 THEN V=V+0.2
100 IF V>15 THEN V=15
110 IF K=138 THEN P=P-4
120 IF P<0 THEN P=0
130 IF K=139 THEN P=P+4
140 IF P>255 THEN P=255
150 SOUND 1,-V,P,1
160 DRAW V*85,P*4
170 GOTO 60
```

Action replay

We can make the computer remember all the movements used to vary the sound and produce the pattern on the screen, and then perform an "action replay" for us. The changing values of V and P need to be stored in arrays. We will call them VS and PS respectively. They must be declared at the start of the program. We will make them capable of storing up to 1000 steps, which should be reasonably adequate:

```
5 DIM VS(1000),PS(1000)
```

(Note that an attempt to use MODEs other than MODE 4 or MODE 5 may leave insufficient memory space.)

We need to be able to count how many steps have been made as the user runs the program, to make sure that the declared limit of 1000 is not overstepped. Rather than having a continuous loop cycling through lines 60 to 170, as we did before, we will put it into an I-loop:

```
55    FOR I=1 TO 1000
         :
         :
170 NEXT I
```

As we may not wish to use the full limit of 1000 steps, we can incorporate an additional check to see if another key has been pressed, and use that as a cue to jump out of the loop and go on to the next part of the program. A suitable key to usc is the RETURN key, since it lies just below the arrow editing keys. When pressed it will return an ASCII code of 13. So we add this line:

```
65 IF K=13 THEN 180
```

which will make the program jump to line 180.

Now for each step I, as well as making the sound and drawing on the screen, we need to store the current values of V and P in the VS and PS arrays:

```
145 VS ( I )=V
146 PS ( I )=P
```

Once this "composing" stage has come to an end, either by reaching the limit of 1000 steps or by pressing RETURN, we go on with the re-run part of the program which will begin at line 180.

First we need to clear the screen, then set the starting point in the middle, as we did at the beginning of the program:

```
180 CLS
190 MOVE 680,520
```

Then we loop through the number of steps required, but this time reading values of V and P from their arrays for the sound and drawing commands, instead of from the keyboard. We will use J as the loop variable this time. The variable I will still have the same value as when its loop was abandoned first time, and so I−1 will be equal to the number of steps that were used. It will therefore be the maximum value up to which the new loop variable, J, will need to go for the replay:

```
200 FOR J=1 TO I-1
210 SOUND 1,-VS(J),PS(J),1
220 DRAW VS(J)*85,PS(J)*4
230 NEXT J
```

Once this has been completed, we can use a dummy GET statement as a cue to allow the user to press any key and do the replay all over again:

```
240 A=GET
250 GOTO 180
```

If this is run with INKEY at line 60, the computer will remember the pauses whilst the user was thinking what to do next. It is probably better to use GET at line 60, which means that values are only remembered when keys are pressed. On replay all of the pauses are ironed out to give a smooth re-creation of the sound picture.

The entire program, with re-numbered lines, will now look like this:

```
 10 DIM VS(1000),PS(1000)
 20 *FX4,1
 30 MODE 4
 40 V=8
 50 P=130
 60 MOVE 680,520
 70 FOR I=1 TO 1000
 80 K=GET
 90 IF K=136 THEN V=V-0.2
100 IF V<0 THEN V=0
110 IF K=137 THEN V=V+0.2
120 IF V>15 THEN V=15
130 IF K=138 THEN P=P-4
140 IF P<0 THEN P=0
150 IF K=139 THEN P=P+4
160 IF P>255 THEN P=255
170 IF K=13 THEN 230
180 VS ( I )=V
190 PS ( I )=P
200 SOUND 1,-V,P,1
210 DRAW V*85,P*4
220 NEXT I
230 CLS
240 MOVE 680,520
250 FOR J=1 TO I-1
260 SOUND 1,-VS(J),PS(J),1
270 DRAW VS(J)*85,PS(J)*4
```

```
280 NEXT J
290 A=GET
300 GOTO 230
```

Here are some designs to help whet your imagination:

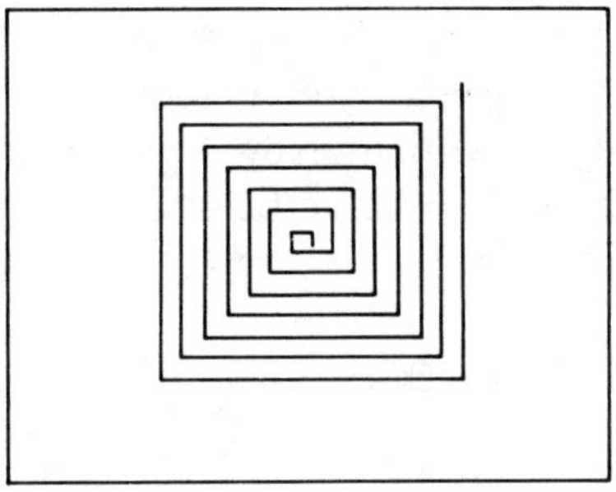

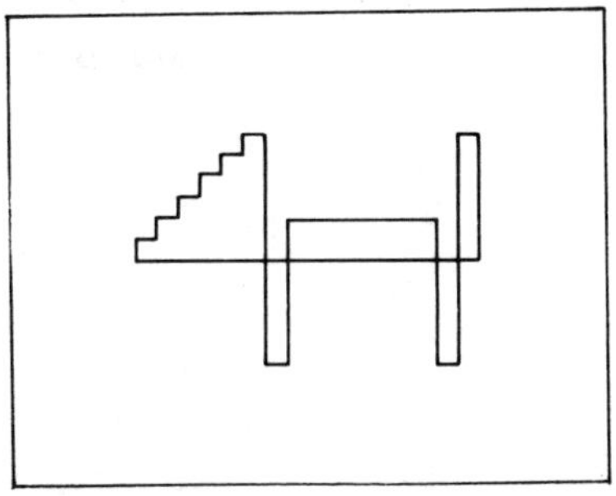

Sound goblins and Indians

goblins

A rather interesting variation is to change the program to read the arrays backwards and so unplot the design back to the initial point, like the action of an invisible sound-gobbling goblin. We must change line 250 to read from high to low:

```
250 FOR J=I-1 TO 1 STEP -1
```

and also instruct the computer to plot these points in black, that is, to unplot them. It is done with this command which sets the graphics colour to 0:

```
230 GCOL 0,0
```

Obviously, the pattern can not be unplotted more than once. An attempt to press a key to repeat the process will only succeed in plotting an invisible set of ghost points. You could try putting in this line:

```
230 GCOL 4,0
```

which will allow the original pattern to be continually replotted—but backwards.

Indians

Reverting once more to the original program as listed on pp.188–189, an intriguing adaptation is to make the movement automatic, or random. Instead of K's value depending on which arrow key is pressed, we can make it assume a random value between 136 and 139 by changing line 80 to this:

```
80 K=135+RND(4)
```

When we run this version of the program we get a resulting pattern which looks rather like examples of ancient Indian art, with music to match.

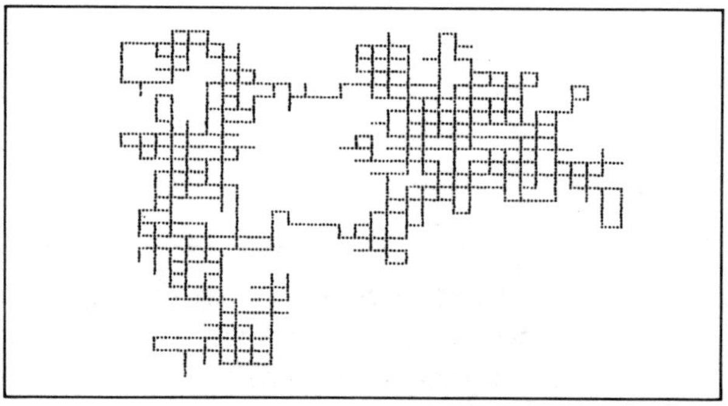

soundstream

Put line 80 back to its INKEY version, and then try out the P+RND(20) amendment as we did before. In this case we will also need to change line 270:

```
260 SOUND 1,-VS(J),PS(J)+RND(20),1
```

When you run the program in this form it is a very simple example of a type of computer-music composing program which is among those in use at the electronic music studios, EMS, in Stockholm, Sweden. The program is called IMPAC and is written by Michael Hinton. It will make the computer deliver a continuous stream of sound which can be controlled by the user as it emerges by using various devices such as knobs, joystick, and a graphics tablet in addition to the main computer keyboard. Having realized a section, it can be replayed, mixed and edited as required. Our simple BBC computer program is limited by its raw sound generators, and as it stands only changes pitch and volume (though it could be extended). The IMPAC system controls a large number of superior sound generators. It will produce a wide variety of sounds ranging, for example, from bell-like sounds to guitar or flute sounds. Its sophisticated control possibilities help the composer to steer his way through cascading fountains of endless musical possibilities.

11 Noise

sound effects, percussion and rhythm

The noise channel

In addition to the three sound channels which we have been using so far, there is a further channel available for making noise sounds. It is useful for trying to copy the sound of percussion instruments, such as drums and cymbals, and for general sound effects. Two different sorts of noise can be produced, known as **white noise** and **periodic noise**.

White noise consists of short, random notes of all pitches occurring so quickly that they blend into a continuous hissing or whooshing sound. You may remember that it was mentioned at the end of Chapter 5. White noise is very common in nature. The sound of the wind in the trees, a waterfall, and the waves on the seashore, are typical examples. To hear what white noise sounds like, type this command straight into the computer. Imagine that you are standing at the foot of a large waterfall:

```
SOUND 0,-15,4,255
```

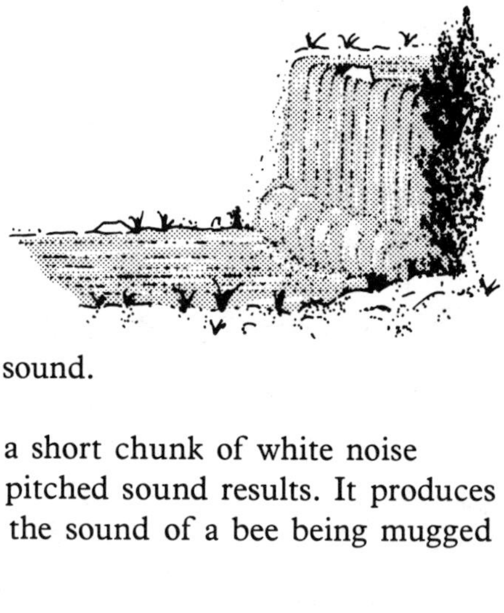

Press ESCAPE to stop the sound.

Periodic noise consists of a short chunk of white noise regularly recycled so that a pitched sound results. It produces a rough buzzing effect, like the sound of a bee being mugged by a model aeroplane:

```
SOUND 0,-15,2,200
```

To produce noise sounds, the same SOUND command is used as for pitched sounds, but the channel number is set to 0. The volume, envelope and duration parameters work exactly as before, but the third parameter, for pitch control, has a smaller range and a different function and is used to select the type of noise required.

The general form of the noise command is like this:

```
SOUND 0,V,P,D
```

V and D are the same as before , but P now takes a value between 0 and 7. The eight different noise types which can be specified by P are:

0 Periodic noise with a high pitch
1 Periodic noise with a medium pitch
2 Periodic noise with a low pitch
3 Periodic noise with a pitch determined by setting channel 1

4 White noise with a higher pitch range
5 White noise with a medium pitch range
6 White noise with a lower pitch range
7 White noise with a pitch determined by setting channel 1

Types 0, 1 and 2 are rather limited, since they produce fixed, unchangeable pitches. They can be used for simple aural cues in general-purpose programming. For example, to produce a squawk when a mistake is made. Type 3 is more useful. It gives a method of producing a different type of pitched sound which is explained on p.199.

Types 4, 5 and 6 are the most useful values. They allow the white noise to be broken up into bands where the sounds are in a higher, middle or lower pitch region, respectively.

High-pitched white noise, type 4, tends to be the most effective. It can be used to copy the sound of higher pitched percussion instruments such as cymbals. Low-pitched white noise, type 6, is more appropriate for drum-like sounds but it does not give such a "clean" effect as type 4.

Type 7, like type 3, is more versatile, though at the expense of losing one of the note channels. It is explained on p.200, where it is used to make clapping sounds.

This short program demonstrates the raw sound of each type of noise in turn:

```
10 FOR P=0 TO 7
20 SOUND 1,-15,P,50
30 NEXT P
```

In this example, since no pitch is specified on channel 1, types 3 and 7 are not giving truly representative sounds.

Noise with envelopes: drums and cymbals

The noise channel works most effectively when used in association with the ENVELOPE shaper, and can produce some quite convincing percussion sounds.

The main characteristic of percussion instruments, which are hit, is that their envelopes have a sharp attack followed by a steep decay. On some instruments, such as a xylophone or a wood block, the sound is dry and dies away immediately. On others, such as a cymbal or a bell, after an initial sharp decay the sound will continue to resonate for some time. A drum-sound lies somewhere in between. Some large gongs have the power to sustain their own sound for a very long time.

A **cymbal** envelope is rather like the piano envelope defined in Chapter 8:

```
10 ENVELOPE 1,1,0,0,0,0,0,0,126,-2,-1,-1,126,100
```

The attack is set as sharp as possible, at 126. The decay begins reasonably steep at −2 until it reaches the decay target of 100 when it becomes less steep with a sustain slope value of −1:

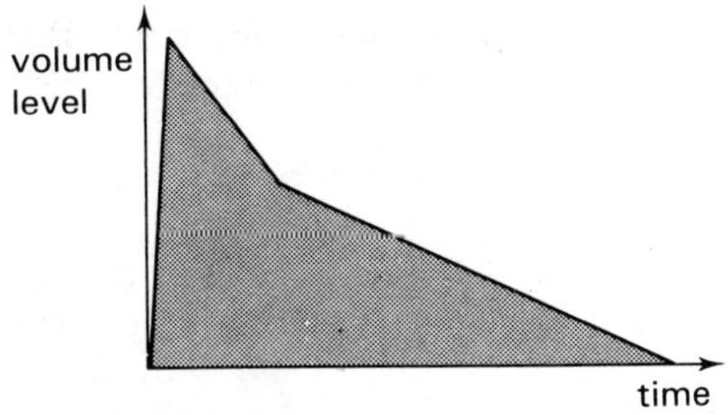

Adding a SOUND statement we get:

```
10 ENVELOPE 1,1,0,0,0,0,0,0,126,-2,-1,-1,126,100
20 SOUND 0,1,4,10
30 GOTO 20
```

Press ESCAPE to stop it.

We will now add a **drum sound**. A slight modification will be made to the cymbal envelope. Since we are now using two envelopes in the same program, we will make the drum envelope number 2:

```
20 ENVELOPE 2,1,0,0,0,0,0,0,126,-2,-3,-1,126,100
```

Most of the values are the same as the cymbal envelope, but at the end of the decay phase the sustain slope has been steepened to -3:

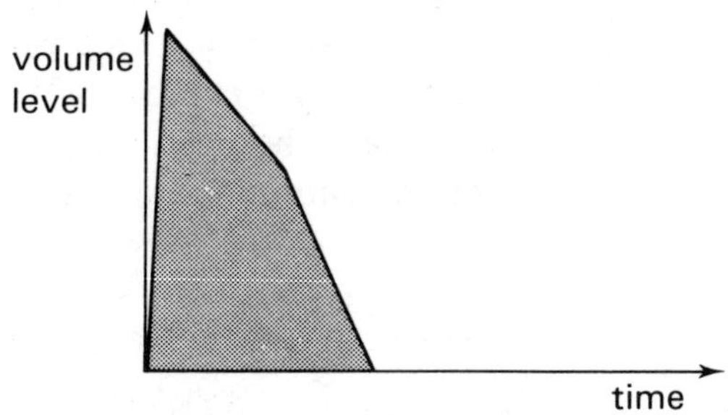

The SOUND statement for the drum note will identify ENVELOPE number 2 in its second parameter position, and low-frequency white noise, type 6, in its third:

```
30 SOUND 0,2,6,10
40 GOTO 30
```

For a more interesting rhythm pattern we will make two short drum notes followed by a longer cymbal crash:

```
10 ENVELOPE 1,1,0,0,0,0,
            0,0,126,-2,
            -1,0,126,100
20 ENVELOPE 2,1,0,0,0,0,
            0,0,126,-2,
            -3,-1,126,100
30 SOUND 0,2,6,5
40 SOUND 0,2,6,5
50 SOUND 0,1,4,10
60 GOTO 30
```

It will produce a rhythm pattern like this:

A wide variety of different rhythms may be generated by changing the order and durations. You could make use of READ and DATA statements as in Chapter 2. To generate a random rhythm, we can replace the durations with this expression:

```
RND(3)*4-4
```

When RND(3) is 2 or 3, the duration will be 4 or 8 respectively, a quaver or a crotchet. When RND(3) is 1, the duration will be 0 and the note will not sound at all. It means that we can loop round a drum SOUND statement followed by a cymbal SOUND statement, yet at the same time have the possibility of two or more notes of the same sound coming one immediately after the other:

```
10 ENVELOPE 1,1,0,0,0,0,
            0,0,126,-2,
            -1,0,126,100
20 ENVELOPE 2,1,0,0,0,0,
            0,0,126,-2,
            -3,0,126,100
30 SOUND 0,2,6,RND(3)*4-4
40 SOUND 0,1,4,RND(3)*4-4
50 GOTO 30
```

More examples of different rhythm patterns appear at the end of this chapter.

Guns, waves and breathing

By varying the shape of the envelope some quite interesting effects may be generated. The classic gun-shot sound has a sharp impact followed by an immediate decay:

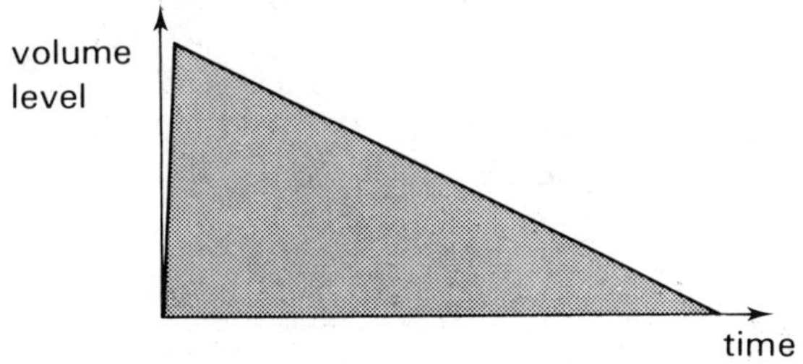


```
10 ENVELOPE 1,1,0,0,0,0,0,0,126,-1,-1,-1,126,0
```

We will use high-pitched white noise and give the sounds a random duration of up to 20 units:

```
20 SOUND 0,1,4,RND(20)
30 GOTO 20
```

We can put the SOUND statement inside a loop which successively reduces the maximum duration of each shot. The gun battle will appear to intensify as time passes:

```
15 FOR D=50 TO 1 STEP -1
20 SOUND 0,1,4,RND(D)
30 NEXT D
```

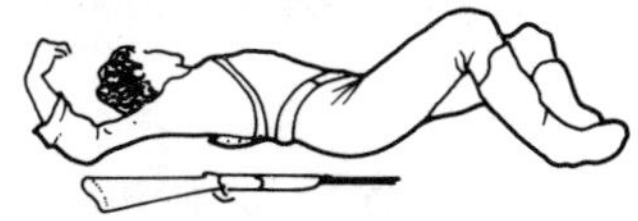

Rather ominously, it comes to an abruptly silent end. The duration of the battle can be extended by reducing the step size. An interesting dimension is added by making the P value vary between 4, 5 and 6. The different noise pitches sound like three different guns involved in the action. Using the expression RND(3)+3 to generate 4, 5 or 6, the "gun battle" program becomes:

```
10 ENVELOPE 1,1,0,0,0,0,
            0,0,126,-1,
            -1,-1,126,0
15 FOR D=50 TO 1 STEP -0.4
20 SOUND 0,1,RND(3)+3,RND(D)
30 NEXT D
```

Reducing the attack slope value to 1 generates sounds which gradually build up in volume. We can get effects like the sound of waves breaking on the seashore. In this example, the time step value has been increased to 2 to stretch the envelope and make it longer:

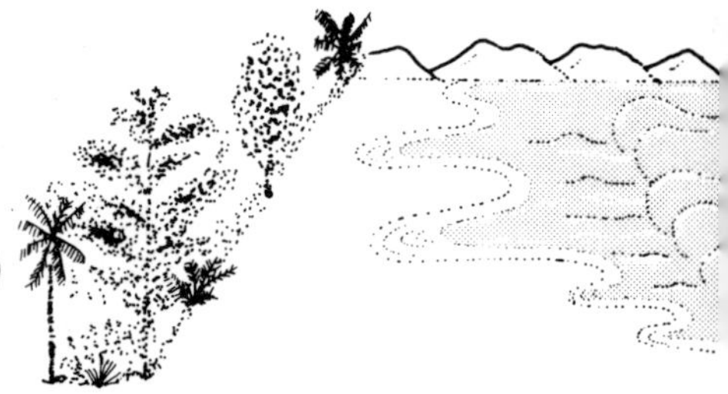

```
10 ENVELOPE 1,2,0,0,0,0,
            0,0,1,-1,
            -1,-1,126,0
20 SOUND 0,1,4,40+RND(60)
30 GOTO 20
```

Making the duration value constant will produce an effect more like heavy breathing. It sounds better if the volume is reduced by decreasing the value of the attack target, last but one in the ENVELOPE statement. Medium pitch noise, value 5, will be used this time. The breathing tends to sound a little laboured, rather like a patient in hospital:

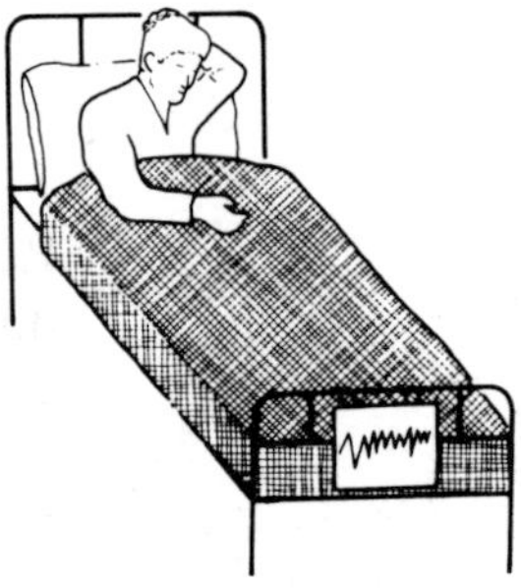

```
10 ENVELOPE 1,2,0,0,0,0,
            0,0,1,-1,-1,
            -1,70,0
20 SOUND 0,1,5,60
30 GOTO 20
```

The pitch envelope does not work with noise. It produces erratic stuttering effects which are not very useful. To change the pitch of the noise in a more controlled way it is necessary to link up with channel 1.

Linking the pitch to channel 1

Linking the pitch of the noise to channel 1 means that two SOUND statements are required for each note, instead of one. The volume level of channel 1 can be set to 0 so that it is not heard. Channel 0 can continue to use its own envelope.

Pitched periodic noise gives an interesting change in sound quality from the square-waves on the other channels. It also ends up producing lower pitches and is a useful way of extending the synthesizer's pitch range downwards. For this example, we will use a familiar envelope shape with a steep initial decay and gentler sustain:

```
10 ENVELOPE 1,1,0,0,0,0,0,0,126,-5,-1,-1,126,100
```

To obtain periodic noise controlled by the pitch of channel 1 we need the P value to be 3:

```
20 SOUND 0,1,3,4
```

The channel 1 sound statement will have a volume level of 0. The pitches will be semitones chosen at random above pitch value 124. When pitched periodic noise is generated in this way, pitch values much below that level produce low notes which are too deep for the computer's own loudspeaker to cope with. They come out as rasping clicks. If you have larger speakers linked to your computer you can try lower values. For now, the channel 1 SOUND statement will be:

```
30 SOUND 1,0,RND(32)*4+124,4
```

Putting the bits together gives this result:

```
10 ENVELOPE 1,1,0,0,0,0,0,0,126,
              -5,-1,-1,126,100
20 SOUND 0,1,3,4
30 SOUND 1,0,RND(32)*4+124,4
40 GOTO 20
```

It produces a sound rather like an electric guitar.

It is worthwhile spending some time exploring the possibilities for substituting this double-channel alternative in other programs in the book. Anywhere strong bass sounds are desirable it is particularly suitable, but it is also a pleasant alternative with higher pitches.

To see what happens when channel 1 is used to control the pitch of white noise, we just need to substitute the number 7 as third parameter in the SOUND statement:

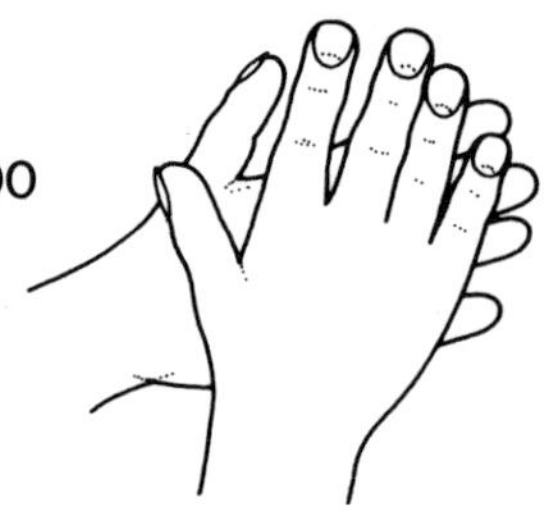

```
10 ENVELOPE  1,1,0,0,0,0,0,0,
              126,-5,-1,-1,126,100
20 SOUND 0,1,7,4
30 SOUND 1,0,RND(32)*4+124,4
40 GOTO 20
```

This produces quite a convincing clapping effect. The random pitch changes correspond to those which occur naturally as a result of slight changes in the size of the air cavity trapped between the hands on each clap.

By changing the shape of the ENVELOPE, making it decay more steeply down to 0, a drier sound is produced. The clapping then sounds as if it is coming from a carpeted living room, rather than the reverberant sports hall effect of the first version:

```
10 ENVELOPE 1,1,0,0,0,0,0,0,126,-8,-1,-1,126,0
20 SOUND 0,1,7,4
30 SOUND 1,0,RND(32)*4+124,4
40 GOTO 20
```

Steam train

To produce a controlled change in volume when envelopes are being used requires the whole ENVELOPE statement to be incorporated inside a loop. The attack target level can then be stepped up or down as required. The envelope will be redefined for each note sounded. We will demonstrate this effect on the noise channel to make the sound of a steam train chugging off into the distance.

We will use an envelope with a fairly gentle attack, and equivalent decay, to get the whooshing sound of each puff of steam:

```
10 ENVELOPE 1,1,0,0,0,0,0,0,3,-3,0,-1,126,0
```

With the "chug" or note duration set to 2, these lines will represent the regular puffing of the train:

```
70 SOUND 0,1,5,2
80 GOTO 70
```

but we start with the effect of the train getting its steam up. A loop will be used to make the "chug" duration longer at the beginning, starting at 20, and then step down one value at a time until it reaches the working speed of 2:

```
20 FOR D=20 TO 2 STEP -1
30 SOUND 0,1,5,D
40 NEXT D
```

Now comes the time for the train to move off into the distance. The ENVELOPE statement will go inside a loop which successively reduces the attack target, AT, down from 126 to 7, the minimum audible level:

```
50 FOR AT=126 TO 7 STEP -1
60 ENVELOPE 1,1,0,0,0,0,0,0,3,-3,0,-1,AT,0
```

```
70 SOUND 0,1,5,2
80 NEXT AT
```

Once the train has reached its most distant point we can leave the engine contentedly chugging away in the distance:

```
90 SOUND 0,1,5,2
100 GOTO 90
```

In this complete version of the program the step size in line 50 has been changed to a fractional amount to stop the train chugging away too quickly:

```
10 ENVELOPE 1,1,0,0,0,0,0,0,3,-3,0,-1,126,0
20 FOR D=20 TO 2 STEP -1
30 SOUND 0,1,5,D
40 NEXT D
50 FOR AT=126 TO 7 STEP -0.4
60 ENVELOPE 1,1,0,0,0,0,0,0,3,-3,0,-1,AT,0
70 SOUND 0,1,5,2
80 NEXT AT
90 SOUND 0,1,5,2
100 GOTO 90
```

Rhythm box

For this program READ and DATA statements will be used to read in lists of duration values which specify a variety of distinctive rhythms. The program will display a menu of rhythm names on the screen from which the pattern required can be selected and heard.

For the first example we will use the unmistakeable rhythm of *Mars* from the opening of Gustav Holst's *The Planets* Suite:

A suitable duration value for the crotchet beat is 12. This will conveniently divide into three making 4 the duration value for each of the triplets at the beginning; and also into half, making 6 the duration value for each of the two quavers. The whole rhythm is then represented by these values:

4 4 4 12 12 6 6 12

At the beginning of the program an appropriate ENVELOPE will be defined. This one works well for a drum-like effect:

```
10 ENVELOPE 1,1,0,0,0,0,0,0,126,-8,-4,-1,126,100
```

A loop will be used to read in each duration value and then make the appropriate sound. One method is to put a number specifying how many notes the rhythm contains at the start of each set of data. The loop is then made to repeat that number of times, as was done in Chapter 2. An alternative method, which we will make use of this time, is to finish each set of rhythm data with a particular value which the program can recognize as marking the end. The value 0 is an obvious choice. It can be tested using a REPEAT . . . UNTIL loop. The appropriate program lines will be:

```
20 REPEAT
30 READ D
40 SOUND 0,1,6,D
50 UNTIL D=0
```

The program will keep looping back to line 20, reading new values of D and setting them in the SOUND statement, until it comes across 0. At that point it will move out of the loop and on to the next line.

We will put in the DATA at line 80:

```
80 DATA 4,4,4,12,12,6,6,12,0
```

As it stands, the rhythm will only be played through once.

To repeat this, the program must be sent back to line 20. As explained in Chapter 2, the computer will not understand that it should also return to the start of the DATA unless it is specifically told to do so with a RESTORE command. Adding these lines, the program becomes:

```
10 ENVELOPE 1,1,0,0,0,0,0,0,126,-8,-4,-1,126,100
20 REPEAT
30 READ D
40 SOUND 0,1,6,D
50 UNTIL D=0
60 RESTORE
70 GOTO 20
80 DATA 4,4,4,12,12,6,6,12,0
```

In order to play other rhythms we can substitute alternative sets of DATA at line 80. Each set should always finish with 0. Other distinctive rhythms we can use are:

Bolero (as in Ravel's *Bolero*)

Using the value 3 for the shortest note, a semiquaver triplet, gives the sequence:

9 333 9 333 9 9 9 333 9 333 333 333

No doubt the side-drum players normally burdened with the task of playing this rhythm throughout a performance would be relieved to know that a computer could do the job for them. Apparently Ravel was inspired to write the piece by the sound of a neighbouring saw-mill.

Habanera (as in Bizet's opera *Carmen*)

Using 4 for a semiquaver gives the sequence:

12 4 8 8

Military

To get the effect of a trill we will use a sequence of eight 1s. A quaver will be 4, giving this sequence:

1 1 1 1 1 1 1 1 4 4

How's your father! All right!

A characteristic rhythm! Our program is not geared up for rests. We can fake it by making the fourth note into a crotchet and ignoring the quaver rest. It produces the same result as the envelope produces very short notes anyway. Using a value of 6 for a quaver gives this sequence:

9 3 6 12 6 12

Bulgarian

Bulgarian folk music uses uneven rhythms (to our ears) in five- and seven-note groups. Using 4 for a quaver gives the sequence:

8 4 8 8

Polonaise (as in Chopin's piano pieces)

Using 3 for a semiquaver gives the sequence:

9 3 6 6 3 3 3 3

Polka

Using 3 for a semiquaver gives:

6 6 9 3

Tango

We have:

6 3 3 6 6 6 6

Rock

Using 3 for a quaver gives:

6 3 6 3 3 3

Boogie

Here, the same two note rhythmic cell is repeated. Only the first two notes need be coded. Since jazz rhythms are interpreted lazily, the dotted pattern comes out like a triplet. Using 3 for a semiquaver/quaver-triplet gives this sequence:

6 3

All of these patterns can be placed in order as a set of DATA statements at the end of the program. Earlier in the program the RESTORE command can be used, followed by a line number, to identify which rhythm DATA to play.

We will now put the "rhythm box" program together. At the beginning the ENVELOPE is defined and the screen cleared. The menu of available rhythms can then be displayed:

```
 20 ENVELOPE 1,1,0,0,0,0,0,0,126,-8,-4,-1,126,100
 30 CLS
 40 PRINT' ' ' "1. Mars"
 50 PRINT"2. Bolero"
 60 PRINT"3. Habanera"
 70 PRINT"4. Military"
 80 PRINT"5. How's your father! All right!"
 90 PRINT"6. Bulgarian"
100 PRINT"7. Polonaise"
110 PRINT"8. Polka"
120 PRINT"9. Tango"
130 PRINT"10. Rock"
140 PRINT"11. Boogie"
```

After the menu has been displayed, an INPUT statement will pick up the user's choice. An appropriate prompt should come first:

```
150 PRINT' ' "Type in the number of the rhythm you" '
             "require followed by RETURN"
160 INPUT K
```

The program can then use the value of K to locate the appropriate set of duration values. The DATA statements will begin at line 240 with line numbers increasing in tens, as usual. If we use the statement:

```
180 RESTORE K*10+230
```

then when K=1, DATA will be read from line 240. When K=2 it will be read from line 250, and so on.

(N.B. Be careful when using a RESTORE statement like this which uses a value worked out when the program runs. If you adapt or extend the program, and RENUMBER the lines, it can muddle things)

The statements to read and play the notes come next, the same as they were before:

```
190 REPEAT
200 READ D
210 SOUND 0,1,6,D
220 UNTIL D=0
230 GOTO 180
```

The lines of DATA follow, each terminating with 0.

One final addition can be made to the program. As it stands, any rhythm will keep repeating indefinitely until the program is stopped by pressing ESCAPE. To request another rhythm it is necessary to RUN the program again. Using the ON ERROR command, as in previous programs, we can make the program jump straight back to the menu whenever ESCAPE is pressed:

```
10 ON ERROR GOTO 30
```

An additional message can be displayed on the screen to explain to the user how to stop the sound:

```
170 PRINT' ' "Press ESCAPE to stop the sound" '
```

When typing in the program remember to test it first and then type in line 10 last. To stop the program you will need to press BREAK and then type OLD to recover it.

The complete "rhythm box" program now looks like this:

```
 10 ON ERROR GOTO 30
 20 ENVELOPE 1,1,0,0,0,0,0,0,126,-8,-4,-1,126,100
 30 CLS
 40 PRINT' ' ' ''1. Mars''
 50 PRINT''2. Bolero''
 60 PRINT''3. Habanera''
 70 PRINT''4. Military''
 80 PRINT''5. How's your father! All right!''
 90 PRINT''6. Bulgarian''
100 PRINT''7. Polonaise''
110 PRINT''8. Polka''
120 PRINT''9. Tango''
130 PRINT''10. Rock''
140 PRINT''11. Boogie''
150 PRINT' ' ''Type in the number of the rhythm you'' '
           ''require followed by RETURN''
160 INPUT K
170 PRINT' ' ''Press ESCAPE to stop the sound'' '
180 RESTORE K*10+230
190 REPEAT
200 READ D
210 SOUND 0,1,6,D
220 UNTIL D=0
230 GOTO 180
240 DATA 4,4,4,12,12,6,6,12,0
250 DATA 9,3,3,3,9,3,3,3,9,9,9,3,3,3,9,3,3,3,3,3,3,3,3,3,0
260 DATA 12,4,8,8,0
270 DATA 1,1,1,1,1,1,1,1,4,4,0
280 DATA 9,3,6,12,6,12,0
290 DATA 8,4,8,8,0
300 DATA 9,3,6,6,3,3,3,3,0
310 DATA 6,6,9,3,0
320 DATA 6,3,3,6,6,6,6,0
330 DATA 6,3,6,3,3,3,0
340 DATA 6,3,0
```

A program of this sort would be useful, say, to a dancing teacher who could select a required rhythm pattern at the touch of a button. The repertoire of rhythms can be considerably extended. It is not too difficult to make the tempo controllable as in other programs in the book.

12

Ethnic sounds

making music from the east, bagpipes and Red Indians using pentatonic scales

The pentatonic scale

The pentatonic scale is simply a scale of five notes, but it is one of the fundamental building blocks of music. When children start singing simple jingles in the playground, or when crowds chant at football matches, they tend to use notes from the pentatonic scale. It can have various forms, but like any scale it is the intervals between the notes which are important. This is one version of it:

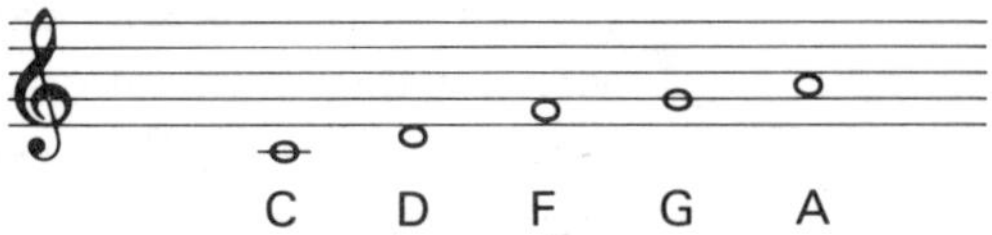

So we get things like:

and

It so happens that the black notes on the piano make up a pentatonic scale. Some of the musical types described in this chapter can be picked out quite easily on the piano just using the black notes, if you feel inclined to try experimenting at the keyboard.

Most of the world's folk music is based on pentatonic scales. We are going to write programs using the pentatonic scale to generate music characteristic of the orient, of bagpipes and of Red Indians.

Storing the scale using an array

When we generate the tunes for these musical types we will simply pick notes from the pentatonic scale at random. We will use an **array** called SCALE to store the values needed by BBC BASIC to give the correct pitches. For our five-note pentatonic scale this will reserve five places known as SCALE(1), SCALE(2), . . ., up to SCALE(5). So if we want the pitch for the fourth note of the scale we will find it by using SCALE(4).

First we need to tell the program that we are going to use an array, what it is called, and how many elements it has got. We do this using a DIM statement:

```
20 DIM SCALE(5)
```

Then we need to put values into the array representing each note of the scale. These will be 101, 109, 121, 129 and 137:

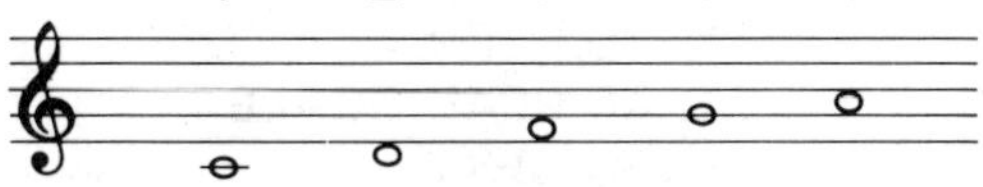

We could have simply used a sequence of assignment statements:

```
SCALE(1) = 101
SCALE(2) = 109
. . . etc.
```

This is not too bad with only five spaces to be filled, but if there were any more it would be hopelessly cumbersome. It is better to use a loop which will cycle through the array one position at a time:

```
30 FOR I = 1 TO 5
40 READ SCALE ( I )
50 NEXT I
```

Here is the required DATA statement containing the scale values:

```
60 DATA 101,109,121,129,137
```

Introducing oriental delights

We will use the pentatonic scale to make some music characteristic of China or Indonesia. Let us extend the pentatonic scale by one note each side so that we have seven notes:

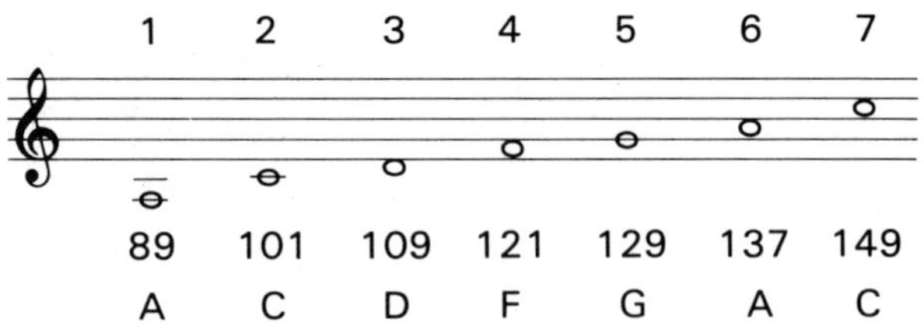

This is still a pentatonic scale. We have simply added an extra A below and an extra C above. To store this we need to make SCALE into a seven-element array:

```
20 DIM SCALE(7)
30 FOR I = 1 TO 7
40 READ SCALE ( I )
50 NEXT I
60 DATA 89,101,109,121,129,137,149
```

but we will only use the top five of these, from 3 to 7, for the melody. (You will find out why later.) To choose a note N from the scale in this range we need to generate a random number between 3 and 7. RND(5) will produce a number between 1 and 5, so if we add 2 to whatever is produced we end up with a number between 3 and 7. This statement will do the job:

```
70 N = RND(5) + 2
```

Having chosen a note from the scale we use SCALE(N) in the pitch position of the SOUND statement to give us the actual pitch value needed.

A suitable envelope to use for these notes is given in this definition:

```
10 ENVELOPE 1,3,0,0,0,0,0,0,126,-10,-5,-2,126,120
```

Now for the rhythm. The melody pattern we are aiming to produce tends to wander up and down in a sequence of regular quavers, and occasionally pauses on a longer note, a crotchet. It might look something like this:

On average we want about one-tenth of the notes to be crotchets and the rest quavers. A suitable duration value for the quavers will be 5 making a crotchet equal to 10.

We could generate exactly nine quavers followed by one crotchet, and keep repeating the pattern. But that would be unnecessarily regular. It is much more fun to use a method which gives less predictable results, breaking the note sequence up into unequal groups, while keeping the general balance of nine quavers to one crotchet.

The RND function when called with 1 as its argument, i.e. RND(1), will produce a decimal number between 0 and 1. Naturally we expect it over a period of time to produce an even spread of decimals from the whole range. Thus one-tenth of the numbers generated will be less than 0.1. We can use this information to construct a test: when RND(1) is less than 0.1 the duration will be 10, otherwise (i.e. most of the time) the duration will be 5:

```
80 IF RND(1) < 0.1 THEN D = 10 ELSE D = 5
```

So having established the duration, we just have to put the pieces together and add the SOUND statement to the program:

```
90 SOUND 1,1,SCALE(N),D
```

and then make the program return to line 70 to choose a new value of N for the next note and keep the process continuing:

```
120 GOTO 70
```

To summarize, here is the program so far:

```
10 ENVELOPE 1,3,0,0,0,0,0,0,126,-10,-5,-2,126,120
20 DIM SCALE(7)
30 FOR I = 1 TO
40 READ SCALE(I)
50 NEXT I
60 DATA 89,101,109,121,129,137,149
70 N = RND(5) + 2
80 IF RND(1) < 0.1 THEN D = 10 ELSE D = 5
90 SOUND 1,1,SCALE(N),D
100 GOTO 70
```

More channels

The sound can be improved by making use of the other channels. We can add a second part which moves in parallel with the first but always down two positions in the pentatonic scale from the melody note. In conventional notation the effect might appear something like this:

To achieve this effect we just subtract two from the value of N, then find out from the scale array what pitch N−2 is. So the SOUND statement for the second channel will be:

```
100 SOUND 2,1,SCALE(N−2),D
```

This is the reason why we made N go from 3 to 7 when we were constructing the melody line above. It leaves room for N−2 to go down to 1 or 2.

The program now works quite well as it is, but since the third channel is available we might as well make use of it.

In this sort of music a little bell-like sound, that of Chinese finger cymbals, may be sometimes heard.

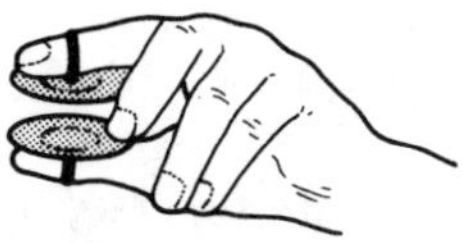

To make this sound, all we need do is generate any note with a high pitch, not necessarily from the pentatonic scale. The expression RND(50)+200 will generate a value between 201 and 250, which should do. We only want the sound to occur occasionally, about every fifth note perhaps. We can use the same technique that we used for working out durations. In this case RND(1) will be less than 0.2 for one-fifth of the time, so the required statement will be:

```
110 IF RND(1)< 0.2 THEN SOUND 3,1,RND(50)+200,D
```

And so the completed program becomes:

The ORIENTAL program

```
10 ENVELOPE 1,3,0,0,0,0,0,0,126,−10,−5,−2,126,120
20 DIM SCALE(7)
30 FOR I = 1 TO 7
40 READ SCALE(I)
50 NEXT I
60 DATA 89,101,109,121,129,137,149
70 N = RND(5) + 2
```

```
 80 IF RND(1)< 0.1 THEN D = 10 ELSE D = 5
 90 SOUND 1,1,SCALE(N),D
100 SOUND 2,1,SCALE(N-2),D
110 IF RND(1)< 0.2 THEN SOUND 3,1,RND(50)+200,D
120 GOTO 70
```

Bagpipe music: Scotch snaps

Scottish bagpipe music uses a pentatonic scale. The sound made by the bagpipe is also close in character to the square-wave sound produced by the computer. This makes it an obvious candidate for our attentions!

Scottish music contains distinctive rhythmic patterns such as a long note followed by a much shorter note:

(as in *Scots wi' a Hay!*)

or its reverse, a very short note followed by a longer one:

(as in *Comin' through the rye*)

This  rhythm is known as a **Scotch snap**. We will make use of these two rhythmic figures to generate our bagpipe music.

In both figures the longer note, a dotted quaver, is three times the length of the shorter note, a semiquaver. If we give the semiquaver a duration value of 3 the dotted quaver will have a duration of 9. So there are two rhythmic combinations we can generate: 9–3 or 3–9. We could have got the program to choose one of these and then defined note durations for the combination it chose, perhaps in an array, or by writing the different alternatives out in full—but that could be clumsy.

We first generate a 3 or 9 at random for the first duration, then the second duration is simply 12 minus whatever the first value was. To generate a 3 or a 9, rather than using an IF . . . ELSE construction where RND(2) provides the two needed alternatives:

```
IF RND(2) = 1 THEN D = 3 ELSE D = 9
```

we can go straight from the 1 or 2 supplied by the RND(2) function to the values 3 and 9 by using the expression RND(2)*6 − 3 :

```
90 D = RND(2)*6 - 3
```

When RND(2) = 1 the expression will equal 3, when RND(2) =2 it will equal 9.

The bagpipe melody

We will use the top six notes of the pentatonic scale as written out on p.212.

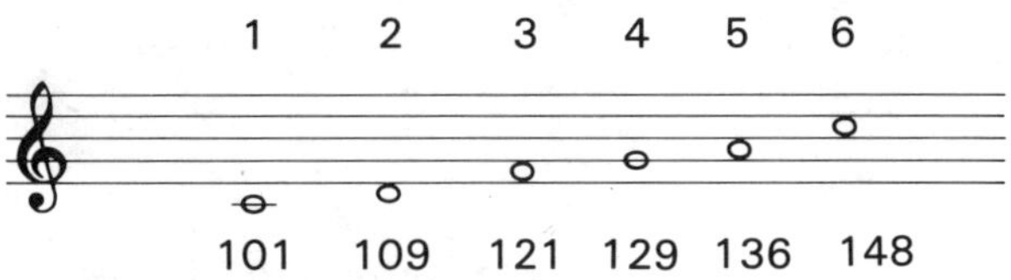


```
10 DIM SCALE(6)
20 FOR I = 1 TO 6
30 READ SCALE ( I )
40 NEXT I
50 DATA 101,109,121,129,136,148
```

For our melody sequence we simply choose a note at random from this array: SCALE(RND(6)).

We will not define any envelope for this program. The bagpipe is unique amongst woodwind instruments in that it manages to keep up an uninterrupted stream of sound from the reservoir of air kept constantly in the bag. As a result the notes move straight from one into the other with no distinguishable gaps. If a bagpipe player attempts to play the same note twice in succession he has a problem, for the second note simply becomes an extension of the first. The same thing will happen in this program. If a note chosen is identical to the one just played it merely sounds like a prolongation of the previous note—although this adds to the rhythmic interest. In the absence of any envelope we will set the V parameter to the maximum value of −15.

Taking into account the duration requirements worked out above, the sound statements will be:

```
100 SOUND 1,−15,SCALE(RND(6)),D
110 SOUND 1,−15,SCALE(RND(6)),12−D
```

You may agree that to the unaccustomed ear bagpipes often seem to sound out of tune. This effect can be deliberately produced by flattening one of the pitch values in the DATA list. We could change the 149 to 148 for example. It is worth experimenting with various possibilities. Obviously it does not make sense to change too many values or the results simply cancel each other out.

Drones

Another important feature of the bagpipe is the set of drones. We can use the spare sound channels to produce a drone which simply sets a pitch and sticks to it throughout. A low F and the C one-fifth above it are a good combination:

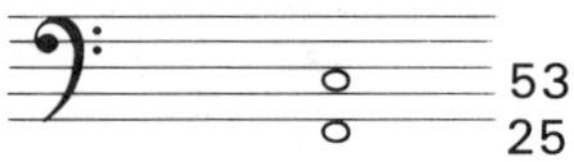

As with some of the melody pitches it gives a better result if these are flattened slightly to 24 and 52. They will have a duration value of 12 in order to last for the same duration as the two melody notes on each cycle:

```
120 SOUND 2,−15,24,12
130 SOUND 3,−15,52,12
```

Since they have no envelope they will not be discernible as new notes starting again each time the statements are encountered afresh, but will appear to sound continuously.

There is a final small feature we can add to the program. You may have noticed how bagpipe drones start by themselves, and then slightly raise in pitch as the melody is introduced. We can write lines into the program to copy this effect. We will begin by making them sound for 100 duration units and use a pitch value slightly flatter than the one the drones eventually settle on to:

```
70 SOUND 2,-15,23,100
80 SOUND 3,-15,51,100
```

To avoid synchronization problems we also need to add a dummy line to make channel 1 sound at zero volume for the same length of time:

```
60 SOUND 1,0,0,100
```

Here is the completed program.

The BAGPIPES program

```
 10 DIM SCALE(6)
 20 FOR I = 1 TO 6
 30 READ SCALE ( I )
 40 NEXT I
 50 DATA 101,109,121,129,136,148

 60 SOUND 1,0,0,100
 70 SOUND 2,-15,23,100
 80 SOUND 3,-15,51,100

 90 D = RND(2)*6 - 3
100 SOUND 1,-15,SCALE(RND(6)),D
110 SOUND 1,-15,SCALE(RND(6)),12-D
120 SOUND 2,-15,24,12
130 SOUND 3,-15,52,12
140 GOTO 90
```

Red Indian music: ostinati and drums

Another type of music using pentatonic scales comes from American Indians. In this case the rhythm of the accompaniment is very important and so will be considered first.

A characteristic pattern is a regularly repeated rhythm like this:

This is known as an **ostinato,** from the Italian word for **obstinate**. As with the bagpipe drones a good result is produced using notes one-fifth apart:

These have pitch values of 13 and 41. We will have to use an envelope in order to separate the notes from each other and make the rhythm perceptible:

```
10 ENVELOPE 1,3,0,0,0,0,0,0,126,–10,–5,–2,126,120
```

A more relaxed pace is appropriate this time so we will use the longer duration value of 8 for a quaver which makes a crotchet 16. To get the pattern we need, we must have one note of length 16 followed by two of length 8. It can be done using a short loop:

```
80 SOUND 2,1,13,16          crotchet, bottom part
90 SOUND 3,1,41,16          crotchet, top part

120 FOR I = 1 TO 2          do this twice
140 SOUND 2,1,13,8          quaver, bottom part
150 SOUND 3,1,41,8          quaver, top part
160 NEXT I                  repeat

170 GOTO 80                 go back and repeat the
                            rhythm indefinitely
```

To add an accent (>) to the crotchet we can use channel 0 to provide a regular drum beat. We will use the same envelope, and low-frequency noise (type 6). It must sound at the same time as the crotchet, but will have a duration value of 32 to make it last for the same time as the crotchet with the two following quavers. It will not actually be heard all this time since the envelope makes the sound die away quite quickly:

```
70 SOUND 0,1,6,32
```

and line 170 needs to be changed to return to line 70 instead of line 80:

```
170 GOTO 70
```

The Red Indian melody

Again notes will simply be chosen at random from the pentatonic scale, but this time the range will be even more limited. We will use only four notes of the scale:

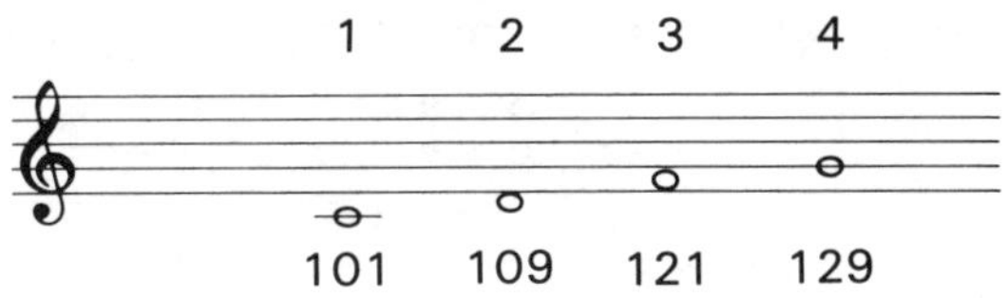


```
20 DIM SCALE(4)
30 FOR I = 1 TO 4
40 READ SCALE ( I )
50 NEXT I
60 DATA 101,109,121,129
```

We want the melody to sound with a continuous quaver movement and so will use a constant duration value of 8. Two channel 1 melody notes will be defined one after the other whilst the crotchet of the accompaniment is sounding. Another channel 1 statement will simply slip into the loop already in the program for the next two quavers:

```
100 SOUND 1,–15,SCALE(RND(4)),8
110 SOUND 1,–15,SCALE(RND(4)),8
    . . .
130 SOUND 1,–15,SCALE(RND(4)),8
```

As with the bagpipes we have used non-enveloped notes with maximum volume here. This contrasts nicely with the enveloped sounds of the ostinato accompaniment, and also introduces welcome variation into the rhythm when identical neighbours happen to be produced.

The INDIANS program

Here is the complete Red Indian music program:

```
 10 ENVELOPE 1,3,0,0,0,0,0,0,126,–10,–5,–2,126,120
 20 DIM SCALE(4)
 30 FOR I = I TO 4
 40 READ SCALE ( I )
 50 NEXT I
 60 DATA 101,109,121,129

 70 SOUND 0,1,6,32
 80 SOUND 2,1,13,16
 90 SOUND 3,1,41,16
100 SOUND 1,–15,SCALE(RND(4)),8
110 SOUND 1,–15,SCALE(RND(4)),8

120 FOR I = 1 TO 2
130 SOUND 1,–15,SCALE(RND(4)),8
140 SOUND 2,1,13,8
150 SOUND 3,1,41,8
160 NEXT I

170 GOTO 70
```

Combining into one program — ETHNIC SELECTION

These three programs can be combined into one larger program, ETHNIC SELECTION. Each program has been redefined as a procedure. A menu is presented on the screen from which the user selects the type of music desired. On cue, the appropriate procedure is called.

Suitable titles have been added to identify which type of music is being played.

```
 10 ON ERROR GOTO 40
 20 ENVELOPE 1,3,0,0,0,0,0,0,126,–10,–5,–2,126,120
 30 DIM SCALE(8)

 40 CLS
 50 PRINTTAB(4,3)"ETHNIC SELECTION"
 60 PRINTTAB(4,4)"_ _ _ _ _ _ _ _ _ _ _ _ _ _ _ _"
 70 PRINTTAB(4,8)"which type of music do you want?"
 80 PRINTTAB(4,15)"1. Oriental"
 90 PRINTTAB(4,17)"2. Bagpipe"
100 PRINTTAB(4,19)"3. Red Indian" ' ' '
```

```
110 A$ = GET$
120 IF A$ = "1" THEN PROCoriental
130 IF A$ = "2" THEN PROCbagpipes
140 IF A$ = "3" THEN PROCindian
150 GOTO 110

160 DEFPROCoriental
170 CLS
180 PRINTTAB(4,10)"Year of the Dragon"
190 PRINTTAB(4,24)"Press ESCAPE to finish"
200 FOR I = 1 TO 8
210 READ SCALE ( I )
220 NEXT I
230 DATA 89,101,109,121,129,137,149,157
240 P = RND(5) + 2
250 IF RND(1)< 0.1 THEN D = 10 ELSE D = 5
260 SOUND 1,1,SCALE(P),D
270 SOUND 2,1,SCALE(P-2),D
280 IF RND(1)< 0.2 THEN SOUND 3,1,RND(50)+200,D
290 GOTO 240
300 ENDPROC

310 DEFPROCbagpipes
320 CLS
330 PRINTTAB(4,10)"Jock's Lament"
340 PRINTTAB(4,12)"or When the Whisky's Gone"
350 PRINTTAB(4,24)"Press ESCAPE to finish"
360 FOR I = 1 TO 6
370 READ SCALE ( I )
380 NEXT I
390 DATA 101,109,121,129,136,148
400 SOUND 1,0,0,100
410 SOUND 2,-15,23,100
420 SOUND 3,-15,51,100
430 D = RND(2)*6 - 3
440 SOUND 1,-15,SCALE(RND(6)),D
450 SOUND 1,-15,SCALE(RND(6)),12-D
460 SOUND 2,-15,24,12
470 SOUND 3,-15,52,12
480 GOTO 430
490 ENDPROC

500 DEFPROCindian
510 CLS
520 PRINTTAB(4,10)"Little Squaw"
```

```
530 PRINTTAB(4,24)''Press ESCAPE to finish''
540 FOR I = 1 TO 4
550 READ SCALE ( I )
560 NEXT I
570 DATA 101,109,121,129
580 SOUND 0,1,6,32
590 SOUND 2,1,13,16
600 SOUND 3,1,41,16
610 SOUND 1,-15,SCALE(RND(4)),8
620 SOUND 1,-15,SCALE(RND(4)),8
630 FOR I = 1 TO 2
640 SOUND 1,-15,SCALE(RND(4)),8
650 SOUND 2,1,13,8
660 SOUND 3,1,41,8
670 NEXT I
680 GOTO 580
690 ENDPROC
```

13

Playing Bach

programming the Prelude no. 1 in C major by J. S. Bach

Musical redundancy

If we want to encode a complete piece of music for the computer to play, anything but the shortest of pieces will involve vast amounts of data and will be tedious to type in. However, most pieces of music involve much repetition. Technically we would say that some music has a high level of redundancy. This is what makes it interesting and enjoyable. As we listen to music our ears recognize familiar note patterns which re-appear, sometimes in slightly different combinations, sometimes as literal repeats. It is rather like examining a small piece of sculpture or jewellery in your hand. As the same object is viewed from many different angles new aspects appear so that it is literally seen in a different light.

This repetition in music can be a great help in encoding a piece to be played on the computer. If we recognize repeated groups of notes and frequently recurring patterns, they need only be encoded once and the repeats written into the grammar of the BASIC program. Sometimes the repetition may not be a precise note-for-note copy of a sequence but might only consist of re-statements of its general shape. This is equally useful.

A piece of music which demonstrates this admirably, and which immediately lends itself to more efficient encoding, is the first prelude from Bach's "48" in C major. This is printed on the following two pages. Even if you cannot read music it should be possible to see from the score that the same up-and-down pattern of notes is repeated throughout.

Prelude no. 1
in C major

J. S. Bach

33,61,81,97,121
53,69,81,101,117
53,81,93,101,117
25,73,89,101,117
29,53,89,101,113,
37,73,97,101,109
33,73,81,97,109
33,69,81,101,117
33,61,81,101,121
33,61,81,97,121
33,65,89,101,125
33,69,81,101,129
33,61,81,101,121
33,61,81,97,121
5,53,81,93,117
5,53,73,89,101,121,101,89,101,89,73,61,73,61
5,49,129,145,157,169,157,145,157,145,129,145,109,121,117,109
149
117
5

Note patterns in Bach's prelude

Let us look at the first bar:

It is immediately obvious that the first and second halves of the bar are identical. The same is true of every bar in the piece except the last three. This gives us an immediate fifty per cent reduction.

The way in which the stems of the notes are joined disguises the fact that the six semiquavers in the top part consist of the same group of three semiquavers played twice. The first bar could be represented diagrammatically like this:

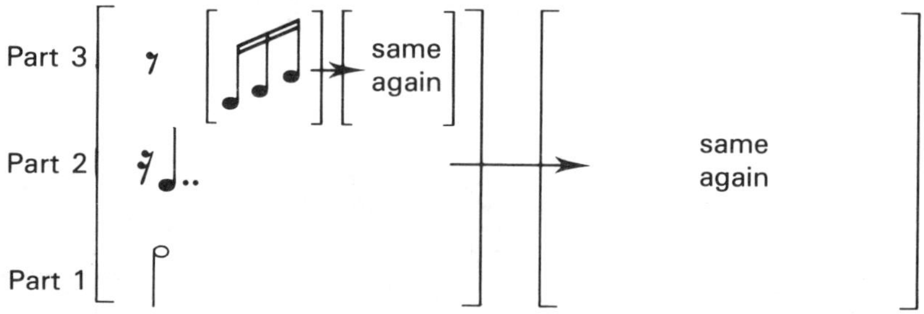

The whole prelude is simply a series of split chords. The chords change bar by bar but the way in which they are split up remains the same. Thus out of a total of 16 notes in each bar there are only five different pitches—the notes of the chord, which need to be specified. The remaining ones are repeats. The rhythm also remains constant throughout. The durations only have to be specified once and come as a consequence of the general structure. To specify pitch and duration for each note in the bar, would require 32 data items. As it is we can make do with 5. So instead of taking more than 30 minutes to type in the data we might manage it in five.

Special provision needs to be made for the last three bars, but even so there is still some repetition here we can identify.

Notice that the prelude is in three parts, or voices, which is useful in fitting it on to the computer's three available sound channels.

Programming the bar pattern

First we will make a decision about durations. Rather than use fixed durations throughout, it would be useful to be able to change the speed at which the piece is played back. We will use D to represent the shortest duration, a semiquaver, so that other durations will be expressed as multiples of D. We can set the value of D at the beginning of the program to vary the speed according to taste. Four is a reasonable value to start with:

```
60 D = 4
```

We will also need an envelope. This one will do. It has rather a twangy sound but is quite good fun:

```
90 ENVELOPE 1,8,1,-1,0,1,1,0,126,-10,-5,-2,126,120
```

For each bar we need to read in the five pitch values which it will be using. We will use an array N and read in values from the DATA statements one at a time:

```
 50 DIM N(5)
120 FOR J = 1 TO 5
130 READ N(J)
140 NEXT J
```

For the first bar the data will be as follows:

```
430 DATA 101,117,129,149,165
```

This is how the data relates to the score:

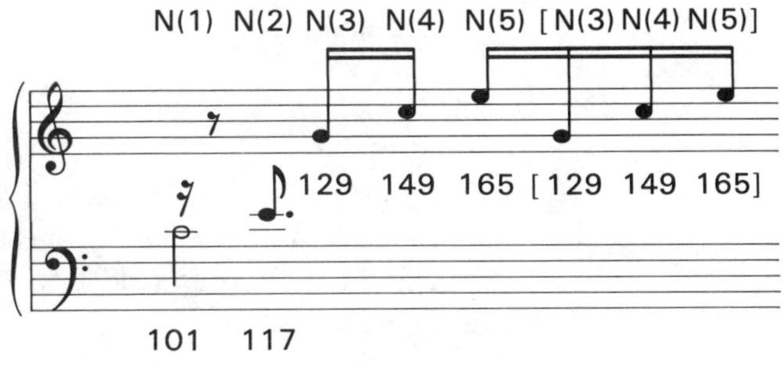

Then we set up a loop which will do the half bar twice. Half a bar is a minim in length so we will use the loop variable M:

```
150 FOR M = 1 TO 2
```

The minim in the bottom part, to be played on channel 1, must be defined first. It is eight times the length of the semiquaver and so has a duration of D *8. Its pitch will be the first value in the N array:

```
160 SOUND 1,1,N(1),D*8
```

Next comes part 2 with a duration of D *7 and pitch stored in N(2). But before it sounds, it has to rest for a semiquaver:

```
170 SOUND 2,0,0,D
180 SOUND 2,1,N(2),D*7
```

Part 3 also has to rest silently for a quaver (D *2) before coming in:

```
190 SOUND 3,0,0,D*2
```

The next three semiquavers in part 3 must be produced twice. Their pitches are in N(3), N(4) and N(5). They will each have a duration value equal to D:

```
200 FOR F = 1 TO 2
210 SOUND 3,1,N(3),D
220 SOUND 3,1,N(4),D
230 SOUND 3,1,N(5),D
240 NEXT F
```

Having completed half a bar we simply return and repeat it.

```
250 NEXT M
```

This finishes a complete bar. The same process is repeated for the first 32 bars. Each time the N array will be re-loaded with five new entries read from the next set of values in the data statement:

```
110 FOR BAR = 1 TO 32
        . . .
260 NEXT BAR
```

The last three bars

Even though bars 33 and 34 do not repeat any of their pitches (at least not in any way suitable for programming) they have the same rhythm and can be usefully incorporated into a loop:

```
270 FOR BAR = 33 TO 34
```

Here is the music for bar 33:

The first note lasts for two minims, D *16. It is a low C, pitch 5, in both bars so it can be written straight into the SOUND statement as such:

```
280 SOUND 1,1,5,D*16
```

We must be careful to remember this when preparing the DATA statements for these last two bars, or the values may go in twice and cause confusion.

We do not need to store any of the following pitch values in an array since they are used only once. They can be read direct from the DATA statements into the temporary variable P. As before, the second part rests for a semiquaver then sounds this time with a duration value of D *15:

```
290 READ P
300 SOUND 2,0,0,D
310 SOUND 2,1,P,D*15
```

The third part, at the top, rests for a quaver, D *2, then the remaining 14 semiquavers can be read and played one at a time:

```
320 SOUND 3,0,0,D*2
330 FOR SQ = 1 TO 14
340 READ P
350 SOUND 3,1,P,D
360 NEXT SQ
```

We repeat for bar 34:

```
370 NEXT BAR
```

The three fixed notes of the final bar can be put straight down as they are. Since only three channels are available we have had to pick out the three most important notes; the Cs at top and bottom, and the E on to which the semiquaver line resolves in the middle:

To observe the pause we use a duration value of D *32:

```
380 SOUND 1,1,5,D*32
390 SOUND 2,1,117,D*32
400 SOUND 3,1,149,D*32
```

We could finish the program there. If we want to keep the piece cycling indefinitely we must RESTORE the data pointer to the head of the list and then we return to the first bar:

```
410 RESTORE
420 GOTO 110
```

The program — PRELUDE

Here is the complete PRELUDE program with all required data written in full. An appropriate screen title has been added at the beginning. Changing the value of D in line 60 to 2 will make the prelude play extra fast, like a "Keytown Kops" effect. Increasing it to 6 will produce a relaxing, leisurely pace; anything more becomes rather dirge like. If D = 1 the rhythm becomes obscured and the sound is simply heard as a series of chords, though it does make the harmonic progressions more readily perceptible. Apparently that is how Bach originally wrote it down.

```
 10 CLS:PRINTTAB(8,10)''Prelude in C major''
 20 PRINTTAB(8,12)''J.S.Bach''
 30 PRINTTAB(8,16)''Arranged for BBC Computer''
 40 PRINTTAB(8,18)''by Kevin Jones''
 50 DIM N(5)
 60 D = 4
 90 ENVELOPE 1,8,1,-1,0,1,1,0,126,-10,-5,-2,126,
               120

110 FOR BAR = 1 TO 32
120 FOR J = 1 TO 5
130 READ N(J)
140 NEXT J
150 FOR M = 1 TO 2
160 SOUND 1,1,N(1),D*8
170 SOUND 2,0,0,D
180 SOUND 2,1,N(2),D*7
190 SOUND 3,0,0,D*2
200 FOR F = 1 TO 2
210 SOUND 3,1,N(3),D
220 SOUND 3,1,N(4),D
230 SOUND 3,1,N(5),D
240 NEXT F
250 NEXT M
260 NEXT BAR

270 FOR BAR = 33 TO 34
280 SOUND 1,1,5,D*16
290 READ P
300 SOUND 2,0,0,D
310 SOUND 2,1,P,D*15
320 SOUND 3,0,0,D*2
```

```
330 FOR SQ = 1 TO 14
340 READ P
350 SOUND 3,1,P,D
360 NEXT SQ
370 NEXT BAR
380 SOUND 1,1,5,D*32
390 SOUND 2,1,117,D*32
400 SOUND 3,1,149,D*32
410 RESTORE
420 GOTO 110

430 DATA 101,117,129,149,165,101,109,137,157,169
440 DATA 97,109,129,157,169,101,117,129,149,165
450 DATA 101,117,137,165,185,101,109,125,137,157
460 DATA 97,109,129,157,177,97,101,117,129,149
470 DATA 89,101,117,129,149,61,89,109,125,149
480 DATA 81,97,109,129,145,81,93,117,129,153
490 DATA 73,89,109,137,157,73,85,109,121,145
500 DATA 69,81,101,129,149,69,73,89,101,121
510 DATA 61,73,89,101,121,33,61,81,97,121
520 DATA 53,69,81,101,117,53,81,93,101,117
530 DATA 25,73,89,101,117,29,53,89,101,113
540 DATA 37,73,97,101,109,33,73,81,97,109
550 DATA 33,69,81,101,117,33,61,81,101,121
560 DATA 33,61,81,97,121,33,65,89,101,125
570 DATA 33,69,81,101,129,33,61,81,101,121
580 DATA 33,61,81,97,121,5,53,81,97,117
590 DATA 53,73,89,101,121,101,89
600 DATA 101,89,73,89,73,61,73,61
610 DATA 49,129,145,157,169,157,145
620 DATA 157,145,129,145,109,121,117,109
```

An automatic prelude

You may have noticed that in moving from bar to bar of the prelude, the notes in each subsequent chord do not change much. Many of the notes stay the same. Those that do change tend to move up or down by one step only.

For example, in going from the first bar to the second, the bottom note stays as it is, the next note up drops down one, the top three notes all go up one. In going from the second to the third bar, the bottom and middle notes drop by one, the remainder stay the same. This is shown by the following diagram:

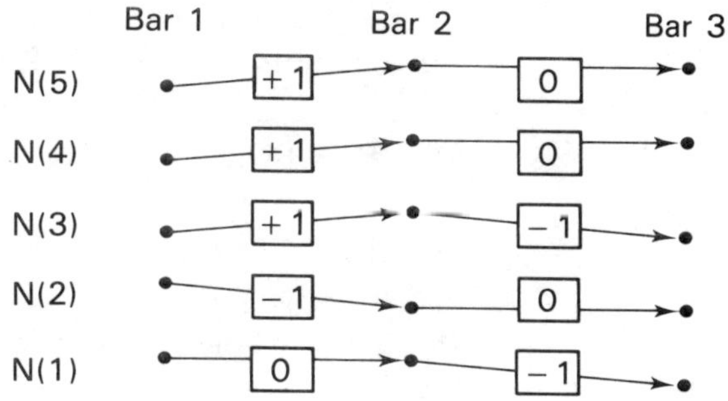

Sometimes only one note changes, as in bars 8 to 9. In fact, as the chord changes from bar to bar, the notes in each position are doing individual random walks (see Chapter 5).

We can use this observation to adapt our program to generate an "automatic" prelude in the same sort of way. We will not make any pretensions that this is an authentic emulation of Bach, but it is quite an interesting experiment. The heart of the program will remain the same, but instead of reading values into the N array from data statements we will make them change according to the rule we have just derived.

Changing the PRELUDE program

So we now set about savaging the PRELUDE program. First of all, we read in the same values that Bach used, for the first bar only. We no longer need line 110 so we put the short data statement in there:

```
110 DATA 101,117,129,149,165
```

Lines 120 to 140 stay as they were, as do lines 150 to 250, but once we have reached the end of this first bar, instead of returning to read new data into the N array for subsequent bars, we change the values in the next few lines of the program.

We continue by first choosing a note in the array at random:

```
270 I = RND(5)
```

The note, or array position, chosen is designated by the variable I. We must then calculate a step size of either −1, 0 or +1 which determines how the note changes. We use the random walk expression: RND(3) − 2:

```
280 S = RND(3) - 2
```

and then change the array's note value at that position accordingly. We multiply the step size by 4 to move it through a whole semitone to the neighbouring note in the chromatic scale:

```
290 N(I) = N(I) + 4*S
```

Having made the change we can return to line 150 to play the next bar with the new set of values:

```
310 GOTO 150
```

This version of the program will change only one note in the chord at a time. To change more, say three notes, we can surround lines 270 and 280 with a loop:

```
260 FOR K = 1 TO 3
      . . .
300 NEXT K
```

We could have made changes occur only on to adjacent notes of the C major scale, but as well as being easier to program, more harmonic interest is generated by allowing changes to occur on to any note of the chromatic scale and some quite interesting chords may result.

The remaining lines of the original program, from 320 onwards, can be deleted.

The AUTOBACH program

Here, then, is the amended program in full with some appropriate changes made to the title display:

```
10 CLS:PRINTTAB(8,10)"Autoprelude"
20 PRINTTAB(8,12)"after J.S.Bach's C major prelude"

50 DIM N(5)
```

```
60 D = 4
90 ENVELOPE 1,8,1,-1,0,1,1,0,126,-10,-5,-2,126,120

110 DATA 101,117,129,149,165
120 FOR J = 1 TO 5
130 READ N(J)
140 NEXT J

150 FOR M = 1 TO 2
160 SOUND 1,1,N(1),D*8
170 SOUND 2,0,0,D
180 SOUND 2,1,N(2),D*7
190 SOUND 3,0,0,D*2
200 FOR F = 1 TO 2
210 SOUND 3,1,N(3),D
220 SOUND 3,1,N(4),D
230 SOUND 3,1,N(5),D
240 NEXT F
250 NEXT M

260 FOR K = 1 TO 3
270 I = RND(5)
280 S = RND(3) - 2
290 N( I ) = N( I ) + 4S
300 NEXT K
310 GOTO 150
```

Some variants

In line 260, if the largest value up to which K can go is increased, perhaps to 5 or above, then more notes in the chord will be changed:

```
260 FOR K = 1 TO 5
```

But notice the following points:

Notes may be changed by a step size of zero. In other words they stay the same.

The same note may be changed twice, but the second change may cancel the effect of the first change.

The same note may be changed twice, but the second change produces a larger interval overall. This is in keeping with the character of the original prelude where changes with greater intervals sometimes occur.

To begin with, the five notes in the chord will move roughly up and down together over a period of time; but if left for long enough the notes will slowly expand to cover a wider pitch range. Alternatively, a few may end up on the same note. They may also cross over each other so that the up-and-down sequence is shuffled. For example, note 2 may finish up lower than note 1.

Changing the expression used for calculating the step size can make the notes only move up:

```
280 S = RND(2) - 1
```

in which case the sounds gradually disappear into the inaudible high-pitched regions—or, they can be forced to move down:

```
280 S = RND(2) - 2
```

so that everything shifts into gruff low pitches. When a pitch limit is reached, for example when the pitch drops below zero, the sound reappears at the top end of the range. Pitches −1, −2, . . . come out sounding at 254, 253, . . . as automatic "wrap-around" occurs. The whole process can be speeded up by increasing the maximum value of K in the K loop at line 260:

```
260 FOR K = 1 TO 10
```

or by reducing the value of D in line 60. We have come a long way from Bach's prelude!

14

Autorock

making music in a contemporary rock style

Outlining the form

A popular musical form which has been used in much recent pop music can be represented by this diagram:

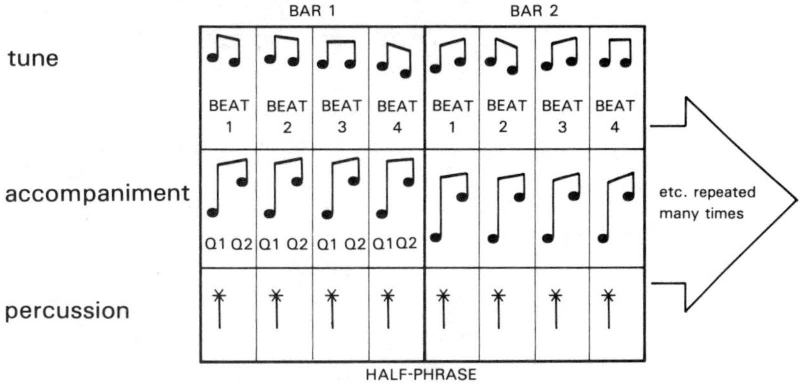

In conventional notation it might appear like this:

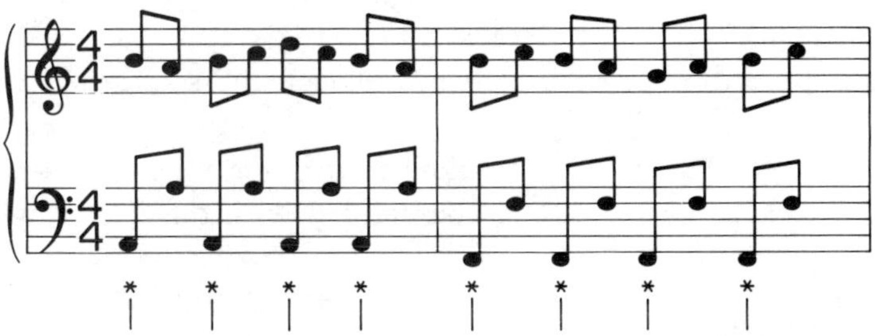

The accompaniment consists of a rocking bass figure of split octaves, with a percussion crash of cymbals or drums on the beat. The melody above it meanders up and down through notes adjacent to each other.

We are going to write a program which will automatically

generate music of this type. The form of the program will be derived from the form of the music.

To make things easier all the notes used will be taken from the C major scale only.

The accompaniment will be based on a range of eight notes:

(Each note that occurs will also be followed by its partner one octave above.) It will change pitch every four beats (once a bar) choosing the note each time from within the specified range.

The melody will have a range of 12 notes:

It will execute a random walk (see Chapter 5) but the starting note for the random walk will be redefined every eight beats (i.e. every two bars).

Percussive accompaniment

This is the easiest part. We will use bursts of white noise, halfway between the sound of a drum and a cymbal.

A suitable envelope for us to use, giving a sharp, clear attack, can be defined with the following statement:

```
20 ENVELOPE 1,2,0,0,0,0,0,0,126,-10,-5,-2,126,120
```

This same envelope will also be used for the melody and accompaniment lines.

So that we can change the speed if required we will use the variable D to stand for the shortest duration, a quaver: 4 is a suitable value to assign to D to begin with:

```
10 D = 4
```

Each burst of noise lasts for two quavers and so will have the duration D *2. The following statements, then, will generate the four bursts of noise for each bar:

```
100 FOR J = 1 TO 4
110 SOUND 0,1,4,D*2
120 NEXT J
```

Defining the scale

The notes will all be chosen from the C major scale. We can store the notes of the scale in an array:

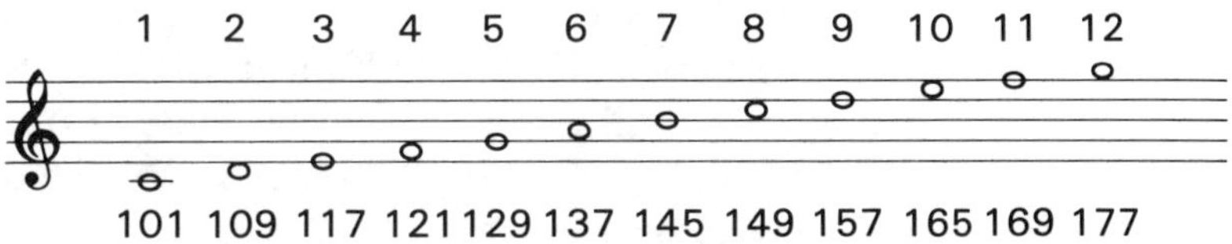


```
30 DIM SCALE(12)
40 FOR I = 1 TO 12
50 READ SCALE ( I )
60 NEXT I
70 DATA 101,109,117,121,129,137,145,149,157,165,
        169,177
```

This array will be used for both melody and accompaniment notes. The notes for the accompaniment will be chosen from only the first eight positions, but the notes for the melody may be chosen from all 12. When the actual pitches for the accompaniment are to be produced, 48 or 96 will be subtracted to make them sound one or two octaves lower.

Accompaniment

The variable B (for Bass) will be used to stand for the note of the scale (between 1 and 8) being used for the accompaniment. Each time it changes, at the beginning of every bar, its value is chosen at random from within this range:

```
150 B = RND(8)
```

Then for each beat in the bar, the bass note is sounded twice, first at the lower octave then at the upper octave. To find the actual pitch to be played the value is read from the SCALE array, then 96 is subtracted the first time for the lower octave, and 48 is subtracted the second time for the higher octave. Channel 1 will be used for accompaniment and so the appropriate sound statements will be:

```
SOUND 1,1,SCALE(B)-96,D
SOUND 1,1,SCALE(B)-48,D
```

It will make the program neater if these two statements can be incorporated into a loop for the two quavers, ready for when the melody notes must be redefined on each quaver at the same time. Since the amount to be subtracted the first time is 96 (i.e. 2 *48) and 48 (i.e. 1 *48) the second time, we will make the loop variable Q (for quaver) start at 2 and go down to 1. Thus the two statements above become:

```
180 FOR Q = 2 TO 1 STEP -1
210 SOUND 1,1,SCALE(B)-Q*48,D
240 NEXT Q
```

Melody

The variable T (for Tune) is used to stand for the note of the scale, between 1 and 12, being used for the melody. A new starting value of T is chosen at random every two bars:

```
130 T = RND(12)
140 FOR BAR = 1 TO 2
      . . .
260 NEXT BAR
```

Inside the two bars, on each quaver, a new value of T is worked out on the "random walk" principle. The expression RND(3) − 2 will produce the values 1, 0 or −1, so when this is added to the old value of T, T will go up or down by one note or remain the same:

```
190 T = T + RND(3) - 2
```

As with the accompaniment, the actual pitch to be sounded is read from the scale array, though this time it stays just as it is without any octave adjustment. Using channel 2 for melody the appropriate sound statement is:

```
220 SOUND 2,1,SCALE(T),D
```

If T gets down to 1 or up to 12 it is possible that it might next become 0 or 13. The computer will then attempt to read the SCALE array with subscripts 0 or 13 which, of course, are not defined and will give an error. We must put in a check to stop this happening. One possibility if the melody hits an upper or lower limit is to make it stay there until a subsequent random decision moves it away again. However, a more interesting result is produced if the melody is forced to jump back into the middle of its range by making T = 6. This is not strictly a random walk, but it makes the statement shorter, sounds interesting, and saves typing in longer alternatives!

```
200 IF T<1 OR T>12 THEN T=6
```

To keep the composing process repeating *ad infinitum* all that remains is to send the program thread back to line 130 to choose another starting value for T:

```
270 GOTO 130
```

A complete, annotated list of the program so far is as follows:

The AUTOROCK 1 program

```
10 D=4                          —set an appropriate note duration
20 ENVELOPE 1,2,0,0,0,          —define a suitable envelope with
   0,0,0,126,-10,-5,             a sharp attack
   -2,126,120
30 DIM SCALE(12)
40 FOR I = 1 TO 12              —set up the SCALE array
50 READ SCALE(I)                 containing the BBC BASIC pitch
60 NEXT I                        values of the C major scale
70 DATA 101,109,117,121,
   129,137,145,149,157,
   165,169,177

130 T = RND(12)                 —choose a starting value for the
                                 melody note
```

140 FOR BAR = 1 TO 2	— repeat the next section for two bars
150 B = RND(8)	— choose a value for the bass note
160 FOR BEAT = 1 TO 4	— repeat this section for four beats
170 SOUND 0,1,4,D*2	— produce the percussive noise sound
180 FOR Q = 2 TO 1 STEP −1	— repeat this section for two quavers
190 T = T + RND(3) − 2	— work out the next melody note on the random walk principle
200 IF T< 1 OR T> 12 THEN T=6	— check to see melody has not crossed the limits. If it has start again mid-range
210 SOUND 1,1, SCALE(B) – Q*48,D	— produce the bass accompaniment note at the correct octave
220 SOUND 2,1, SCALE(T),D	— produce the melody note
240 NEXT Q	— next quaver
250 NEXT BEAT	
260 NEXT BAR	
290 GOTO 130	— go back and repeat it all again

Now, having worked out the basic form of the program, there are a number of refinements and improvements that can be made.

Adding a third part

So far we have only used the noise channel and two of the three available note channels, but why not make use of the spare channel 3. To add a completely independent part would be complicated, but the third channel can be usefully employed doubling up one of the other parts. This gives it a more interesting timbre or sound quality. Usually in this sort of music the accompaniment is given prominence, so it is reasonable to double this part. If we do this at the upper octave by adding 48 to each note value, our channel 3 sound command will be:

```
230 SOUND 3,1,SCALE(B) – 48*Q + 48, D
```

If we had doubled at the lower octave, by subtracting 48, we would risk going off the end of the lower pitch limit.

Alternatively we could have doubled the melody at the octave in the same sort of way, but this is not as effective:

```
230 SOUND 2,1,SCALE(T) + 48, D
```

Retrieving a realization

It can be very frustrating to hear the computer generate an interesting piece and realize that because it has been produced randomly, there is no way of repeating it. It has disappeared for ever. But all need not be lost. As pointed out in Chapter 6, the BBC BASIC random number generator has a facility for enabling a random sequence of numbers to be repeated by calling the RND function with a **negative** argument. Each time this same argument is used, it resets the random number generator to generate a particular sequence based on that argument. So to start, we set X to a value:

```
90 X = 432172
```

and then call the random number function with the negative of that number in order to reset it:

```
110 K = RND(-X)
```

K is simply a dummy variable used to enable us to call the RND function. Now, whenever the program is run, it will produce the same result. To get a different output we change the value of X in line 90. To save changing the program each time we can use an input statement:

```
90 INPUT X
```

Numbers up to 2,147,483,647 can be used giving us a total of over two billion different random number sequences; that is over two billion variations of this musical form!

Alternatively, we can still get the computer to choose X at random to give us a different and unpredictable result each time the program is run:

```
90 X = RND(1000000)
```

Then when a particularly good sequence emerges we can stop the program and get the computer to print out the current value of X which will still be in its memory:

```
PRINT X
```

Repeating phrases

The continuous, relentless flow of changing sounds can soon become boring. Most music has a high level of repetition; to reflect this fact we can split our piece up into repeating phrases. The starting melody note is redefined every two bars; we will call this a half-phrase (HF). Two half-phrases will go to make up a phrase. So the form of each phrase will look something like this:

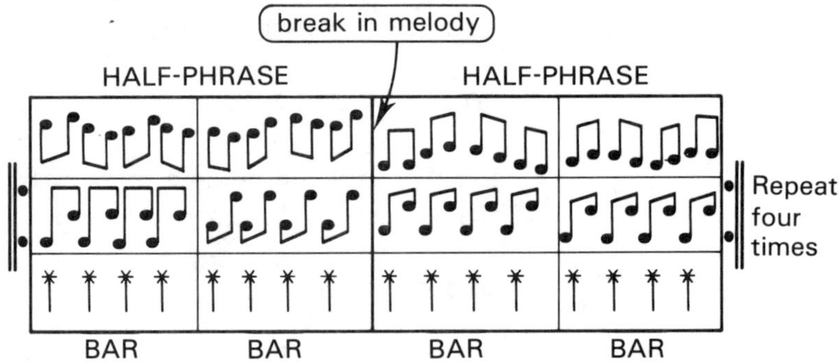

In this way the two half-phrases form a balanced pair, a statement and an answer, which is a common musical arrangement.

One way to achieve the desired repetition is to store all the note values as they are generated the first time in a large array so that they can be read from the array on each repetition; but this is a tedious and unnecessary method. It is much easier to use the fixed random number sequence facility which we used above.

Each time the phrase is repeated the random number is reset so that it follows an identical sequence:

```
90 X = RND(1000000)         — new random sequence initiated
100 FOR PHRASE = 1 TO 4     — four phrases repeated
                              identically
```

```
110 K = RND(-X)          — random number reset to the
                           same value
120 FOR HF = 1 TO 2      — two different half-phrases
130 T = RND(12)          — melody reset to a different
                           value
140 FOR BAR = 1 TO 2     — two bars
      . . .                      etc.
260 NEXT BAR
270 NEXT HF
280 NEXT PHRASE
290 GOTO 90
```

This version of the program will now repeat four identical phrases, then generate a different phrase repeated four times, and so on.

Changing the tempo

The constant tempo can also be varied very easily by changing the value of D at random. Suitable values for D are 3, 4, 5 and 6. These can be generated with the line:

```
80 D = RND(4) + 2
```

If the tempo is to remain constant throughout, line 290 can remain as it is. To change the tempo with each new group of phrases it should become:

```
290 GOTO 80
```

Line 10 is now redundant, of course, and can be removed.

Building up a form

Music usually has a regular form where, for example, a particular section may keep recurring interspersed with sections of different material. This gives a chorus, or refrain-type structure. Capital letters can be used to stand for different sections of music. For example, the repeated section may be called A, other sections of different material B and C. Thus the form just described would be represented by the sequence:

A B A C A

To get our program to generate forms like this, we can incorporate the bulk of the program into a **procedure** (see p.106) called with an argument X, in brackets. Any call of the procedure with a particular value of X will always produce the same result. We can use three different arguments A, B and C to represent the sections of the music.

We will give the procedure the name PROCsection since it generates a section consisting of four identical phrases. Constructing the procedure is easy. We frame the appropriate lines of the program with DEFPROC and ENDPROC statements:

```
90 DEFPROCsection(X)
      . . .
290 ENDPROC
```

Now the program up to line 290 deals with initializations and definitions. The action part of the program will begin at line 300. We will adjust line 80 to send the thread of action in the right direction:

```
80 GOTO 300
```

If we are going to be able to retrieve any particular realization we need to start by calling the RND function with negative argument. Since X has been gobbled up into the procedure we will use the variable N (for number) here. (Good programmers could have declared X a local variable in the procedure, but it does not really matter.)

```
300 N = RND(1000000)
310 K = RND(-N)
```

We also need to reassign a value to D:

```
320 D = RND(4) + 2
```

Values can be assigned to A, B and C representing the different sections:

```
370 A = RND(1000000)
380 B = RND(1000000)
390 C = RND(1000000)
```

Then the procedure can be called with the arguments in an appropriate sequence to represent the form:

```
400 PROCsection(A)
410 PROCsection(B)
420 PROCsection(A)
430 PROCsection(C)
440 PROCsection(A)
```

Other form patterns could be used: A B A B A C A etc.

Finally, the program may simply end:

```
480 END
```

The pattern could be repeated:

```
480 GOTO 400
```

Or a fresh, new sequence could be generated:

```
480 GOTO 320
```

Adding a pause

If the pattern is being repeated, or a new sequence generated, a pause can be included at the end of the sequence. The easiest way to do this is to use an INKEY statement. The computer will wait for the time specified by the argument, in hundredths of a second. It is reasonable to relate this pause length to the value of D: slower realizations will have a longer pause, faster realizations a shorter pause. Z, like K, is merely a dummy variable allowing us to call the INKEY function:

```
450 Z = INKEY(D*128)
```

Changing the key

The continuous use of C major becomes a little wearing after a while. Changing to a different key is simply a matter of adding a constant value to each note as it is generated. In that way all the interval relationships between the notes remain the same, which is what matters.

There are twelve different possible keys. One of these is chosen at random. Because there is a difference of 4 between the values of any two adjacent notes, the amount to be added to each note must be a multiple of 4:

```
KY = RND(12)*4
```

The lowest value generated by the program as it stands is 5, but we can if necessary go as low as 1. To make full use of the available range the amount to be added to each note, KY, can go as low as −4. The minimum value of the expression RND(12)*4 is 4, so if we subtract 8 it will achieve the desired effect:

```
330 KY = RND(12)*4 - 8
```

All the SOUND statements inside the procedure need to be changed to add KY to each pitch specified on channels 1, 2 and 3:

```
210 SOUND 1,1,KY + SCALE(B) - 48*Q,D
220 SOUND 2,1,KY + SCALE(T),D
230 SOUND 3,1,KY + SCALE(B) - 48*Q + 48,D
```

Varying the percussive accompaniment

More character can be given to the music by varying the percussive accompaniment of unchanging high-frequency noise used so far. Alternative pitch values can be used in the SOUND statement at line 170. Reasonable sounds are given by the values 3, 4, 5, 6 and 7. (The other possibilities, 0, 1 and 2 do not work so well.) To give the noisy sounds more of a characteristic shape a better result is achieved by varying the P value according to the beat. For instance:

```
170 SOUND 0,1,8 - BEAT, D
```

or another possibility:

```
170 SOUND 0,1,BEAT + 2, D
```

Even more variety can be achieved by setting up a four-element array R (for Rhythm) to store a pattern which can be repeated for each bar. Firstly line 30 must be adapted to reserve the array space:

```
30 DIM SCALE(12),R(4)
```

The elements in the array need to be assigned. Values between 3 and 7 will be generated:

```
340 FOR I = 1 TO 4
350 R ( I ) = RND(5) + 2
360 NEXT I
```

And finally, line 170 is adjusted to read the appropriate element from the array:

```
170 SOUND 0,1,R(BEAT),D*2
```

With tempo, key and noise channel changes, the program will probably work better without the pause in line 450. So here is the complete amended version of the program as it now stands.

The program — AUTOROCK 2

```
 20 ENVELOPE 1,3,0,0,0,0,0,0,126,-10,-5,-2,126,120
 30 DIM SCALE(12),R(4)
 40 FOR I = 1 TO 12
 50 READ SCALE ( I )
 60 NEXT I
 70 DATA 101,109,117,121,129,137,145,149,157,165,
        169,177
 80 GOTO 300

 90 DEFPROCsection(X)
100 FOR PHRASE = 1 TO 4
110 K = RND(-X)
120 FOR HF = 1 TO 2
130 T = RND(12)
```

```
140 FOR BAR = 1 TO 2
150 B = RND(8)
160 FOR BEAT = 1 TO 4
170 SOUND 0,1,R(BEAT),D*2
180 FOR Q = 2 TO 1 STEP -1
190 T = T + RND(3) -2
200 IF T<1 OR T>12 THEN T=6
210 SOUND 1,1,KY + SCALE(B) - 48*Q, D
220 SOUND 2,1,KY + SCALE(T), D
230 SOUND 3,1,KY + SCALE(B) - 48*Q + 48, D
240 NEXT Q
250 NEXT BEAT
260 NEXT BAR
270 NEXT HF
280 NEXT PHRASE
290 ENDPROC

300 N = RND(1000000)
310 K = RND(-N)

320 D = RND(4) + 2
330 KY = RND(12)*4 - 8
340 FOR I = 1 TO 4
350 R(I) = RND(5) + 2
360 NEXT I
370 A = RND(1000000)
380 B = RND(1000000)
390 C = RND(1000000)

400 PROCsection(A)
410 PROCsection(B)
420 PROCsection(A)
430 PROCsection(C)
440 PROCsection(A)
460 GOTO 320
```

Extending the program

There are many ways in which this program may be extended.

Musically, the accompaniment pattern could be varied, perhaps playing fifths instead of octaves, or performing fast arpeggios, or simply just staying on the same note. The third part could be made to execute its own random walk, or to do something silly like playing completely unrelated random notes in a high octave as a twinkling background.

It should not be difficult to generate a screen display representing visually, the sounds being played. It could either be a rough diagrammatic parallel, like the illustrations at the beginning of this chapter, or an accurate rendering in formal musical notation.

Many of the decisions could be made to depend on a user's responses with prompts to decide such things as tempo and key. A number of accompanying percussive patterns might be suggested until the user finds something he likes and instructs the computer to use it. The computer could present various alternative phrases from which the user can select and define his own form combinations.

15 Process music

setting up automatic musical processes and leaving them to run

Musical processes

In recent years **automatic** musical processes have come to feature more in the work of many composers. An example of such a process is where a composer starts with a small group of notes:

and then repeats them, adding an extra note on the end:

The process continues in the same way, each time repeating the previous group and adding an extra note:

Processes like this are not new. Composers have made use of such devices throughout history. What is new is the extent to which they are now sometimes used. The French composer Messiaen frequently uses processes in his compositions, usually in developed combination with other musical ideas. More radical composers such as Steve Reich and Terry Riley have made a single, simple process the basis of a whole composition.

Where a process is being applied logically and consistently to develop musical material a computer is an obvious candidate for assistance. Process music performed by live musicians can often end up being cruelly exhausting to play.

It is not difficult to program the process we have just described, and it can produce quite an effective result.

An expanding process program

We first need an envelope for the sounds:

```
10 ENVELOPE 1,4,1,-1,1,1,2,1,60,-4,-1,-1,126,100
```

We will work out a note sequence first and store it in an array. Having established the sequence, we can then play note 1, followed by notes 1 and 2, then notes 1, 2 and 3, and so on until the whole sequence is played through in its entirety.

This core sequence will be worked out at random. It will need a maximum length. We will make it capable of containing up to 50 notes. Two arrays are required to store the sequence, one for pitch values, P, and another for durations, D. These arrays must be DIMensioned at the start of the program:

```
20 DIM P(50),D(50)
```

Next we determine a length for the source sequence between 1 and 50 notes long. We will use the variable T, for Total length:

```
30 T=RND(50)
```

The notes in the source sequence will be determined at random each time the program is run. We will use chromatic pitches roughly within a two-octave range, from 48 to 148. The duration values will be 1 or 2, for a quaver or a crotchet. A loop will cycle through notes one at a time until the source sequence length, T, has been reached, working out appropriate values to put in the P and D arrays:

```
40 FOR N=1 TO T
```

```
50 P(N)=RND(25)*4+48
60 D(N)=RND(2)
70 NEXT N
```

When the program runs, the "composing" time taken to set up these arrays is barely perceptible.

We can now start making the sounds. Beginning with a value of 1, we will need to increase the group length, L, of notes played back from the array by one step at a time until it reaches the full length of the source sequence, T. An outer loop will do that job. Inside that will go another loop to play notes from 1 up to the current group length, L:

```
80 FOR L=1 TO T
90 FOR N=1 TO L
      :
110 SOUND 1,1,P(N),D(N)*7
      :
130 NEXT N
140 NEXT L
```

The duration values of 1 or 2 are multiplied by 7 to give a reasonable tempo. The sound quality may be enhanced a little by doubling up (or rather trebling up) on the other channels:

```
100 FOR C=1 TO 3
110 SOUND C,1,P(N),D(N)*7
120 NEXT C
```

We now have three NEXT statements following straight after each other in lines 120 to 140. They can be slimmed down on to one line:

```
120 NEXT C,N,L
```

The final version of the program now looks like this:

```
10 ENVELOPE 1,4,1,-1,1,1,2,1,60,-4,-1,-1,126,100
20 DIM P(50),D(50)
30 T=RND(50)
40 FOR N=1 TO T
50 P(N)=RND(25)*4+48
```

```
60  D(N)=RND(2)
70  NEXT N
80  FOR L=1 TO T
90  FOR N=1 TO L
100 FOR C=1 TO 3
110 SOUND C,1,P(N),D(N)*7
120 NEXT C,N,L
```

Reversing the process, speeding up and deliberate mistakes

The composition *Les Moutons de Panurge* by American experimental composer Frederick Rzewski makes use of the same process we have just programmed. In the case of his piece, an exact score of notes to be played is supplied, but the instructions for playing it are the same: first note alone, followed by notes 1 and 2, followed by 1,2,3 and so on. But he goes a bit further. Once the performers have got as far as playing the entire sequence, they are then instructed to continue the process, but this time successively missing off the first note each time the group is repeated, until it eventually becomes a single, final note.

It is not difficult to extend the program we have, so that the sequence will carry on to undo itself in the same way. We use exactly the same loops again, but this time, instead of making N count from the 1st to the Lth note each time, it will start at the Lth note and read up to T, the end of the sequence:

```
130 FOR L=1 TO T
140 FOR N=L TO T
150 FOR C=1 TO 3
160 SOUND C,1,P(N),D(N)*7
170 NEXT C,N,L
```

In Rzewski's score the musicians are also instructed to increase their speed gradually. This effect can be copied by making the tempo factor, 7 so far, depend on the value of L.

The first time, in line 110, we can replace 7 with the expression:

```
(7-L/25)
```

When L is 1 at the start of the sequence, the value of the expression will still be 7. But as L increases it will decrease until it equals 5 when L is 50.

Similarly, in the reverse section, at line 160, we can replace 7 with the expression:

```
(4-L/25)
```

This will begin at 4 and work its way down to 2 when L=50. Lines 110 and 160 will accordingly become:

```
110 SOUND C,1,P(N),D(N)*(7-L/25)

160 SOUND C,1,P(N),D(N)*(4-L/25)
```

Rzewski's composition is meant to be performed by a number of players in unison. Making allowances for human fallibility, he recognizes that some players are bound to make mistakes and get lost. An important feature of the work's ethos is that players are instructed not to worry, but carry on regardless.

The computer, on the other hand, is stubbornly, and boringly reliable. None the less, we can mischievously incorporate random "mistakes" into our program by inserting additional lines which make the program pause occasionally. When this happens the channels get out of synchronization:

```
105 IF RND(7)=1 THEN A=INKEY(100)

155 IF RND(7)=1 THEN A=INKEY(100)
```

It produces quite a comical effect as one channel is left behind and appears to be struggling to keep up with the others. Eventually the buffers sort themselves out as other channels are gagged for equivalent periods. The trailing channel has a chance to catch up and they all get back into stride again.

Separating the channels out into different octaves helps to make the effect clearer. It can be done by adding 48*(C-2) to the pitch value in the SOUND statements, lines 110 and 160.

Here is the amended program in full:

```
10 ENVELOPE 1,4,1,-1,1,1,1,2,1,60,-4,-1,-1,126,100
20 DIM P(50),D(50)
30 T=RND(50)
40 FOR N=1 TO T
50 P(N)=RND(25)*4+48
60 D(N)=RND(2)
70 NEXT N
80 FOR L=1 TO T
90 FOR N=1 TO L
100 FOR C=1 TO 3
105 IF RND(7)=1 THEN A=INKEY(100)
110 SOUND C,1,P(N)+48*(C-2),D(N)*(7-L/25)
120 NEXT C,N,L
130 FOR L=1 TO T
140 FOR N=L TO T
150 FOR C=1 TO 3
155 IF RND(7)=1 THEN A=INKEY(100)
160 SOUND C,1,P(N)+48*(C-2),D(N)*(4-L/25)
170 NEXT C,N,L
```

Phase loops: Glass and bamboo

Another process favoured by some contemporary composers makes use of phased loops of notes. In such a process two or more short musical motifs are defined so that they each contain a different number of notes.

One motif might have four notes for example:

and another, five:

The two motifs are then repeated many times, simultaneously. Because they are of different length, they do not link up exactly but move in and out of step:

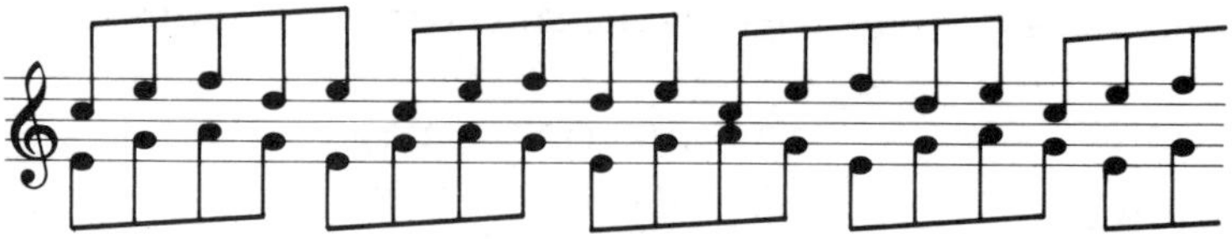

The motifs only match up again after 20 notes. It is rather like building a wall where the bricks are of different length on each row:

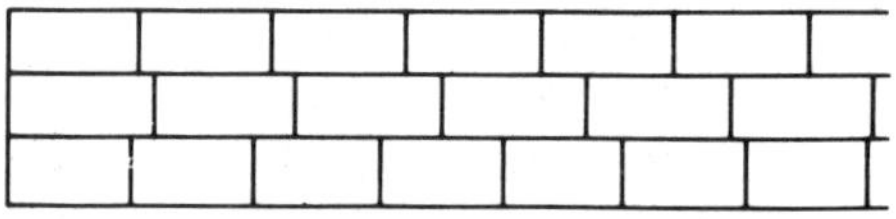

What begins as a minor miss-match gradually becomes larger until the cycle is completed and it matches up again. Steve Reich, and other composers, have used the technique in making music with electronic tape. It is possible to set up simultaneous tape loops which are slightly different in duration. At first it will not be noticeable, then the difference will gradually become more rhythmical and pronounced. If the difference is slight enough, they may not get back into phage again until an hour has elapsed.

With larger numbers of simultaneous loops even more complex patterns may be produced.

This idea of out-of-phase loops is nothing new in music. It formed the basis of the isorhythmic motets of medieval composers such as Machaut (*c.* 1300–1377). To generate some of their musical lines they would often use a rhythmic motif (known as the **talea**) and a melody motif (known as the **color**) containing different numbers of notes. Repeating and combining the two patterns, they would link up differently each time.

For example, this three-note rhythm motif:

combined with this four-note melody motif:

will produce this 12-note phrase:

Melodic phase patterns and processes are a strong feature of music by the American composer Philip Glass whose work has recently begun to gain wide recognition. Their influence can also be seen in the music of pop musicians such as Mike Oldfield.

Further afield, in the musical island of Bali, these effects are a common feature of everyday life. The bamboo poles which help to irrigate the fields tilt backwards and forwards producing a resonant clunk. Neighbouring groups of poles, exhibiting worthy solidarity, will tilt at different speeds and produce rhythmically phased sound patterns. This sound gave rise to a style of playing in Balinese xylophone orchestras known as the **Gamelan Anklung**.

Moiré patterns

The aural effect of phased loops is directly parallel to the visual effect of moiré patterns which appear when two different grids are superimposed. The interference patterns which occur when the lines do not quite match up form wavy contours, like zebra skins. The effect can be seen when net-curtain folds over itself, or when one comb is moved around close behind another.

The computer will produce moiré effects very easily as it attempts to plot sloping lines on to the rectangular grid of the graphics screen. This short program is an example. It draws lines which radiate from a fixed point above the top of the screen to a point which moves across the bottom of the screen:

```
10 MODE 0
20 FOR X= -500 TO 1780 STEP 4
```

```
30 MOVE 640,2000
40 DRAW X,0
50 NEXT X
```

Different effects can be produced by changing the step size, and by using different colours in MODE 1 or 2:

```
10 MODE 1
20 FOR X= -500 TO 1750 STEP RND(50)+4
30 MOVE 640,2000
40 DRAW X,0
50 NEXT X
60 GCOLO,RND(8)+1
70 GOTO 20
```

Moiré music

To make a moiré music program we will use the three channels to play different length loops simultaneously. The program will choose how long each loop is to be, and what notes it contains, so that we get a different result each time the program is run. We cannot use BASIC programming loops to cycle round each melody loop, as we have done before, since they will not have the same length. The beginnings and ends will match up differently each time. Instead, we have to keep count of which note number we are up to in each loop every time a sound is made. Once a loop limit has been reached the counter can be set back to 1 to start playing and counting from the beginning of the loop again.

A two-dimensional array, RIF, will be used to store the note values for each loop. We will use the term riffs for the melody loops (they are similar to the riffs we came across in Chapter 2), since it helps to avoid confusion when talking about programming loops.

RIF consists of three-note lists, one for each channel's riff. We will let each riff contain up to 20 notes making RIF's dimensions 3 by 20. Two other three-element arrays are required to hold values for each channel. L will store the number of notes in each riff, in other words, each riff's Length. N will be used to hold the current note Number being sounded in each loop, once we get to that stage.
A fourth array SC will be used to store the pitch values of the major scale, as before. The arrays are all declared at the start of the program:

```
10 DIM SC(8),RIF(3,20),L(3),N(3)
```

Next we define an appropriate envelope and read scale values into the SC array, as we have done before:

```
20 ENVELOPE 1,1,0,0,0,0,0,0,126,-1,-1,-1,126,120
30 FOR I=1 TO 8
40 READ SC ( I )
50 NEXT I
60 DATA 0,8,16,20,28,36,44,48
```

We now need to choose a riff length and work out the notes for each channel. We will use a loop to work through each of the three channels in turn:

```
70 FOR C=1 TO 3
```

The riff length can be chosen between 8 and 20 notes long:

```
80 L(C)=7+RND(13)
```

Another loop will be used to work out values for each note. It will step up from the first note to the riff length L(C) which was just established:

```
90 FOR J=1 TO L(C)
```

Each note will be stored at position (C,J) in the RIF array, meaning the Jth note on the Cth channel. Its value is chosen at random from the SC array:

```
SC(RND(8))
```

In order to hear the three parts distinctly we can make channel 2 play its notes one octave higher and channel 3, two octaves higher. Channel 1 will stay where it is. In other words we need to add 0 , 48 or 2*48. We use the same method as earlier and add (C−1)*48 to the pitch value. The full expression to calculate the note value will look like this:

```
100 RIF(C,J)=SC(RND(8))+(C−1)*48
```

We now close the J-loop:

```
110 NEXT J
```

While still inside the C loop, the "current" note number held in the N array can be set to its starting value of 0:

```
120 N(C)=0
```

and then we will close off the C-loop:

```
130 NEXT C
```

Everything is now ready to start playing the riffs. The instructions will be in an endless loop which keeps returning to line 140 after each of the channels' notes has been sounded. We will put the necessary statements inside another short loop to deal with each channel in turn:

```
140 FOR C=1 TO 3
```

We first update the current note number for that channel's riff:

```
150 N(C)=N(C)+1
```

and then check to see if it has yet reached the end of the riff. It will be checked against the riff-length value for that channel stored in the L array. If it has, then it is reset back to 0:

```
160 IF N(C)>L(C) THEN N(C)=0
```

Now the sound can be made by looking up the note value N(C) at the appropriate position in the RIF array:

```
170 SOUND C,1,RIF(C,N(C)),4
```

The duration is kept at a constant value of 4 for the time being.

The C loop can be closed off, and the program sent back to line 140 to repeat the process again:

```
180 NEXT C
190 GOTO 140
```

The complete program looks like this:

```
 10 DIM SC(8),RIF(3,20),L(3),N(3)
 20 ENVELOPE 1,1,0,0,0,0,0,0,126,-1,-1,-1,126,120
 30 FOR I=1 TO 8
 40 READ SC ( I )
 50 NEXT I

 60 DATA 0,8,16,20,28,36,44,48
 70 FOR C=1 TO 3
 80 L(C)=7+RND(13)
 90 FOR J=1 TO L(C)
100 RIF(C,J)=SC(RND(8))+(C-1)*48
110 NEXT J
120 N(C)=0
130 NEXT C
```

```
140 FOR C=1 TO 3
150 N(C)=N(C)+1
160 IF N(C)>L(C) THEN N(C)=0
170 SOUND C,1,RIF(C,N(C)),4
180 NEXT C

190 GOTO 140
```

Press ESCAPE to stop it.

Key and tempo changes

The program can be extended in several ways. A simple improvement is to make the tempo change every time the program is run. As in earlier programs we can replace 4 by D, in line 170, and put in an extra line at the beginning to work out a value for D:

```
 65 D=1+RND(3)
      :
170 SOUND C,1,RIF(C,N,(C)),D
```

Another interesting variation is to let the process play for a while and then transpose or shift all the notes up by a fixed interval. The key will appear to have changed, though the melody patterns will be the same. This produces quite a pleasing effect. We will use P to stand for the value of the pitch shift, making it an exact number of semitones within an octave range:

```
135 P=RND(12)*4
```

The core of the program will then be put inside another loop which will allow the generation of a random number of notes, say up to 300, before returning to line 135 to choose a new P value and change the key:

```
137 FOR K=1 TO RND(300)
```

The SOUND statement will need to be changed to incorporate the addition of P to the pitch value:

```
·170 SOUND C,1,RIF(C,N(C))+P,D
```

At the end of the program we close the K-loop and send the program back to line 135 to choose another P value:

```
190 NEXT K
200 GOTO 135
```

Before listing the revised program we will make one additional modification. We will surround the K-loop with yet another loop. This one will permit the generation of up to 11 sections in different keys before going back to the beginning of the program to start again. A new tempo and completely fresh riffs will be defined. This outer loop will be called Q:

```
132 FOR Q=1 TO RND(11)
        :
200 NEXT Q
210 GOTO 65
```

In the following revised version, some of the lines have been combined and renumbered:

```
 10 DIM SC(8),RIF(3,20),L(3),N(3)
 20 ENVELOPE 1,1,0,0,0,0,0,0,126,-1,-1,-1,126,120
 30 FOR I=1 to 8:READ SC ( I ) :NEXT
 40 DATA 0,8,16,20,28,36,44,48

 50 D=1+RND(3)
 60 FOR C=1 TO 3
 70 L(C)=7+RND(13)
 80 N(C)=0
 90 FOR J=1 TO L(C)
100 RIF(C,J)=SC(RND(8))+(C-1)*48
110 NEXT J,C

120 FOR Q=1 TO RND(11)
130 P=RND(12)*4
140 FOR K=1 TO RND(300)
150 FOR C=1 TO 3
160 N(C)=N(C)+1
170 IF N(C)>L(C) THEN N(C)=0
180 SOUND C,1,RIF(C,N(C))+P,D
190 NEXT C,K,Q

200 GOTO 50
```

Shorter loops and wider pitches

Varying the maximum loop length, set in line 70, will change the style of the music. Try reducing it to 7 or even less, for example:

```
70 L(C)=RND(7)
```

This will give short riffs and produce quite a different effect. It sounds like music by the composer Janacek which often contains short, repeated motifs. He is most well known for his operas, such as *The Cunning Little Vixen* where these sounds are used to reflect the calls and cries of the forest creatures.

Another possibility is to extend the pitch range of each riff so that riffs overlap and mingle with one another, giving an impression of even more parts. The scale array will need to be increased in size, for example to 15, and additional values read in:

```
10 DIM SC(15),RIF(3,20),L(3),N(3)
        :
30 FOR I=1 TO 15:READ SC ( I ) :NEXT
40 DATA 0,8,16,20,28,36,44,48,56,64,68,76,84,92,96
```

At the note selection stage values up to 15 can now be used:

```
100 RIF(C,J)=SC(RND(15))
```

The +(C−1)*48 factor previously at the end of the statement can be left in or out. Try it both ways, it works equally well.

The other loop limits may also be reduced to make the program change key or redefine riffs more frequently. Some quite radical changes in the resulting sound may be produced.

You may also like to try programming medieval **talea** and **color** patterns like those described on p.260.

To conclude, here is a version of the moiré music program which generates different screen patterns at the same time as the music is played. Try it out in different MODEs, 0, 1 or 2. The music generating part of the program has been split up into two procedures, PROCriffchange and PROCriffplay. Their structure has been modified slightly. Before, the SOUND statement came inside loops of random length which changed the key or defined new riffs when they were completed. This time, cues are incorporated inside the playing procedure to trigger the same changes, but at random time intervals. It makes it easier to co-ordinate the music with the screen display. Again, the size of the random check values can be reduced to make changes happen more frequently:

```
 10 DIM SC(15),RIF(3,20),L(3),N(3)
 20 FOR I=1 TO 15:READ SC ( I ):NEXT
 30 DATA 0,8,16,20,28,36,44,48,56,64,68,76,84,92,96
 40 ENVELOPE 1,1,0,0,0,0,0,0,126,-1,-1,-1,126,120
 50 PROCriffchange

 60 MODE 1
 70 FOR C=0 TO 3:VDU 19,C,RND(8)-1,0,0,0:NEXT

 80 FOR K=10 TO 600 STEP K
 90 S=RND(50)+4
100 GCOL 0,RND(8)-1

110 FOR X=0 TO K STEP S
120 IF TIME>D*2 THEN PROCriffplay:TIME=0
130 MOVE 640-K,512+K
140 DRAW 640-X,512-X
150 DRAW 640+K,512-K
160 DRAW 640+X,512+X
170 DRAW 640-K,512+K
180 NEXT X

190 FOR X=0 TO K STEP S
200 IF TIME>D*2 THEN PROCriffplay:TIME=0
210 MOVE 640+K,512+K
220 DRAW 640-X,512+X
230 DRAW 640-K,512-K
240 DRAW 640+X,512-X
250 DRAW 640+K,512+K
260 NEXT X,K

270 GOTO 60

280 DEFPROCriffchange
290 P=RND(12)*4
```

```
300 D=2+RND(3)
310 FOR C=1 TO 3
320 L(C)=4+RND(6)
330 N(C)=0
340 FOR J=1 TO L(C)
350 RIF(C,J)=SC(RND(15))
360 NEXT J,C
370 ENDPROC

380 DEFPROCriffplay
390 IF RND(200)=1 THEN PROCriffchange
400 IF RND(30)=1 THEN P=RND(12)*4
410 FOR C=1 TO 3
420 N(C)=N(C)+1
430 IF N(C)>L(C) THEN N(C)=0
440 SOUND C,1,RIF(C,N(C))+P,D
450 NEXT C
460 ENDPROC
```

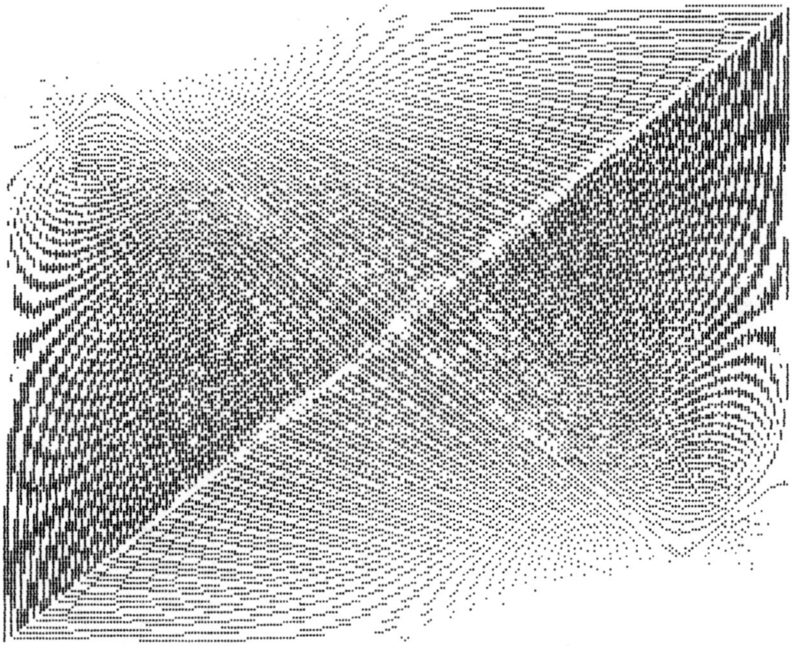

Appendix: Music on the Electron

Many of the programs in the book will work successfully on the Electron, but its sound capabilities are very limited compared to the BBC computer. In particular:

- it will only produce one channel of sound
- it has no control over volume, the sound is either on or off, so as a result:
- there is no amplitude (volume) envelope, but it does have the same pitch envelope
- the tuning of the higher pitches is rather doubtful;
- noise sounds are limited

These general points are considered first, then ways of adapting programs for the Electron are discussed chapter by chapter.

Channels

Although it can only produce one channel of sound at a time, in order to be consistent with BBC BASIC, the channel number can be specified as 1, 2 or 3. If an attempt is made to play on all three channels simultaneously chaotic splutterings result. It is normally best to keep to channel 1.

Most of the programs in the book use just one channel and will work on the Electron, though it is necessary to take into account envelope and tuning adjustments. In some cases channels have been doubled-up merely to achieve a more interesting sound quality. It is a simple matter to remove any doubling-up statements.

Sometimes a crafty re-arrangement will enable a three-voice program to work on a single channel and still produce an acceptable result. The Bach *Prelude* in Chapter 13 is an example.

Volume

As with the channel number, the same range of values can be used on the Electron as on the BBC computer, but they will not necessarily make any difference.

Any value in the range −15 to −1 will make a sound at a constant volume level. A value of 0 is used for "silent" notes, or rests. Envelope numbers 1, 2, 3 or 4 are also acceptable for this parameter, though as explained below, they will only affect the pitch of a note.

Amplitude envelope

The lack of an amplitude envelope means that it is not possible to obtain different instrument-like sounds. It also means that notes are not separated from each other. A note with the same pitch as its predecessor will be heard as an extension of the first note, not as a separate, new note. It sometimes means that rhythms are confused.

The easiest way to solve this problem is to put a SOUND statement which plays a dummy note at zero volume and with zero duration after each note-making SOUND statement:

```
SOUND 1,0,0,0
```

The time taken by the program to process the command is enough to introduce a gap between notes.

A pitch envelope can be defined on the Electron, just as on the BBC computer.

Tuning

If the regular tuning scale of four pitch values per semitone is used on the Electron, some of the higher pitches will be out of tune. Such notes are usually slightly sharp, but the effect does not seem to follow a consistent pattern.

Where programs work out pitch values automatically, in multiples of 4, it is best to keep to lower notes which are more in tune. Where fixed pitches are read in, to define a major scale for example, it may sometimes give better tunings to "bend" some values slightly to the next pitch value down. An example of this is given when a method of adapting the Bach *Prelude* in Chapter 13 is discussed below.

Noise

The noise sounds produced by the Electron are rather different to those made by the BBC computer, and are very limited.

Notes on how well the material in each chapter suits the Electron, and suggestions for ways of adapting programs follow:

Chapter 2: Tuning up

The first few programs work just as they are. Note particularly the point about introducing a rest between adjacent notes of the same pitch, on p.17. It is especially relevant to the Electron since it cannot generate amplitude envelopes.

The section on envelopes does not apply. If you happen to include one of these envelopes in an Electron program it will still run, but will not make any difference to the sound. Envelope number 1 can be used in a SOUND statement even if no envelope has been defined. It will simply produce the maximum volume all the time, just as if −15 had been used. In fact, on the Electron, it probably makes sense to use the value 1 as a standard volume setting for "on" most of the time. Be careful though, because if a pitch envelope definition is lurking in the computer's memory from an earlier program, it might be used in error.

As pointed out previously, a dummy note statement should be included to separate neighbouring notes of the same pitch. For the *Sailor's Hornpipe* this line should be added:

```
45 SOUND 1,0,0,0
```

The last section in the chapter on chords and two-part music will not apply on the Electron.

Chapter 3: Random selection

Most of the chapter will also work on the Electron without any need for alteration. Any references to random channel numbers should be ignored; always keep to channel 1.

Chapter 4: Steps and glissandi

With the exception of the last section, everything works on the Electron.

By changing one digit in the last program, p.67, the Electron can be made to sound as if it is producing two separate channels. Instead of specifying channel 2 in line 30, use channel 1 again, so that the program looks like this:

```
10 FOR P=0 TO 255
20 SOUND &11,-15,P,1
30 SOUND &11,-15,255-P,1
40 NEXT P
50 GOTO 10
```

The Electron's single sound channel then switches rapidly from the pitch specified in line 20 to the pitch specified in line 30, then back to the pitch in line 20, and so on.

It could be represented like this:

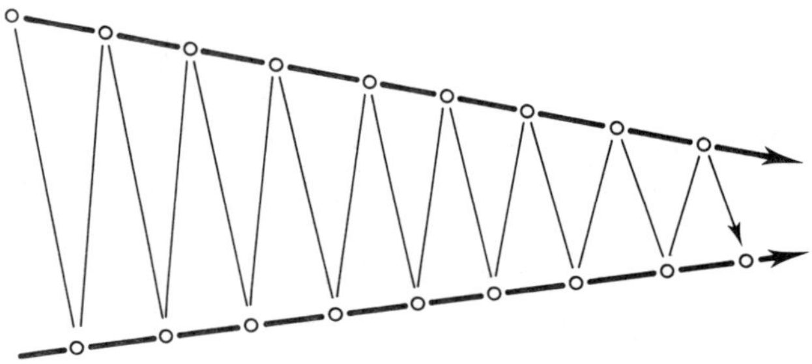

This happens so quickly that the ear does not have time to register the switching and only hears the general trend of the resulting ascending and descending glissandi slopes.

Chapter 5: Walking

Pages 68 to 74 work well on the Electron, but pages 75–79, where three parts are used, will not work. You can try substituting &11 for &12 and &13, as was done previously, but the result is not as good as with the glissandi in Chapter 4. The effect with just two channels is slightly better and is worth trying with the plotting commands.

Pages 79 to 91 will work effectively. Again, instead of using an envelope, add a SOUND 1,0,0,0 statement after any other SOUND statement.

Chapter 6: Melody rules

The musical parts of the chapter will work on the Electron but when it comes to displaying the melody movement on screen, the colour coding will not work as the Electron has no Mode 7. If you are familiar with the BBC and Electron's graphics commands you should not find it too difficult to work out an equivalent display in Mode 2, say.

Chapter 7: Aural training

Nearly all of the program will work adequately on the Electron, though the tuning is worse than on the BBC computer. Notice that the "simultaneous interval" option will not apply. Those lines can be removed and the variable S set permanently to 1 in the PROCplay procedure.

Chapter 8: Envelopes

Pages 135 to 147 concerning the amplitude envelope, will not apply. The Electron's fixed version of the amplitude envelope, if set up for the BBC computer, would have the following A, D, S, R, AT and DT values:

```
126,0,0,-126,126,0
```

However, pages 148 to 155, on the pitch envelope, apply equally to the Electron. Notice that the Electron "amplitude envelope" values, as set out above, have been used on these pages anyway, in order to keep a note sounding at full volume throughout, to enable us to hear a pitch envelope's full effect.

When defining an envelope for the Electron, the last six values can be any numbers at all. Six zeros are adequate. If you are expecting to run the same program on a BBC machine at some stage, in order to get exactly the same sound the amplitude envelope values given above should be used.

Chapter 9: Organizing the keyboard

A few modifications are required in this chapter since the Electron keyboard has a different layout.

The first two sections apply unchanged. The higher notes at the bottom of the chart on page 169 need to be changed to take into account the different location of the arrow editing keys. From note number 19 it will read:

number	note	key	ASCII code
19	F#/G♭	–	45
20	G	↑	139
21	G#/A♭	←	136
22	A	↓	138
23	A#/B♭	→	137
24	B	COPY	135

There are now only 24 notes available (and there is also no TAB key on the Electron). Line 60 must be changed to read 24 instead of 27 values into the N array. The list of DATA values must also be adapted. The lines will become:

```
60  FOR I=1 TO 24
70  READ A
80  N(A)=I
90  NEXT I
100 DATA 9,49,81,50,87,69,52,82,53,84,54,89,85,56,
         73,57,79,80,45,139,136,138,137,135
```

Pages 172 to 177 which suggest envelope changes and doubling-up channels for different stop effects, will not work on the Electron.

Chapter 10: Etchamus

This works on the Electron, but notice that there will be no variation in volume level. The ← and → arrows will only affect the line being drawn on the screen and not the sound. In all other respects, the suggested amendments work successfully.

Chapter 11: Noise

The noise channel on the Electron is rather limited. Since any effective use of noise really requires an amplitude envelope, it is scarcely worth bothering with.

Chapter 12: Ethnic sounds

These programs are really beyond the Electron's capabilities. The basic melody line for each program can be generated, but accompanying figures on other channels will not work.

Chapter 13: Playing Bach

It would seem from looking at the music that Bach's *Prelude* will only work on three channels. In fact it is possible to fake quite a reasonable Electron version on one channel. This is because no two notes actually begin at the same time. The three channels are only used together in order to sustain one or two notes whilst others play over them. By making each note have the basic semiquaver duration, D, and removing all the sustains and balancing rests, everything can be played on one channel. Since channel 3 is used for the existing semiquavers, we will keep to that as our single channel number. It involves fewer alterations. The changed lines in the body of the program will be:

```
160 SOUND 3,1,N(1),D
170
180 SOUND 3,1,N(2),D
190
     :
280 SOUND 3,1,5,D
     :
300
310 SOUND 3,1,P,D
320
     :
380 SOUND 3,1,5,D*32
390
400
```

Notice that lines 170, 190, 300, 320, 390 and 400 are removed altogether. The last note might sound rather lonely. You could try settling on one of the other pitches in the last chord to see if you prefer the sound.

When you run this Electron version you may notice that some of the higher notes sound appreciably out of tune. In fact, they tend to be sharp. Reducing their pitch values by 1 will give better tuning. For example, replace the high F's value of 169 with 168 each time it appears in the DATA list.

The AUTOBACH program will work with equivalent alterations. Lines 160 to 190 should be changed exactly as they are above.

Chapter 14: Autorock

This will not work on the Electron.

Chapter 15: Process music

The first process described will work, but ignore suggestions to double-up channels to improve the sound quality. Also, of course, the out-of-step channel effect will not be possible.

The moiré music process requires three channels and so will not work on the Electron.

Index